Rural Banks
for
Rural Development

RURAL BANKS FOR RURAL DEVELOPMENT

MAJOR DR. GOURI PRASAD MOHAPATRA,
M.A., L.L.B., Ph.D.
Reader in Economics
Science College, Hinjilicut (Ganjam).

Discovery Publishing House
New Delhi - 110002
INDIA

Reprinted - 2018

First Published - 1997

ISBN: 978-81-7141-380-5

Rural Banks for Rural Development

Published by:

DISCOVERY PUBLISHING HOUSE PVT. LTD.
4383/4B, Ansari Road, Darya Ganj
New Delhi-110 002 (India)
Phone: +91-11-23279245, 43596064-65
Fax: +91-11-23253475
E-mail: discoverypublishinghouse@gmail.com
sales@discoverypublishinggroup.com
web: www.discoverypublishinggroup.com

Printed at:
Infinity Imaging Systems
Delhi

Dedicated
to
Late R.N.Mohapatra
(Father)
&
Smt. K.B.Mohapatra
(Mother)

Contents

Preface

Rural Development has been considered as the sine qua non of National development and social welfare. Lending from rural development through financial institutions for increasing the standard of living of the weaker sections of the poplulation has been a policy level direction ever since the major commercial banks were nationalised. The Regional Rural Bank being a specific bank for priority sector, has been playing a development role in the rural sectors of each district of India since its date of inception i.e. from October 2nd 1975. It provides cheap money capital to the needy rural artisans, farmers and self employed persons of the undeveloped, neglected and unbanked area of each district of India. The Regional Rural Bank is powerful primary instrument for redistribution of income in rural area. It aims to strengthen the rural economy by improving the financial infrastructure and to generate new income with the expansion of productive employment.

The present thesis is an in-depth study of a Regional Rural Bank (Rushikulya Gramya Bank in Ganjam district of Orissa) at work in one of the districts in the state of Orissa. It highlights the National policies, problems and suggests the measures to be taken for the existence and viability of the tailor-made financial institution, designed specifically for the upliftment of the rural poor in India at the district level.

The present study is basically a research work undertaken by the author for the award of Ph.D. Degree of Berhampur University under the supervision of Dr. Narasing Prasad Patro, Retired Professor of Post Graduate Department of Economics of Khallikote (Autonomous) College, Berhampur, Ganjam, Orissa.

I express herewith my deepest gratitude to my honourable professor Dr.N.P.Patro for his inspiring guidance, meticulous care, constant supervision and invaluable suggestions in the preparation of this thesis. As my former teacher, he initiated me into the study of Rural Banking and with indulgent care, sustained my interest in the subject. It is needless to say that this unstinted assistance and supervision has led to the completion of the research project. I also express my thanks to the authorities of Berhampur University for permitting me to publish the work.

In the process of this research work, I have received assistance, help, co-operation and encouragement from various organisations, officials, colleagues, students and other individuals. They are too numerous to mention each one of them specifically. I am thankful to all of them for their goodwill and encouragement. Specifically, Prof. C.V.J.Rao, has gone through my thesis and made necessary correction in the language of the manuscript. I express my gratitude to him.

I record herewith my sincere gratefulness to my parents, warm appreciation for my wife Mrs. Meerabai Mohapatra, my daughters Priti Priyadarshani, Subhra Subhadarshani and my son Sibasish (Pinkula) for bearing with patience all the inconveniences during the course of my research work without the least demur.

While all those mentioned have helped to bring out the work in its present form, I alone am responsible for the short comings and errors of judgement that might have inadvertently crept in.

Major. Dr. Gouri Prasad Mohapatra.

List of Abbreviations

ACP	:	Annual Credit Plan
AAP	:	Annual Action Plan
ARDRS	:	Agricultural Rural Debt Relief Scheme.
ACRC	:	Agricultural Credit Review Committee.
BDO	:	Block Development Officer
CDP	:	Community Development Programme.
CRAFICARD	:	Committee to Review Arrangements For Institutional Credit for Agriculture and Rural Development.
CRR	:	Cash Reserve Ratio.
CGS	:	Credit Guarantee Scheme.
DICGC	:	Deposit Insurance and Credit Guarantee Corporation.
DCB	:	Demand, Collection, Balance.
DWCRA	:	Development of Women and Children in Rural Areas.
DIC	:	District Industries Centre.
DRIS	:	Differential Rate of Interest Scheme.
DDM	:	District Development Manager.
DCP	:	District Credit Plan.
DRDA	:	District Rural Development Agency.
DPAP	:	Drought Prone Area Programme.
DDP	:	Desert Development Programme.
ERRP	:	Economic Rehabilitation of Rural Poor Programme.
FSS	:	Farmer's Service Societies.
HYV	:	High Yielding Varieties.
HADP	:	Hill Area Development Programme.
IADP	:	Identified Area Development Programme.
IRDP	:	Integrated Rural Development Programme.
IBA	:	Indian Banker's Association.
IDA	:	International Development Association.
IDBI	:	Industrial Development Bank of India.
JRY	:	Jawahar Rojagar Yojana.
KVL	:	Khadi and Village Industries.
LAMPS	:	Large Sized Agricultural Multipurpose Co-operative Societies.
LT	:	Long Term.

LBO	:	Lead Bank Officer.
MNP	:	Minimum Need Programme.
MT	:	Medium Term.
MF	:	Marginal Farmer.
NRB	:	National Rural Bank (Proposed).
NABARD	:	National Bank for Agricultural and Rural Development.
NS	:	Non-schematic.
NREP	:	National Rural Employment Programme.
OSFC	:	Orissa State Financial Corporation.
OSCSTD	:	Orissa Scheduled Caste and Scheduled Tribe Development.
OSAO	:	Other than Seasonal Agricultural Operations.
PACS	:	Primary Agricultural Co-operative Societies.
PLDB	:	Primary Land Development Banks.
PLCP	:	Potential Linked Credit Plan.
PS	:	Priority Sector.
RRB	:	Regional Rural Bank.
RGB	:	Rushikulya Gramya Bank.
RLEGP	:	Rural Landless Employment Guarantee Programme.
RBI	:	Reserve Bank of India.
ST	:	Short-term.
SLDB	:	State Level Development Banks.
SAA	:	Service Area Approach.
SESEUY	:	Self Employment Scheme for Educated Unemployed Youths.
STs	:	Scheduled Tribes.
SCs	:	Scheduled Castes.
SLR	:	Statutory Liquidity Ratio.
SCH. LOAN	:	Schematic Loans.
SAO	:	Seasonal Agricultural Operations.
SSI	:	Small Scale Industries
SF	:	Small Farmers.
SBI	:	State Bank of India.
SCFCC	:	Scheduled Caste Finance Cooperative Corporation Ltd.
TRYSEM	:	Training of Rural Youth for Self-Employment.

1

An Overview of the Study

The present work constitutes an in-depth study of a Regional Rural Bank at work in one of the districts of the State of Orissa. This tailor-cut institution, designed specifically for the uplift of the rural poor was inducted into the field of rural finance in India in the mid-seventies of this century. It was particularly meant to provide the nucleus of rural finance in a region which is administratively designated as a district.

Following the policy prescription for creation of this innovative institution in India, the Rushikulya Gramya Bank, i.e., the RRB under the present study, was started in 1981. The Andhra Bank which is a nationalised commercial bank has sponsored it and in this capacity it lays down the policies, the procedure of working and also the broad frame-work of functioning of the newly designed institution.

In the present work an attempt has been made to thoroughly analyse the working of the Rushikulya Gramya Bank with its wide net-work of branches spread over the entire district so as to ascertain the measure of success it has attained in the fulfillment of the avowed objectives as also to pinpoint its short-comings.

With the rural economy of Ganjam District as the back-drop, the present chapter provides a study of the evolution of the concept of rural development in the county and the role of the different financial institutions in the provision of the credit inputs for accelerating the growth of the rural sector of the economy.

An attempt has been made in this chapter to explain the genesis and growth of rural financial institutions and the need for establishing the RRBs in the county is examined. The chapter as it advances spells out the scope of the study, hypotheses adopted for testing, the methodology applied and the limitations of the study. At the end the chapterisation plan of the study is stated.

In India rural development is considered as the sine-qua-non of over-all development of the national economy. All-sided development of the country can not be accomplished without bringing about a radical change in the traditional scenario of the rural economy. Seventy six percent of the population lives in rural area (according to 1991 census) and the rural sector subscribes variously to the economic development of the country such as (1) product contribution in terms of growing flow of increased food grains, (2) factor contribution in the form of labour and raw materials, (3) market contribution means of expanding industrial goods within the country through a rapid increase in farm generation of rural population, and (4) foreign exchange contribution by the export of primary goods.

The rural economy of India is characterised by under-utilisation of land, labour, water, mineral, capital and abundant man-power resources. There is scarcity of capital, dearth of investment-opportunities and disguised unemployment. Vicious circle of poverty is a common feature of the rural sector of India. Thus, it was realised soon after independence that the programmes of rural development for increasing production, employment and generating new income in rural sector are an essential requisite of economic planning.

In the post-independence period. India has adopted the policy of economic planning to initiate growth, to build a strong and self-reliant economy, to raise the standard of living of the masses and to create a social system based on equity and justice. Since the formal launching of the five year plans in April 1951, the planning process has grown in depth and sophistication[1] and currently the 8th five year plan is under implementation. As a part of the planning process, the foundation for rural development in this country was laid with the introduction of CDP (Community Development Programme) in 55 pilot blocks on 2nd October 1952 which had the following objectives.

(a) Area development-with a minimum all-round progress.
(b) Self-help programme - people's participation in full measure.
(c) Development of the whole community with special emphasis on the weaker and the under-privileged in rural India.

For area development, administrative units called 'Blocks' and the block development offices with an outfit of extension Officers were created. At the end of the first five year plan, 1,200 blocks had already come into existence[2].

The term "Community Development" became very popular in countries where development programmes like mass education, village improvement and community organisation had been taken up. Each country which took up community development programmes emphasised different aspects in defining them. Some gave importance to the economic and social development, while others, concentrated on the methods of implementation.

Community development has been defined as an attempt in the direction of developing healthy leadership from the base of the structure of the growing domestic society. India's community development programme has been also defined as a method by which people who live in villages are involved in helping to improve their own economic and social conditions and thereby become effective working groups in programmes of national development[3]. It is a process of change from the traditional way of living, as a method by which people can be assisted to develop themselves on their own capacity and resources, as a programme for accomplishing certain activities in fields concerning the welfare of the rural people ; and as a movement for progress with a certain ideological content[4].

The entire rural India is at present divided into 5,004 blocks. A block now covers an area of about 620 square kms with 100 villages and a population of about 1,00,000[5]. The community development projects try to give effect to an intensive and comprehensive programme covering all aspects of rural life, e.g., agriculture, rural industries, education, housing, health, recreation, etc., and aim at utilising under a democratic set-up, the surplus labour force in rural areas for the development process.

The community development programme could give benefits to a limited group of people, mainly to those rural people who were better endowed with land resources. But no creative rural framework could be achieved as an out-come of the programme.

In early 1956, the Planning Commission appointed a committee, known as the committee on plan projects. This committee studied the individual schemes of the Government of India and suggested methods for improvement of these programmes.

The concept of Panchayati Raj for decentralised administration was put forward by Balwantray Mehta Committee in 1957. Which studied community development projects. Panchayati Raj as a part of the community development Programme took its shape in 1959. It was the brainchild of late Prime Minister Pandit Jawaharlal Nehru. It has decentralised the political and economic institutions in a three-tier structure, i.e., the local governing bodies at the village level, the Panchayats and the district Boards at district level. But in course of time the importance of these local bodies was lost due to the Panchayat elections which led the idle minds of village people to nasty political activities and corrupt practices.

The Panchayati Raj programme were again stimulated during the administration of Prime Minister Rajiv Gandhi. At present in most of the states the elected bodies of Panchayat Samities are functioning to meet the various socio-economic needs and problems of the rural people.

In order to accelerate rural development and uplift the rural poor importance was laid on the C.D. programme for increasing production and productivity in the agricultural and allied sectors. Food was given top priority in the year 1951 and it was a year of peak food imports. The country was being drained of a large volume of valuable resources which could have been utilised for other useful purposes. The following activities with top priority on food were included in the C.D. Programme in the year 1952 : (1) High yielding varieties (ii) Fertilizers and manures (iii) Irrigation (iv) agricultural implements (v) milch and draught cattle (vi) Other farming operations which included reclamation of *usar* and acidic soils, cultivation of vegetables, and plantation of orchards (vii) Small scale industries and (viii) Subsidiary occupations[6].

From time to time in the rural development programmes that were pursued by the State and Central Government agricultural and artisan sectors were encouraged. At the same time, importance was also laid on village planning, education, functional literacy, public health and sanitation, road and communication facilities, and on such other activities which are meant for the uplift of the rural population, especially the rural poor.

While CDP attempted to promote uniform rural development over the whole country without consideration for the peculiar problems of any region, the Identified Area Development Programme (IADP) suggested concentration in the selected neglected districts of the country for overall development. During the fourth five year plan the green revolution was the slogan of rural development and under 'Garibi Hatao' programmes the rural poor were given special consideration. The green revolution was introduced with technological changes using the HYV seeds, fertilizers and mechanisation in irrigation.

Programmes like Food for work culminated in National Rural employment Programme (NREP) for the generation of primary employment and supplementary employment for the unemployment and the underemployed, followed by Rural Landless Employment Guarantee Programme (RLEGP) with accent on development of landless labourers. For small farmers development agency were initiated. Minimum Needs Programme (MNP) was introduced in the fifth five year plan.

Programmes like Hill Area Development were designed to remove hostile environment factors regarding development of such areas. In Drought Prone Area Programme (DPAP) and Desert Development Programme (DDP), emphasis was laid, among other things, on water and moisture conservation.

Several land reform legislations were enacted in respect of tenancy, distribution of ceiling surplus land, consolidation of land-holdings and abolition of intermediary tenure. Effective implementation of land reforms through regular monitoring is ensured[7].

The integrated Rural Development Programme (IRDP) was launched in 1978-79. A multiplicity of agencies for the uplift of rural poor was replaced by one single Integrated Programme (IRDP) which became operative throughout the country[8]. The IRDP is specially designed as a poverty alleviation programme for the rural poor. This programme is carried out through the District Rural Development Agency (DRDA).

In the sixth plan period the Programme Evaluation Organisation of the Planning Commission found some deficiencies in the final implementation of the IRDP. Following this, in the seventh plan high priority was given to direct rural employment programmes.

Indira Awaas Yojana was added as an important component of rural employment programme. All wage - employment programmes have been merged into Jawahar Rozagar Yojana (JRY). The setting up of Technological Mission for Drinking Water and Related Water Management in 1985 gave a new thrust to rural water supply programme.

All the above rural development programmes aimed to remove rural poverty and poverty in general and to generate employment opportunities and thereby for the creation of additional income. The fundamental objective of Rural Development implies the enrichment of the economic base so as to ameliorate the standard of living of the rural population.[9]

Thus, the basic problem of rural development in India is rural poverty. The anti-poverty programmes have to be area and community specific, in order that their benefits may be wide spread. They have to off-set the uneven effects of economic progress on the poor in different areas. During 1977-78, it was estimated that nearly 51.2% of the total rural population was below the poverty line and the same has come down to 40% by 1984-85.[10] Poverty is essentially a macro-problem and its eradication needs both macro as well as micro-level treatment with greater emphasis on the latter. The problem of rural poverty is stupendous, complex and wide-spread having economic and political ramifications. In Orissa about 66% of the population still remained below the poverty line by the year 1977-78[11].

Rural poverty can be alleviated by injecting credit and capital to the target people e.g., the landless labourers, marginal farmers, rural artisans, small entrepreneurs, small traders and professionally self-employed workers and such others. It is to be performed by the financial institutions like co-operatives, commercial banks and regional rural banks and Government. On the other hand, the non-institutional sources providing credit in the rural sector are the village money - lenders, relatives etc.

Before independence, there was an undeveloped and uncoordinated credit structure which was prevailing in India. The unscrupulous village money lenders and the landlords were playing a pivotal role in the flow of finance to agriculture and the rural sector of the economy. The wealthy people in the villages were exploiting the poor farmers and artisans by extracting high interest rates. Thus wealth got concentrated in the hands of a few people while the majority groups of rural poor lived a precarious life.

Efforts to build up institutional financing for agricultural sector started with the passage of the co-operative credit societies Act in 1904 which aimed at freeing agriculturists from the grip of money lenders and enabling them to secure production credit to the extent required by them at relatively cheap rates of interest.

The Co-operative Societies Act of 1912 brought into existence a federal cooperative structure with higher level financing institutions to provide guardianship and financial and technical support to the village level organisation so as to enable them to meet the credit requirements of millions of scattered farmers and artisans.

During the great depression of 1929-33, the co-operative movement received a rude shock. Agricultural prices fell sharply and the cultivators, hard pressed by the heavy burden of debt, showed practically no interest in the co-operative movement.

In 1937, the newly established Agricultural Credit Department of the Reserve Bank of India stressed the importance of multi-purpose co-operative societies. During the second World War the co-operative movement gained considerable momentum due to the rise in the prices of agricultural products.

After independence the co-operative movement came to be considered as the kingpin of development planning. But a review of its working by the All India Rural Credit Survey Committee (1954) appointed by RBI reveals that the co-operative and the Government lending to the agricultural sector accounted for only three percent of the total agricultural credit and the share of commercial banks was less than one percent.[12] The Governments - both States and Central played in this respect only a marginal role. This committee recommended co-operative credit societies as the most appropriate agency for supply of credit to the rural sector. The Central Government and the RBI made special efforts to strengthen the co-operatives.

The cooperative credit structure consists of two wings i.e., short-term and long-term credit wings. The short-term wing is federal in character, based on three-tier pattern with the apex bank at the state level, Central co-operative banks at the district level and co-operative credit societies at the village level.

The long term credit structure is either unitary or federal in character with State Land Development Banks (SLD Banks) as the apex institution at the state level and Primary Land Development Banks (PLD Banks) or branches of SLDBs at the taluk/block level.

The field level co-operative institutions which provide credit to individual borrowers consist of (i) primary agricultural credit societies providing both short-term and medium-term credit to their members and (ii) PLDBs or branches of SLDBs dispensing long-term credit to their members. At the grass root level, Large sized multi-purpose societies (LAMPS) and Farmer's Service Societies (FSS) have been set up to provide the package of services required. These are base-level institutions like the primary co-operative agricultural credit was not much satisfactory and the major weakness of the co-operative credit structure are summarised [13] These are given below :

(i) Almost 10-15 percent of the PACS are dormant.

(ii) Credit co-operatives, at each stage of the three-tier, have demonstrated marked having dependence on external sources of finance, among which the more important are borrowings. As on 30th June 1985, the proportion of borrowings to the total working capital of the co-operative undertaking was 16.3

percent in case of State Co-operative Banks 29.1 per cent in case of Central Co.op. Banks and as high as 70.6 percent in case of PACs. Further, a sizable proportion of even the share capital of the co-operative comes from the Government. Thus, in case of resources, co-operatives are heavily dependent on the Government and other refinancing agencies. The aforesaid are all India averages, the position is still worse in a majority of the States.

(iii) Because of their strong socio-economic position and their stranglehold over the rural economy, large landowners have managed to corner a very sizable proportion of the loans disbursed by the co-operative credit institutions. For instance, in 1982 small and marginal farmers, i.e., farmers having holdings of less than five acres, received only 31.2 percent of the total loans advanced by the PACS while owners of holding measuring more than five acres received 65.4 percent. The share of agricultural labourers, rural artisans etc., has always been negligible. Thus, the benefits of co-operative credit have not been adequately passed on to the weaker sections of the rural society. Prior to the establishment of Regional Rural Banks, the rural poor continued to depend on the non-institutional sources of credit.

(iv) It has been observed that adequate control over the end use of the credit has not been exercised. Quite often than not, the proceeds of the loans are used for unproductive purposes.

(v) There are considerable regional disparities in the amounts of loans disbursed by co-operatives. In 1982-83, the States of Andhra Pradesh, Gujarat, Haryana, Kerala, Madhya Pradesh, Maharastra, Punjab and Rajasthan together accounted for about 80 percent of the total credit disbursed by the co-operative societies in the country as a whole.

(vi) The PACs have suffered from incompetent, ignorant and non-performing managements. Most of the PACs are weak both financially and managerially and suffer from inadequate business, heavy overdues and faulty and inefficient managements. As at the end of June 1985, in the case of PACs, the overdues constituted as high as 40.9 percent of the loans outstanding. In the matter of central co-operatives one-third of the loans outstanding were overdues. Heavy incidence of overdues has led to the cessation of the process of credit recycling thus crippling these institutions of their capacity to grant loans.

(vii) Some of the co-operative credit institutions in the States like Gujarat, Maharastra and Punjab have faced the problem of ungainful utilisation of founds. In the absence of adequate avenues for deployment of resources within their territorial jurisdictions, they are forced to keep their surplus resources in the form of deposits with commercial banks. This situation, paradoxically, prevails side by side with the co-operative banks in other states which are hard-pressed for want of adequate resources for meeting their legitimate requirements; and,

(viii) The co-operatives in this country have been receiving Government support and patronage from the very beginning. However, following the recommendation of the All India Rural Credit Survey, the co-operatives have been given since mid fifties large-scale financial support in various forms by the Government in the name of state partnership. This means, in practical terms, the ruling party's and the government bureaucrats' control over the co-operatives. This development has led to the following consequences.

(i) Politicisation of the movement.
(ii) Officialisation of the management.
(iii) Lack of accountability, and
(iv) End of democratic control.

However, after the advent of new technology, the credit needs of agricultural sector increased beyond the capacity of co-operatives. Thereafter, commercial banks were inducted into the field of agriculture in particular and in the rural sector in general. This was done following the policy of 'Social Control' over banks which was adopted in 1967. The process was further intensified with the nationalisation of 14 major commercial banks in 1969.

The main objectives of nationalisation of the banks were :

(a) Widening the branch network of banks particularly in the rural and semi-urban areas.

(b) Greater mobilisation of savings through bank deposits.

(c) Re-orientation of credit flows so as to benefit the hitherto neglected sectors such as agriculture, small-scale industries and small borrowers.

Therefore, bank nationalisation resulted in the wider availability of banking facilities and brought about a change in the lending pattern by directing increasing volume of credit flow to the desired sectors and making the banks and effective instrument of economic development.

With a view to achieving the objectives of social control and nationalisation several steps have been taken since 1969. These are as follows :

(1) Under successive branch licensing policies banks were required to open offices in rural and semi-urban areas with a view to increase the coverage of branch network outside metropolitan and urban areas.

(2) Banks were required to lend a certain proportion of the net bank credit to the priority sectors which included agriculture, small-scale industries and small business. Under the over-all target, sub targets were fixed for credit to specific sectors such as agriculture and for weaker sections of the society.

(3) With a view to ensure deposit mobilisation in rural and semi urban areas RBI has taken steps to ensure that the rural areas maintain a credit deposit ratio of 60 percent[14].

(4) Specific targets were also laid down for bank participation in poverty alleviation programmes such as IRDP.

(5) In determining the lending rate structure of banks, an element of cross subsidisation was built into it. While large borrowers

paid higher rates of interest, certain other sectors of the economy paid lower rates of interest.

(6) With a view to meet more effectively the credit needs of the weaker sections in the rural areas, Regional Rural Banks as separate institutions were set up in the mid seventies.

(7) Formulation of district Credit plans and annual action plans through the Lead Banks of the district have been initiated so as to ensure that credit made available by banks was dovetailed with development plans.

(8) To prevent large borrowers from pre-empting credit from the banking system, the Credit Authorisation Scheme was introduced.

(9) Every bank was asked to formulate a credit plan for the bank as a whole each year so that the objectives of overall monetary and credit policy could be achieved.

(10) The branches of the banks were allotted with a service area and they are liable to meet the credit requirements of the area and for its economic development. They are to make economic surveys and to estimate the credit needs of their command areas.

The service area approach is expected to contribute to an orderly and planned development of credit in the target area and help intensify supervision of credit use, recovery of loans and harmonising the efforts of banks in providing credit for rural development activities with those of other development agencies.[15]

Since the time of social control of commercial banks and subsequent nationalisation of major commercial banks in 1969, there has been a significant transformation in the role of banks in accelerating rural development by providing credit and also other extension services through their wide net-work of branches, the banking system has an important role to play in pumping the external capital funds into the capital scarce rural areas.

In the modern economy "Banks are to be considered not merely as dealers in money, but more realistically the leaders in development. Similarly, banks are not just the store houses of the country's wealth but are the reservoirs of resources necessary for economic development."[16]

The number of banking offices in India in 1935 was 946, of which 160 branches were of the imperial Bank, the remaining being accounted for by other banks. This gave roughly one bank office for every three lakhs of population.[17] When the commercial banks were nationalised in June 1969, there were 8,262 bank offices. The number of bank offices rose to 57,197 in June 1989, with the share of rural branches rising from 1,860 (or 22.5 percent of the total) to 32,577 (57.0 percent of the total)[18] The average population served by bank offices was three lakhs in 1935. 5,000 in 1969 and 12,000 in the year 1988 (September)[19]. By the time of nationalisation, the number of Bank branches (As on 30.12.69) were 14 in Ganjam district with Rs. 3.48 crores of deposit and Rs. 0.63 crores of advances. The credit deposit ratio was 18.10%. On the other hand, as on 31.03.90, there were 247 branches of 17 scheduled commercial Banks, 75 branches of RGB, 32 branches of Co-operative Banks with total deposit of the Banks of the district at Rs. 218.94 crores and total advances of Rs. 171.06 crores. The credit deposit ratio as on the said period was 71.13% and advances to priority sector constituted 78.16% of the total Bank advances of the district[20].

Banking has to play the role of an effective catalyst agent of socio-economic change in the country. Equality and social justice, inter alia constitute the guiding principle of our five year plans and these are sought to be promoted through increased emphasis on rural development and extending assistance to the weaker sections of the society. Banks are contributing their mite to agricultural and rural development by extending support to (i) 20 point programme (ii) Integrated Rural Development Programmes (IRDP) and Self Employment Scheme for Educated Unemployed Youth (SESEUY). During 6th plan 16.6 million families have been provided financial assistance by the banks to the tune of Rs. 3,102 crores under IRDP.[21]

The post nationalisation era witnessed phenomenal growth in banking in quantitative and qualitative terms and as well as their spatial expansion into almost every nook and corner of the country with a special bias for the rural and backward regions, and persons with small means and economically and socially backward. Systematic efforts were made to bring about a change in lending pattern of banks. Certain activities like agriculture, small scale industries, small business etc., were brought under the priority category.

The concept of priority sector lending was evolved to ensure that the assistance from the banking system flowed in an increasing measure to the vital sectors of the economy and according to national priorities. This concept has been reviewed by the Government of India and Reserve Bank of India from time to time and Banks have been directed to channelise their lending accordingly.[22]

Since 1972, banks have asked to extend at least one percent of net bank credit under differential rate of Interest Scheme (DRI) advances to the weaker sections of the society at a concessional rate of interest of four percent per annum. Thus the rural branches of the banks being the agents of rural development are mainly engaged in implementation of agricultural and poverty alleviation programmes and extending credit to the doorsteps of needy beneficiaries at a concessional rate.

There is a phenomenal growth in bank branches since 1969 which facilitated the banks efforts to mobilise deposits and bring these rural deposits into the organised banking system. The basic aim of expansion of banking facilities to unbanked and undeveloped rural areas is to reduce the glaring disparities in the matter of bank offices and to make available credit to the identified priority sector borrowers and other weaker sections of the society.

In the Ganjam district of Orissa, the banking sector in rural area comprises the public sector and private sector banks. Co-operative Banks, Co-operative Land Development Banks and Regional Rural Banks. The State Financial Corporation has also a role in the financing of the large-scale non-target group and for the economic development of the residents of the district.

The public sector commercial banks were expected to co-ordinate and supplement the effort of the co-operative credit structures. But, it is observed from experience that the entry of commercial banks in the field of agricultural and rural finance did not make any dent on the problem due to their unsuitable organisational set up with reference to the rural areas of the country. The high paid bank staff neither like to stay in the rural areas nor did they show their involvement in village life and to improve the economic life of the villagers through their profession.

The commercial banks in the rural sector, instead of providing more credit to the agricultural sector, supplementing the co-operatives, mobilised substantial savings, specially from the wealthier population of the rural areas and channelised them into urban areas and metropolis for profitable investment. The Lead Bank scheme was introduced to bring about a proper co-ordination between co-operatives and commercial banks and to correct the lapses of commercial banks in the field of rural finance. But, inspite of all these, measures, it was noticed that the banking activities of commercial banks were lopsided and haphazard. The disbursement of credit by the commercial banks was high in some parts and low in other parts of the country. Besides, people having larger securities and greater influence in rura! areas received better facilities and benefits from the commercial bank branches of the rural areas. The needy and poor masses could not get the benefit of rural commercial banks.

After about five years of bank nationalisation. It was felt that the commercial banks failed to play the role of an agent of rural development and in getting a structural change in the economy of rural India and the methods of operation of Commercial Banks could not be changed to the desired extent.

The need for evolving a hybrid type of credit agency which combines the resource orientation of the commercial banks and the rural orientation of the co-operatives has been expressed in the reports of some of the committees, which have looked into the problems of rural credit.

The Government of India appointed in 1975 a Working Group under the Chairmanship of Sri M. Narasimham which recommended the setting up of state sponsored, regionally - based and rural oriented banks called Regional Rural Banks (RRBs). They were meant to combine the local feel and familiarity with several problems which the co-operatives possess and the degree of business organisation ability to mobilise deposit, access to central money markets and a modernised outlook which commercial bank have.[23]

The creation of Regional Rural Banks in our country in 1975 as an institution of rural credit has come to be regarded as a major innovation in the field that would have far-reaching effects on the extension of banking facilities to the rural areas. It is devised as a potentially powerful policy instrument for achieving rural development mainly through the development of rural poor.

Objectives of RRBs

Under the RRB Act, 1976, regional rural banks were to be set up mainly with a view to develop the rural economy by providing resources for the purpose of development of agriculture, trade, commerce, industry and other productive activities in the rural areas, credit and other facilities, particularly to the small and marginal farmers, agricultural labourers, artisans and small entrepreneur, and for matters connected therewith and incidental thereto.[24] "The RRBs by design and operation score over the commercial banks for further extension of banking facilities to the rural areas in view of their comparatively lower cost structure, a greater degree of rural orientation due to locally recruited staff, simpler forms and procedures for advancing loans, a higher credit deposit ratio and most important a clearly defined task of meeting all the credit requirements of only the specified weaker sections of the rural society both for agricultural and allied purposes and for non-agricultural (including manufacturing and trading) as well as for consumption purpose. On this last-mentioned ground, the RRBs definitely score over the co-operative institutions of rural credit including those operating at the grass-root level".[25]

The Union Government promulgated the RRBs ordinance on 26th September 1975, while the first ever plan for establishment of 'Rural Banks' was put forward by Bangal National Chamber of commerce.[26] The chamber had suggested that such banks should be sponsored by scheduled banks of five year standing which should subscribe 50% of the capital of each rural Bank. However, nothing substantial was done to implement the idea.[27]

The sponsor banks' role and responsibility in the development of RRBs have not been spelt out. But, in general, they are expected to :

(a) subscribe to its share capital as specified in the act of RRB.

(b) to recruit and train the personnel of the RRB during its initial period, the RRB may also ask the sponsor bank to send its officers and other staff on deputation for specified periods.

(c) to provide managerial and financial assistance as mutually agreed upon ; and

(d) to provide general counselling and support to their RRBs and oversee their activities so that they are in a position to achieve their corporate objectives.

The RRBs which are basically scheduled commercial banks, are different from the existing commercial banks in the following points:

(a) their area of operation is limited to a specified area comprising one or more districts in a state.

(b) the beneficiaries of their loans and advances have been pre-determined.

(c) their lending rates will not be higher than the prevailing lending rates of co-operative societies in the concerned state.

(d) the salary structure of employees in the RRB is prescribed by the Union Government and it is equal to the salary structure State Government employees of the concerned state as per section 17(1) of the RRB Act of 1976. But at present the salaries of the RRB employees have been made equal with other nationalised Banks and the RRBs are no more a lower cost Banking Organisation. This change in the salary structure has disturbed the basic objective of RRB as a lower cost banking organisation and the same has happened due to the nation-wide demand of the RRB employees.

The RRBs resources come from the share capital. Subscribed by the State Government, Central Government and from the sponsor bank, secondly from the deposits, thirdly from the borrowing and the finances from NABARD and sponsor bank.

The Dantwala Committee in the year 1977 reviewed the affairs of RRBs in its structural and functional aspects. The committee recommended that RRBs should from an integral part of the rural credit structure. It recommended that while establishing new RRBs, priority be given to areas served by weak Central Co-operative Banks. Further the committee suggested that the RBI, instead of the Union Government, should be the share-holder and local participation should be provided both in the share capital as well as in the management.

The Dantwala Committee has recommended that with a view to avoid wasteful competition in servicing the rural poor, eligible rural business of commercial banks may be transferred to RRBs in a phased manner.[28]

The Working Group on Multi-agency Approach to agricultural finance under the chairmanship of C.E. Kamath has made some relevant observations on the role of regional rural banks. It noted the existence of RRBs as a part of the multi-agency approach to finance agriculture which has now become an accepted fact. The Kamath Group has called the setting of Regional Rural Banks as a 'recent development of significance in the rural credit field.' According to it, the role of the RRB is to 'supplement and not to 'supplant the other institutional agencies in the field.[29]

The RRBs being the district-level organisations, can be trusted to take banking closer to the rural house-holds and ensure more effective supervision over the end-use of credit.

RRBs like any business organisation must earn profit for survival and success. The viability of RRBs was in doubt much before their establishment. A number of RRBs have shown poor financial viability in their operation even after several years of their existence "The number of loss making RRBs rose substantially from 100 in 1983 to 154 in 1985. Which constituted 82 percent of the total RRBs."[30] "The accumulated losses of RRBs increased from Rs. 9.8 crores in 1982 to Rs. 31.7 crores in 1984 and as high as Rs. 126.3 crores in December 1987. Of the total 196 RRBs as many as 124 (63 percent) have eroded their share capital and reserves. A state-wise analysis of such banks shows that Uttar Pradesh has a maximum of 24 such banks followed by Madhya Pradesh with 20, Bihar and Rajastan 12 each, Andhra Pradesh Karnataka 10 each, Orissa 8, West Bengal 6 and Gujarat 5."[31] In Orissa of 9 RRBs, 6 incurred losses during the year 1983 and by March 1990, their condition did not improve. The losses of RRBs in Orissa was 68.80 lakhs during 1983 and had risen up to Rs. 886.17 lakhs in the year 1989-90. By March 1990, the accumulated losses of RRBs of Orissa was Rs. 2784.59 lakhs.[32] Huge losses of most of the RRBs are being viewed with concern as these have raised doubts about the viability of maintaining such network of rural banks.

The costs of rural banking are high. Due to low levels of rural savings, deposits per branch are usually inadequate and lending takes some time to develop. The ratio of bank accounts and transactions to the volume of funds is normally very high and raises the costs. The rural lending is risk-prone. The bankers must constantly endeavor to improve the efficiency of their operations; costs can be reduced only over a period of time with the development of business.[33]

No doubt the RRBs are incurring losses but the monetary losses of RRBs may be disregarded for a while keeping in view the socio-economic benefits received from the RRBs as an agent of rural development in respect of the target groups. In the process of rural development role played by the RRBs is quite significant. It is necessary to develop the RRBs into dynamic and progressive institutions for the economic development of the rural sector and to provide leadership in co-ordination with co-operatives and various other district level agencies engaged in the common task. The Kelkar Committee in 1986, the Agrawala Committee in 1987 and the RRB bill passed in December 1987 have led to amendments for the benefit of the employees and the RRBs are functioning for achieving the socio-economic objectives.

There is a phenomenal growth of RRBs in branch expansion since 1975. By the end of March 1990, 29 banks sponsored 196 RRBs covering 372 districts of the country through their 14443 branches. The total deposits of the RRBs in India by the said period was Rs. 415051.79 lakhs and advances made was Rs. 355403.72 lakhs and the credit deposit ratio was 86 percent. In Orissa there were 9 RRBs with 819 branches covering all the districts of the state and the total deposit was Rs. 15031.47 lakhs in 1459148 accounts and similarly the RRBs have outstanding credit for Rs. 22590.93 lakhs in 1153016 accounts. The credit deposit ratio was 150 by the end of March 1990.[34]

The RBI is the licensing authority of RRBs for their branch expansion. In the matter of identifying the district for the establishment of new RRBs on the basis of proposals, the steering committee on RRBs takes into account various factors such as (a) the branch gap i.e., the number of additional offices as per the RBI's branch licensing policy (b) the percentage of small and marginal farmers, holdings to total holdings, (c) the percentage of scheduled castes/scheduled tribes and also tribal population to total population (d) the percentage of agricultural labourers in district districts, etc. Besides, the prospective viability of the RRB taking into account the credit gap in the area is also an important consideration for recommending any new proposal. The performance of demand collection and Balance (DCB) in the district is also taken into account as reflected in the audit classification of D.C.B. its overdues position. Short-term loans per hectare sanctioned etc. In otherwards, areas/districts where a new RRB can·become a viable proposition, generally weighs with the committee in identifying districts for the establishment of new RRBs.[35]

The steering committee is headed by the Chairman of NABARD. Chairman of Public Sector Banks, top officials of Ministry of Finance and the Chairman are also represented in the committee. The actual implementation of the recommendations of the steering committee is done by the NABARD in consultation with the Government of India.[36]

The NABARD is the main source of refinance to the RRBs. Thus the credit planning of RRBs is generally a joint exercise of the Government of India, Government of the States, RBI, NABARD, sponsor Bank and concerned RRB.

The sponsor bank, which is invariably the lead bank of the district has a deep involvement not only in the overall management but also in the financial control of the RRB (sponsored by the concerned scheduled commercial Bank).

The institution of RRB is therefore a socio-economic movement, and as concluded by Dantwala Committee "this institutional innovation" is designed to "strengthen the internal credit structure". Further, "such an institution is needed to make good some of the inadequacies in the existing rural credit system and the RRBs should become an integral part of the rural credit structure.[37]

By December 1991, there were 75 branches of RGB functioning in different blocks of the district. Annexure I of the thesis presents the branch list of RGB. The RGB in Ganjam district has no branch in Dharakote and Nuagada blocks. As such out of 29 blocks, the RGB has now covered only 27 blocks of the district. [38]

The Table 1.1 indicates the grip of RGB over the area of operation in terms of branch expansion and increasing trend of business over the decade. From the table it is seen that in the year 1981, it had 7 branches with 30 adopted villages and per branch deposit and advance was Rs. 565,000 and Rs. 161,000 respectively. In the year 1990-91 the number of branches increased to 75, the total number of adopted villages to 1817 and deposits and advances increased to 2011,000 and Rs. 2212,000 respectively. Similarly the businesses of 1981 was for Rs. 726,000, which has increased to Rs. 4223,000 by the year 1990-91. This shows the increasing rate of RGB in the Ganjam district. However the details of the performance of RGB and its role in the rural economics will be studied in-depth in the latter part of the thesis.

TABLE - 1.1

The Rushikulya Gramya Bank (RGB) from 1981 to 1991

(Amounts in Thousands of Rupees)

Year	*No. of Branches of RGB*	*No. of Village adopted*	*Deposit per Branch*	*Adv. Per Branch*	*Business Per Branch*
1	2	3	4	5	6
1981	7	30	565	161	726
1982	25	250	369	374	744
1983	36	342	401	540	941
1984	52	482	403	620	1023

(Contd.)

Table 1.1 (Contd.)

1	2	3	4	5	6
1985	68	702	456	638	1094
1986	68	702	662	865	1527
1987	69	709	978	1165	2143
1988-89	75	1833	1149	1560	2709
1989-90	75	1817	1622	1925	3547
1990-91	75	1817	2011	2212	4223

Source : Annual reports of RGB - 1990-91

Importance of The Study

The importance of the study is to pinpoint the difficulties in the working of this institution in Ganjam district as well as to examine its performance, achievements and handicaps, while contributing towards the uplift of the rural poor in the district in terms of generating income output and employment.

Ganjam is not a backward district in Orissa but in certain parts of the district development is not very much in evidence. Illiteracy and ignorance still prevail in the district, specially in case of the target group people. RGB being an agent to help the target group is to be judged on the basis of macrolevel and microlevel study of the performances of the bank in the district.

The performances of RGB will also be judged by making comparisons with the other financial institutions. Which also participate in lending to the rural sector of the district.

The Scope and Objective of the Study

The present study constitutes an attempt at a critical evaluation of the role of Rushikulya Gramya Bank as a source of Rural Credit in Ganjam district. As such, it would study in-depth the organisation and working of the bank in the context of mobilisation and disbursement of credit to farmers, agricultural labourers, artisans and other sections of rural population of the district.

The period covered under the study in 1981 to 1991. This is a sufficiently a long period during which definite trends are bound to emerge. Concrete benefits of its credit - oriented services will have crystalised by the end of the period. This reference period as such will permit comprehensive analysis of the working of the institution. However, in trying to give a correct perspective to some aspects of the study sometimes the temporal boundaries have been exceeded and data pertaining to years outside the reference period considered.

The main objective of the study is to assess the multidimensional role of the bank in the field of rural development in Ganjam district. This broad objective resolves itself to certain specific objectives which are given below.

(1) to examine the soundness of the organisation and management to effectively discharge the assigned task.

(2) to assess the role of the bank in the provision of credit to effectively implement rural development programmes in the district.

(3) to analyse the correctness of the procedures and practices followed by the bank for free flow of credit to the rural sector for income generation and employment creation and for fulfilments of such other avowed objectives.

(4) to recommend suitable remedies for its short comings, both functional and organisational.

(5) to evaluate the performance of RRBs in the district and to examine the viability of the same in the rural sector.

(6) to examine the nature and extent of loan overdues and the problems of recovery.

(7) to investigate the factors responsible for non-payment of loans.

(8) to study the role of RRB of the district in comparison to other financial institutions of the district.

(9) to provide credit to the villagers although they do not fulfil the criteria of creditworthiness as per commercial banking rules.

(10) to know the extent of credit utilisation by the beneficiaries and the impact of loans on their living standards.

(11) to find out the role of RRB credit in different sponsored poverty alleviation programmes.

(12) to find out the problems of RRB staff and their efficiency in administration and application of credit.

Hypotheses

The thesis will examine the following hypothesis :

(1) The credit needs for rural development cannot be effectively met without tailor-cut, specially designed banking institutions like the Regional Rural Bank.

(2) That it is not enough to provide credit on easy, convenient terms and at lower rates of interest to create sustained growth in the rural sector which would secure distributive justice, there is need for proper credit disbursement on a selective basis and also for monitoring of bank-financed activities and timely repayment of loans.

(3) That use of credit will be effective when provided as per planned assessment of requirements prepared in consonance with rural development programmes.

(4) That there is a need for proper co-ordination of the working of rural credit agencies for planned supply of credit to the rural sector.

These hypotheses will be tested by making a case study of the RGB in Ganjam district and to state its role in the field of rural credit in comparison with the commercial banks and co-operatives in the district.

The policies of the Government, the behavior of the borrowers in respect of the rural credit will be observed the present "service area approach" and the "credit reliefs" by the Government of the state puts enormous strains on financial institutions in the field of lending. The Regional Rural Banks being the institutions for rural credit and rural development can being remarkable positive changes in the rural sector, if the constraints in their functioning can be removed. As such the arguments of the thesis will be to find out the constraints on its functioning and to suggest remedial measures to the bank as well as to the Government, because credit is the key factor for rural development.

Methodology

The study will follow both the deductive and inductive methods in its process of research. The functioning of some of the RGB branches will be examined on a sampling basis in order to reach inductive conclusions so as to know about the functioning of the Rushikulya Gramya Bank in Ganjam district. Whereas the policies, statements, financial performances of RGB and the CDP etc. at the district level, state level and national level will be taken as premises so as to draw deductive conclusions in order to evaluate the functioning of Rushikulya Gramya Bank in Ganjam district. The deductive conclusions will be compared with the inductive conclusions. The comparison will enable us to state our findings, suggestions and conclusions.

This research work is in the nature of a case study of a RRB in Ganjam district. It is worth mentioning that the present work is the first ever full length research work on Rushikulya Gramya Bank. However two dissertations for M. Phil. degree were found on the RGB at Berhampur University.

The work will use the historical method to assess the working of other financial agencies in the past as also the role of this bank in rural development of the district since its inception. The functioning of some of the RGB branches will be examined on a sampling basis in order to reach inductive conclusions. In this respect the primary data and beneficiaries by personal interviews in the form of questionnaire method.

There is a wide use of the secondary data collected from the RGB head office, branches and from the lead Bank. The District credit plans from 1981 to 1991 were used as a main source of secondary data. In addition to that the statistics from NABARD. District level organisations, Bureau of Statistics, previous writings, Government policies, reports and returns from official sources and published books in this line are to be used as the sources of secondary data.

There are some works undertaken on the Regional Rural Bank elsewhere. Some of them were referred to by the scholar as the available literature for the study. The Rural Banks for Rural Development by Charan D Wadva, Rural Banking in India by M.L. Verma, Handbook on personnel management and industrial Relations for Rural Banks by Anil K. Khandewal, Financial performance of Regional Rural Banks by M.R. Vyas, are some of the specific works in the field. On the other hand there are a number of books found on agricultural and rural development, which were used for reference. There are articles found in the periodicals of IBA Bulletin, RBI Bulletin, Kurukshetra, Yojana, etc. on Rural Banks.

However, the present study is the first attempt of its kind in Ganjam district. Every region has peculiar characteristics. The Banks are so designed as to have the necessary adaptability to tackle the peculiar problems. The findings of the present study are bound to be different from the findings of similar works taken up elsewhere.

Limitations of the Study

The study broadly covers the period 1981 to 1991. It takes into account the performance of the RRB in the district and it is confined only to the rural poor consisting of small and marginal farmers, landless and agricultural labourers, rural artisans, small entrepreneurs, small businessmen, retail traders and professionally selfemployed persons, those who constitute the target groups of the weaker section. Specific case studies are made for answering the question of viability, and income generation of the beneficiaries of Jarado branch of Purusottampur block and Sikiri branch, and Samarjhola branch of the Hinjili block of Ganjam district.

The Plan of the Study

The first chapter states at the outset what the work constitutes. In this connection it traces the origin and genesis of rural development in India. The present concept of rural development has been elaborated and the steps for the promotion of such development are described. In this context the different rural development programmes like community development to IRDP, the social control of banks, the role played by co-operatives, and the establishment of RRBs for the benefit of target groups are highlighted. The importance of the study, scope and objectives, hypotheses, methodology, limitations and the plan of the study are explained.

In the second chapter, an attempt has been made to present the socio-economic features and the characteristics of the rural economy of the district.

The third chapter starts with a description of different credit agencies in Ganjam district and their role in rural credit in the district. There after the problems in estimating the credit and the methods used by the Lead Bank and the District Credit Plan are discussed. In this context the theoretical model and practical difficulties in estimating the credit are presented.

The fourth chapter analyses threadbare the coverage and lending operations of RGB and the techniques of the lending policies.

This chapter is broadly divided into three sections :

Section-A Lending in Agriculture

In this section the lending of RGB in agriculture and allied activities are discussed and the role played by RGB is to be judged by comparing the lendings of other financial agencies and by assessing the contribution of RGB in the District credit plan from 1981 to 1991.

Section-B Lending in Industries and Service Sector

This section will deal with the lending operations of RGB in the same way as discussed in section-A.

Section -C Lending in Government Sponsored Programmes and in the Priority Sector

This section specifically deals with the priority sector advances and lending under the different sponsored schemes particularly in RGB. Towards the end of the chapter the conclusion provides the findings and makes suggestions.

The fifth chapter spells out the capital structure and sources of capital of RGB. The different sources of capital of RGB are elaborated in this chapter. In this context it deals with share capital, deposit mobilisation, refinance and borrowings and the recovery for recycling for business. The profit and loss of business is to be analysed to find out the efficiency of the bank in business. The profit is a main source of capital for RGB to do business. This chapter also concludes with findings and suggestions.

The impact of RGB finance on income and employment generation is studied in Chapter six. This chapter deals with the constraints of RGB in general highlighted through particular case studies. In this chapter both the primary and secondary data are considered. Interview and Questionnaire method are followed in respect of a few branches of RGB in Ganjam district. At the end of this chapter the conclusion has been derived on the basis of the observations.

The seventh chapter being the last chapter of the thesis presents the overall summary of the work and conclusions with findings and suggestions.

References

1. Ojha, P.D. (Deputy Governor. R.B.I.), "Banking and Economic Development in India" *Reserve Bank of India Bulletin*, Vol. XLI, No. 1 January 1987, p. 14.

2. Desai, Vasant, "Committee Development, *A Study of Rural Economics*, Bombay, Himalaya Publishing House, January 1983, p. 595.

3. Thekkamalai, S.S., *Rural Development and Social Changes*, Sangeeta Printers, 1983, p. 21.

4. Desai, Vasant, *Op-cit*, p. 591.

5. Ghosh, Alok, *Indian Economy its Nature and Problem*, Calcutta, The World Press Private Limited, 1987 (Silver Jubilee Edition), p. 170.

6. Singh, V.B., (Doctoral Work-*Mimeograph*) : "A study on the Co-operative credit and its impact on C.D. Programmes in selected districts of U.P.", Allahabad University, 1976, p. 9.

7. India 1990, Edited by Research and Reference Division Ministry of Information and Broadcasting, New Delhi, Government of India, p. 447.

8. Ghosh. Alok, *Op. cit*, p. 170.

9. Panda, Prabhakar, "Rural Development - Some important aspects of the role of Banks." *Orissa Review*. November 1981, Govt. of Orissa Publication, Bubaneswar, p. 21.

10. Sethy, S. Basudev, "Some issues on Rural Developments", *The Journal of Indian Institute of Banks*, Vol. 59. No. 3, July - Sept, 1988, p. 80.

11. Bureou of Statistics, office records, Bubaneswar, Orissa, (enquiry).

12. Ojha, P.D., (Deputy Governor, RBI), "Agriculture Credi Institutions : India, their structure and role in development", *RBI Bulletin*, Vol. XL, No. 2, February, 1986, p. 150.

13. Lal, G.S (Edited), "Rural Finance : The Multi-Agency Approach", *The Journal of Banking Studies*, Vol. X, No. 3, July - September, 1987, p. 165.

14. Rangarajan. C, (Deputy Governor, R.B.I.), "Banking Development since 1947", *RBI Bulletin*, Vol. XLIII., No. 1, January, 1989, p. 21.

15. Ojha, P.D. (Deputy Governor, R.B.I) "Regional Development and the Role of Banks", *RBI Bulletin*, Vol. XLIII, No. January 1989, p. 30.

16. Syndicate Bank, "The Role of Banks in National life", Manipal. 1968, p. 4.

17. Rangarajan, C, *Op. Cit*, p. 19.

18. Annonymous, "Two Decades of Bank Nationalisation : Report on trend and progress of Banking in India", *RBI Bulletin (Supplement)*, July - June, 1988 - 89, p. 7.

19. Regional Office, Andhra Bank, Berhampur, Ganjam (Enquiry).

20. Panigrahy, Nalinikanta (Lead District Manager - Andhra Bank), "Post Nationalisation of Banking Scenarios", *Ganjam - 90* Smaranika of Industrial exhibition, May 1990, Berhampur.

21. Ojha, P.D, (Deputy Governor, RBI), "Banking and Economic Development in

India : Problems and prospects", *RBI Bulletin*, Vol. XLI, No. 1, January, 1987, p.16.

22. Ibid. p. 16.

23. "Report of the committee to review arrangements for institutional credit for agriculture and Rural Development" CRAFICARD, RBI Publication, p. 106.

24. Lal. G.S., (Edited), "The Rural Finance - The Multi-Agency Approach" *The Journal of Banking studies*, Vol. X, No. 3, July - Sept., 1987, p. 175.

25. Wadva, Charan. D, "Overall assessment of the working of RRBs in India", *Rural Banks for Rural Development - An Analysis of Working of Regional Rural Banks in India with two case studies*, Bombay, Delhi, Madras, Calcutta, The Macmillan Company of India Limited 1980, p. 164.

26. Rural Banking Enquiry Committee, p. 71.

27. Khandelwal, Anil K, *Hand Book on Personal Management and Industrial Relation for Rural Banks*, Jaipore (Rajasthan) Rawat Publications, 1987, p. 3.

28. Patel A.R., "Flow of Credit Rural Credit", *Rural Economy in India*, (Edited by N.L. Murty and K. V. Narayana), Delhi, Mital Publications, 1989, p. 195.

29. Wadva, Charan D, *Op. cit*, p. 206.

30. Abdul, Noorbasa and M. Jyoti, "Viability of Regional Rural Banks - case study, *Yojana*, Vol. 33, No. 9, May (16 to 31), 1989, p. 18.

31. Jethwaney, Sonika, "Regional Rural Banks - a review", *Indian Banks Association Bulletin*, Vol. X, No. 12, December 1988, p. 246.

32. RRB Statistics, 1989 - 90, Bombay, NABARD.

33. Malhotra, R. N, (Governor - RBI), "The Role of Banking in Rural Development", *RBI Bulletin*, Vol. XL, No. 9, Sept. 1986, p. 561.

34. RRB Statistics 1989-90, Bombay NABARD.

35. Government of India : Report of Working Group on Rural Banks, 1986, p. 34.

36. Khandewal, Anil K., *Op. cit*, p. 7.

37. Vyas M.R., "Credit Deployment", *Financial Performance of Regional Rural Banks*, Jaipore (Rajastan) Arihant Publishers, 1991, p. 13.

38. RGB, Head Office source as on 31.12.91 (Enquiry)

2

The Rural Economic Scene of Ganjam District of Orissa

Any study of the role of a financial institution in the economic development of an area should be done with reference to the economic condition of the said area by analysing various features, such as, the demographic characteristics, physical features, climatic conditions, resource position, infrastructural facilities, rate of industrialisation, percapita income, etc. This chapter attempts to state the broad features of the rural economy of Ganjam district.

Scheme of rural development are intended mainly to reduce poverty and economic inequalities among the people. The banks play a major role in the promotion of rural development through provision of adequate, timely and cheap credit. Unless the concerned banks and planners of credit have the necessary information regarding the scope for development of various aspects of rural economy and their constraints, both institutional and socio-economic, in the process of exploitation of available resources, rural development cannot take place. With this end in view, in the following paragraphs an attempt is made to present the socio-economic profile of Ganjam district in Orissa.

Till 1936, Ganjam district was under the Madras presidency. When the province of Orissa was created on 1.4.1936, Ganjam became one of the six districts.[1] The name Ganjam is derived from the Persian words "Ganj-i-am", which means Granary of the world.[2] The district is rich in agricultural resources.[3]

Ganjam district is the third largest district of the state. It lies between 18° 46' North and 20° 17' North Latitudes and between 83° 48' East and 85° 11' East longitudes.[4] It lies in the southern most part of the state and is bounded in the north by the districts of Phulbani and Puri, in the east by the Bay of Bengal and Puri district, in the south by the Srikakulam district of Andhra Pradesh and on the western side by Koraput and Phulbani districts. The district head-quarters is at Chatrapur, which is 140 Kms away from the state capital Bhubaneswar.

Administrative Set-Up

The district is divided into four sub-divisions, namely (1) Chatrapur (2) Berhampur (3) Bhanjanagar (4) Paralakhemundi.[5] Out of the 75 branches of RGB are found in Paralakhemundi Sub-division (at present known as Gajapati district). The Ganjam district is subdivided into 14 Tahasils, 29 blocks and 466 Grama Panchayats.[6]

Each Sub-division is administered by a Sub-divisional Officer, each Tahasil by a Tahsildar and each block by a block development officer. There are 18 Notified Area Councils and two Municipalities in the district by 31.3.92.[7]

Under Chatrapur Sub-division, the tahasils are (1) Chatrapur, (2) Kodala, (3) Purushottampur and (4) Khallikote. The tahasils of Berhampur Sub-division are (1) Berhampur, (2) Konisi, (3) Chikiti (4) Digapahandi. In Bhanjanagar sub-division, the tahsils are (1) Bhanjanagar, (2) Buguda, (3) Aska and (4) Surada. In the Parlakhemundi Sub-division (now called Gajapati District) the tahsils are (1) Paralakhemundi, and (2) R. Udayagiri. The eight blocks of Bhanjanagar Sub-division are (i) Bhanjanagar (ii) Bellaguntha (iii) Surada (iv) Sheragada (v) Dharakote. (vi) Buguda, (vii) Jaganathprasad, (viii) Aska. Similaraly the Chatrapur Sub-divisions has eight blocks (i) Chatrapur, (ii) Ganjam (iii) Kallikote (iv) Kodala (v) Polosora, (vi) Purusottampur, (vii) Kabisurya Nagar and (viii) Hinjilicut. The Berhampur Sub-division has six blocks i.e. (i) Rangeilunda, (ii) Kukudakhandi (iii) Digapahandi (iv) Sanakhemundi (v) Chikiti and (vi) Patrapur. In the same way, the Parlakhemundi Sub-division has seven blocks. They are (i) Paralakhemundi, (ii) Kasinagar, (iii) Gumma, (iv) Rayagada, (v) R. Udayagiri (vii) Nuagada, and (vii) Mohana. Thus the district with

29 blocks, 14 Tahasils and four Sub-divisions is being administered by a collector or District Magistrate.

Demography

"As per the 1981 census, the total population of the district is 26,69,899 (1991 Census, 31,40,477) which covers 10.13% of the total population of the state. The growth rate of population over 1971 census is 15.65%. In the entire district the percentage of urban population is 14% and that of rural population is 86%. 26,69,899 persons of the district live in an area of about 12531 sq. kilometers and as such the density of population comes to 213 persons per sq. km. This is comparatively higher than the state's density of 169 persons per sq. km. The sex ratio i.e., number of females per thousand males is 1031 which is much more than the state average of 981 females per thousand males. Thus the district has more number of females compared to males.

Out of the total population of 26,69,899 persons, scheduled caste and scheduled caste and scheduled tribe population constitute 4,01,116 and 2,53,034 persons respectively. Percentage wise the S.Cs constitute 15.02% and the S.Ts 9.48% of the total population.[8]

The trend of urbanisation in this district compared to the districts is remarkable with 20 nos of towns and the density of urban population is 3,79,996.[9]

Table 2.1 indicates the literacy position of Ganjam District.

TABLE - 2.1

The Literacy and General Education of the District (As per 1981 Census)

1.	Percentage of literacy in general	30.78
2.	Percentage in male literacy	45.15
3.	Percentage of female literacy	16.87
4.	Percentage of urban literacy	51.69
5.	Percentage of rural literacy	27.29
6.	Number of colleges (Affiliated to Berhampur University as upto 1986)	20.00
7.	No. of schools (1981-82) (High Schools, M.E. Schools & Primary Schools)	36.50

Source : Andhra Bank, Regional Office Ganjam, Berhampur (GM), (Enquiry).

At present, the Bhanja Swakhara Samiti of Ganjam district has taken up the literacy programme under the Chairmanship of the District Magistrate. The Samiti has set the target of total literacy for Ganjam district by 15th August 1992. It is claimed that this movement has increased the literacy rate in the district to a great extent but this claim appears to be exaggerated. The programme has very little impact on the poor of both the urban and the rural areas as they are more in need of food and work for their very existence.

The Occupational Pattern of the District and the Unemployment Position

As per 1981 census the total workforce was 9.277 lakhs which works out to 34.75% of the total population. Further break-up of workforce when compared with the total workforce consists of 42,14%, cultivators, 32.46% agricultural labour; 3.39% engaged in household industry and the remaining 22.02% belong to other categories.[10]

"The organised sector provides employment to 4.76% of the total workforce. There are about 61,552 educated unemployed as on 31st March 1992. Out of this, diploma holders constitute 810 persons. It is estimated that 1.40 lakhs were either underemployed or unemployed in the organised sector.[11]

Physical Features

Physically, the district may broadly be divided into two divisions:

(i) Coastal Plains in the east.

(ii) Hill and table land in the west.

In Ganjam district, the hills are very close to the sea. The coastal Plains in the east contain more fertile and irrigated land. Towards the centre and south, it is hilly with beautiful well-watered vallies. The south eastern portion is fertile. The extreme north-east is occupied by a portion of the famous Chilka lake. The Tableland of the west is a continuation of the good range of eastern ghat.

(a) Hills

The northern plateau which contains hills ranging in height from two thousand feet to 4.5 thousand feet to 4.5 thousand feet lies between the hill range of Balliguda in north and R. Udayagiri in the south. The southern Plateau lies between R. Udayagiri and Parlakhemundi Plains. These two plateaus are the home land of Kondhs and Saoras (ST). The southern plateau contains some of the highest hills, namely Singha Raja Parbat (4,534 feet) Mahendragiri (4,923 feet) and Debagiri (4534 feet)"[12]

(b) Rivers

The rivers of the districts are Rushikulya, Badanai, Mahendratanaya, Bansadhara, Bahuda, Hadabhangi, Ghodahada, Dhanei and Baghua. Rushikulya is the largest river which is about 160 kms long. It starts from Daringibadi in Ballguda Sub-division of Phulbani district. It is joined by Badnai at Aska and enters the sea at Ganjam. the Ghodahada is the main tributary of Rushikulya. These rivers mostly remain dry in summer but during the rainy season they cause occasional floods. In October 1990, due to the overflow of heavy rain water, the rivers of Ganjam district caused a serious flood, seriously disrupting the economy of the district. Aska, Hinjilcut, Purusottampur, Kodala and Ganjam blocks were greatly affected by the floods and the rural agricultural economy of these blocks was much damaged. The years old Aska bridge, other bridges and communication were destroyed and the marketing of rural and agricultural productions was seriously affected. The district has a coast line of 60 kms.

(c) Soil and Rocks

The district has alluvial soil in the eastern part, laterite soil in the west and small patches of black cotton soil at the centre. The geological formations in the district are alluvial, newer dolerites archun comprising igneus, bloom land, laterites, gondwanas, cadapab, metamorphic rocks of sedimentary origin.[13]

(d) Climate

The district is characterised by an equal temperature althrough the year, particularly in the coastal regions. The winter starts from

December and lingers till February. It is followed by Summer from March to May. The districts receives rain through the south west monsoon from June to September. The month of October and November constitute the post-monsoon transition period.

The table 2.2 presents the year-wise rainfall of the district.

TABLE - 2.2

(Rain Fall - mm)

		1989 (cm)	*1990* (cm)	*1991* (cm)
(a)	Normal rainfall	118.92	118.92	118.90
(b)	Actual average rainfall	121.92	191.91	141.00

Source : PLCP of Ganjam (NABARD) Bhubaneswar 1993-94. p. 40.

The rainfall generally increases from the coastal towards the interior hilly tracts of the district. The annual rainfall of the district starts from the second week of June and ends in early October. On an average the district has 65 rainy days in a year, but this , of course, varies from year to year. The relative humidity is high throughout the year specially in coastal areas. Winds are fairly strong particularly in coastal regions in summer and monsoon months.[14]

(e) Economic Minerals

The economic minerals found in the district are abrasive and grinding materials, clay, limestone, manganese, monazite, sand, tale black-sand consists of ilmentele, monozile, iron, Garet, rutile, quarter, and sillmarile. M/S Indian are Earth Limited, Government of India undertaking has taken exploratory work near the sea-beach area of Chatrapur.

(f) Forest

There are 5099 sqr kms of forests land that constitutes 40.69 percent of the total geographical area of the district.[15] The area under reserve forests is 37.5% of the total forest area during 1974-80. The major portion of forest of the district is located in Parlakhemundi, Rayagada, and Bhanjanagar area.[16]

The forests are rich in timber, bamboo, subaighas, gum, resin, oil seeds, ivory, honey,, tamarind and other forest products. A large number of tribal people of the district depend upon bamboo and other minor forest products for their livelihood. Kendu leaves are one of the major commercial products of the Orissa forest. "This district has witnessed the highest sale proceeds of forest products."[17] Various wild animals such as elephant, tiger, panther, Cheetal, Sambar, Bear, Deer, monkey are found in the forests of the district.

Fisheries

Ganjam is potentially rich in inland and brackish water fisheries. It has a coast line of 60kms with 26 fishing villages. Available inland water resources are 16,749.68 hects. Besides this, the district has 195 small reservoirs covering an area of 18,510 hects. The area developed till 31st March 1992 under inland fisheries was 4,961.11 hects. The Brackish Water Fisheries Development Agency had surveyed the area and found that an area of 2,738.59 hects was suitable for brackish water prawn culture in the five blocks viz.. Chatrapur, Chikiti, Ganjam, Khallikote and Rangeilunda. The area developed till 31st March 1992 under Brackish Water Fisheries was 1114 hects.[18] By 1989-90 Prawn culture constituting 395.03 hects. For quality seed supply, government of India has established modern prawn seed production Hatchery at Gopalpur in 1989-90.[19]

The total number of fishermen in the district is estimated at 20,000.[20] the production of marine fish in the district was 6008 mt tons in 1984-85 which increased to 8799.29 mt tons during 1987-88.[21] The people of Ganjam district have already adopted the latest technology and are well conversant with the modern methods of intensive and extensive fish culture.

Live Stock

The live stock resources of the district are comparatively high and the district has got a good scope for utilisation by engaging the people in industrial activities. Supply of hides, skin bones and horns provide ample scope for handicraft artisans of the district. As a matter of fact, as per 1977 census 3,78,113 nos. of hides and skin were available.[22]

TABLE - 2.3

The Number of Animal and Birds of the Districts

(As per 1991 census)

SL. No.	Animal / Birds		No. of Animals
1.	Plough Animals (Nos. 4,10,332)		
		(a) Plough Bullocks	3,43,592
		(b) Plough Buffalos	66,730
2.	Dairy Animals (Nos. 3,96,970)		
		(a) Cattle	3,49,701
		(b) Bullocks	47,269
3.	Small animals (Nos. 4,75,510)		
		(a) Sheep	1,30,484
		(b) Goat	2,91,445
		(c) Pig	35,581
4.	Poultry Birds		4,77,249

Source : DDM, NABARD, Berhampur and PLCP (Ganjam) 1993-94, p. 41.

There are two veterinary hospitals, 45 veterinary dispensaries, 271 Live Stock aid Centres, with A.I. facilities at 100 centres and one cattle breeding farm in operation in the district. An Indo-Swiss Project is functioning in the district since 2nd March 1991 to provide training to the farmers and animal husbandry staff and to provide infra-structure facilities in this regard. There is a Govt poultry Farm at Bhanjanagar catering to the needs of the small poultry farms.

Representing in Central and State Government

Out of 147 Assembly constituencies of the state the district (undivided district elects 15 MLAs and two MPs to the Parliament. The people of Ganjam district are politically conscious.

Agriculture

(a) Pattern of Land Utilisation and Cropping

Ganjam district is divided into three agricultural divisions i.e., Berhampur, Aska and Parlakhemundi. "The agro-climatic condition is most suitable and ideal for development of horticulture crops suitable and ideal foe development of horticulture crops particularly in high elevated regions and various fields crops in the plateaus and coastal regions of the district."[23]

The net area sown in the district is showing an increasing trend over the period. The area was 4.80 Lakh hectares in the year 1988-89. It has increased to 5.385 lakh hectares during 1991 Khariff and likely to go upto 5.403 hectares during 1992 Khariff.[24]

The pattern of land utilisation is presented below in table - 2.4.

TABLE - 2.4

Pattern of Land Utilisation (As on March 1992)

(a)	Geographical area	:	12531 sq. Kms
(b)	Net area sown	:	5,38,500 hects.
(c)	Fallow land	:	7,000 hects.
(d)	Land not available for cultivation	:	5,000 hects.

Source : DDM, NABARD, Ganjam, Berhampur, Orissa.

The district has a lower percentage of net area sown compared to the figures for the state and is slightly below the national average. This is because (a) the percentage of area under forests is slightly higher than the state average and is far above the national average (b) the area miscellaneous trees, crops and groves is comparatively large in this district because of the exuberant growth of cashew, apple, coconut, bamboo etc. along the coastal stretch (c) the large number of absolutely rocky hillocks shown across agriculture throughout the eastern portion of the district. otherwise plain fertile and green.

The principal crops of the district are paddy, Ragi, Mung, Biri, Til, Groundnut, Kulthi, sugarcane and chillies. The harvest area during 1983-84 has been estimated to be 2.72 lakh hectares. The food crops constitute 65% while the non-food crops account for the rest. The paddy cultivation constitutes 80% of the total cultivated area.[25]

The details of achievements under the major crops with production particulars for 1991 are presented below in table 2.5.

TABLE - 2.5

Cropping Pattern of the District (during Kharif 1990-91)

SL.	*Crops*	*Area (hects)*	*Production in M.T.*	*Productivity kgs / hact.*
1.	Rice	2,87,940	7,03,988	2,445
2.	Other cereals	81,526	71,701	880
3.	Total pulses	49,747	27,963	562
4.	Groundnut	40,500	30,375	750
5.	Other Oil Seeds	24,615	10,328	419
6.	Vegetables	38,746	2,59,645	6,960
7.	Spices	2,576	3,310	4,283
8.	Fibres	7,008	7,008	1,000
9.	Sugar cane	5,466	38,282	7,000
10.	Other crops	420		
	Total	5,38,544		–

Source : PLCP, Ganjam NABARD, 1993-94, p. 30.

The chief food crop paddy which constitutes 60% to total area under cultivation. "The chief cash crops are sugarcane, patato, groundnuts, mustard, etc."[26]

(b) Land Holdings

The following table 2.6. gives the pettern of land holdings in the District.

TABLE - 2.6

Pattern of Land-holdings in Ganjam District.

	Size of Holdings (in Acres)	*Individual Holding no.*	*Holding Area*	*Joint Hol-ding No.*	*Area*
1.	Below 1.00	2,37,367	1,11,175	528	249
2.	1.00 - 1.99	68,586	93,299	344	482
3.	2.00 - 3.99	35,567	91,492	188	488
4.	4.00 - 9.99	11,974	66,927	101	565
5.	10.00 and above	964	12,678	-	-
		3,54,458	3,75,571	1,161	1,784

Source : District Credit Plan (1988-90) and Annual Action Plan - 1988, Ganjam, p. 9.

Hence the percentage of Marginal Farmers is 86.44% which is relatively higher than the relevant state average.

(c) Irrigation

Since Agriculture is the mainstay of the district, in fitness of things, irrigation has a priority in agriculture activities and in agriculture credit. The percentage of net area irrigated to the net area sown in the district by 1980-81 was 54.17.[27], while for the state it is about 44.22% and of the National average is 58.45%.[28] The major source of irrigation in the district is river Rushikulya. There are a number of Major/medium irrigation projects in the district irrigating an ayacot of 2.20 Lakh hectares. The major and medium irrigation projects in the district with their irrigation potential are given in the Table 2.7

TABLE 2.7

The Major Medium Irrigation Projects of Ganjam district.

S. No.	Name of the Project	Irrigation ayacot in Hect.
1.	Rushikulya Irrigation system	61,231.09
2.	Jayamangala system	7,349.75
3.	Hiradharbharti system	7,349.75
4.	Dhanei system	3,741.04
5.	Baghua system - I	2,885.50
6.	Bahuda system	7,738.67
7.	Ghodahada system	7,738.67
8.	Ramanadi system	1,321.24
9.	Daha system	4,760.08
10.	Salia (Ganjam Portion)	2,005.78
	Total	1,06,121.57

Source : Annual Credit Plan, Ganjam, Andhra Bank 1991 - 92. p. 11.

The major sources of irrigation in the district are the canals and dugwells. The ground water exploitation in the district is yet to reach 65% level. In order to exploit 65% of the groundwater potential, it needs 24,500 dugwells, 2620 STWs/bore walls, 60 deep tube wells/450 RLPs and 29,750 pump sets.[29]

Twenty blocks out of the district are identified for dryland farming under National Watershed Development Programme in the district.[30] The district has 11,655 hectares of canals, 81,235 hectares of tanks, 12,487 hectares of wells and 19,827 hects of irrigation from other sources.[31]

(d) Horticulture

The district has four horticulturists stationed at four sub-divisional headquarters. The activity under cashew and coffee is looked after by the Soil Conservation Department. For promotion of rubber, the rubber board has opened its Regional office at Berhampur alongwith a small demonstration farm. Coffee Board is also having an office to provide all requisite extension support to the farmers. Sericulture Department has a massive infrastructure in the district. Besides this, five fruit nurseries are working for the benefit of the farmers. In the Hinjilicut block the betelvine is the commercial horticulture crop and it has an extensive market outside the state.

(e) High Yielding Varieties (HYV)

The Agricultural Department of the district has an ambitious programme to bring more area under high yielding varieties. They are holding demonstrations at various centres to educate the farmers for adoption of HYV. Therefore, there is rapid change from traditional varieties to high yielding varieties in the districts. The Programme undertaken by Agriculture Department boosted the agricultural production in the district. By 1981-82 the area under HYV was 164000 hectares and the yield rate of HYV by the same year was 5.25 quintals per hectare.[32]

(f) Consumption of Fertilizers

With the increasing use of HYV of crops the consumption of fertilizers is also going up in the district. The consumption of fertilizers per hectare of cropped area was 23 kg for Ganjam district, while 14 kg for the state of Orissa and 45 kg for India as a whole during the year 1983-84.[33]

The fertilizers consumption was 57 kg per hectare during 1991-92[34] in Ganjam district. By December, 1988, there were 241 stores of fertilizers belonging to co-operative and agricultural department. The total most private dealers of fertilizers was 1007 in number.[35]

(g) Agricultural Production Credit

The advent of a HYV technology implied that larger credit is to be supplied to the farm sector to adequately translate the new technology into practice. The table 2.8 presents the target and achievement of production credit in Ganjam district from 1989 - 90 to 1991 - 92

TABLE - 2.8

Production Credit Estimates and Achievements in the district

(Rupees in Lakhs)

	1989-90	1990-91	1991-92
Target	2079	1847	1555
Achievement	1681	938	1022
% of achievement	81	51	6

Source : NABARD, Bhubaneswar

It is seen from the table 2.8 that despite increase in area, the production credit is not increasing correspondingly and the targets for production credit are reducing year after year. The shortfall in achievement during 1990-91 was due to heavy floods and the only reason for deficit in achievement during 1991-92 was due to heavy defaults in this sector. As against a demand of Rs. 49.94 crores under agriculture and allied activities as on 30th June 1991, the overdues account is 83%.[36]

Sericulture

Sericulture was first started in Rayagada, R. Udayagiri and Mohana blocks during the 6th plan period. But it gained momentum only after grounding of the Bivoltine Sericulture Development Project at Chandragiri in 1987. Intensive development of sericulture has been taken up in R. Udayagiri and Mohan blocks under ERRP and IRDP till 31.3.90. Mulberry plantation has been done in 602.5 acrs. of land through 772 beneficiaries most of whom belong to ST community Training in silk Work has been impoarted to 55 mulberry growers. Cocoon production started during 1988-89. The production of cocoon in 1989-90 was 15500 kgs valued at Rs 8.5 lakhs.[37]

Infrastrctural Facilities

(a) Markets

There are two regulated markets in the district i.e., one at Hinjlicut and the other at Parlakhemundi. In addition, there are five marketing societites existing in the district. There are five fertilizers stores at regional level abd 488 stores at primary level of the co-operative department.[38]

(b) Roads, Railway and Ports

The National Highway No.5 from Madras to calcutta Passes through Ganjam district connecting Berhampur, Chatarpur, Ganjam, Khallikote (Part) and Chikiti (Part). There is a total stretch of 3366 kms road maintained by different organisation.[39]

The total length of broad guage railway line in the district is 79 kms (Howrah - Madras) and narrow gauge railway line is 45 kms from Nuapada to Gunupur.[40] There is one small port at Gopalpur-on-sea.

(c) Power / Electricity

The district gets power supply from the Machkund Hydro-electricy grid. There is one 132 KV sub-station at Rayagada and one at Therubali which supply power to Gunupur and Parlakhemundi through 33 KV feeder transmission lines. There are five more 132 KV sub-station at Berhampur, Ganjam, Mohana, Kotinada (Aska) and Chatarpur for distribution of power in this district. Under the Rural Electrification Programme so far 3055 villages have been electrified under rural Electrification Corporation (REC) Scheme.[41]

The Table 2.9 presents relevant information on the generation and consumption of electricity in the Ganjam district.

TABLE - 2.9

The Generation and Consumption of Electricity in Ganjam District.

Sl. No.	*Items / Quantity*	
1.	Total Genration of Electricity of the district.	11 (MVA)
2.	Total consumption	98347 Thousand (KWH)
3.	Total domestic consumption	18451 Thousand (KWH)
4.	Total industrial consumption	64393 Thousand (KWH)
5.	Other purposes	15503 Thousand KWTT

Sources : Andhra Bank, Regional Office, Berhampur, Ganjam (Enquiry)

(d) Post and Telegraphs

As per the information availaible, upto 31.3.88, there are 780 post offices and 78 telephone/telegraph offices in the ditrict with a divisional office at Berhampur. The total number of telephone exchange was 26 and the number of telephone connections were 2400. There were 37 public call offices.[42]

(e) The Financial Institutions of the District

As on 31 March 1992, there were 143 branches of commercial banks with the C.D. ratio of 54 and 75 branches of RGB (RRB) with the C.D. ratio of 102. There were two central Co-operative Banks with 27 branches with the C.D. ratio of 105. The district has five branches of Land Development banks for providing the medium and long term loans.[43]

The number of Bank offices per lakh population by December 1983 for Ganjam district was 5.4 while it was 5.3 and 5.6 for Orissa and India respectively. The per capita Bank deposit by December 1983 for Ganjam district was Rs. 274/- while it was 286/- and Rs. 897/- for Orissa and India respectively. Similarly the per capita Bank advances by December 1983 for Ganjam district was Rs 133/- while it was Rs. 299/- and Rs 603/- for Orissa and India respectively. The bank credit for agriculture by June 1981 in Ganjam district was Rs. 112/- while it was Rs. 126/- and Rs. 245/- for Orissa and India.[44]

The banking system in the district has spread into the rural sector and does not remain confined to the urban sector. In Ganjam district the population per branch was 29,000 in 1979 and this has improved to 19000 per branch in 1982. The lead Bank kept the objective to reduce the population per branch to 17000 by March 1985.[45]

The following (Table 2.10) is deposit and advances of the Banks and Co-operatives of the district for 1989-90 and 1990-91.

TABLE - 2.10

Deposits/Advances of all Banks (Ganjam Dist.)

(Amounts in Lakhs)

	(1989-90)		(1990-91)	
	Deposits	Advances	Deposits	Advances
Commercial Banks	20,872.70	12,416.76	23,732.58	13,851.01
R.G.B	1,259.81	1,450.79	1,552.82	1,665.40
Co-operative	1,394.19	2,751.09	1,568.19	2,639.97

Source : PLCP, Ganjam, NABARD, Bhubaneswar, (1993-94), p. 42.

The Andhra Bank is the lead Bank and the sponsor Bank for RGB, (RRB) in the district. It has the responsibility of formulating the district credit plan and the annual credit plans and to estimate the credit. As the lead Bank it has to co-ordinate the village level to block level plans at the district level by following the Service - Area Approach.

Industries

The Ganjam district is industrially back-ward in comparison to other coastal districts. However there are a few important large scale and medium scale industries operating in the district, as shown in Table No. 2.11 and 2.12. The table 2.11 provides the information on the ancillary and medium scale industries established in Ganjam district.

TABLE - 2.11

Ancillary and Medium Scale Industries of Ganjam district

Sl. No.	Name & Address of the Unit	Project
1.	M/s Gold Star Battery, At/Po : Ankuspur	Battery
2.	M/s. Kishore Industries, I.E. Berhampur	Nuts and Bolts
3.	M/s. Madhusree Chemicals, Ganjam	Barium Carbonate.
4.	M/s. Kasinagar Jute Mill, Kasinagar.	Jute twine.
5.	M/s. Taratarini Bakelite Elec. Acessories, Saru Junction	Bake lite fittings.
6.	M/s. J.D. Chemicals Ganjam	Alum.

(*Source* : District Industry Centre, Berhampur, Ganjam)

Table 2.12 provide the information on the large scale industries of Ganjam district, their investment capital, employment generation capacity and their products.

TABLE - 2.12

Large Scale Industries of Ganjam district (Investment amounts and employment creation)

(Rs. in Crores)

Sl No.	Name of the Industries	Location	Product	Invst (Rs.Crores)	Employment
1.	M/s. Jayasree Chemicals (P) Ltd. Ganjam	Ganjam	Caustic soda Hydrocloric Acid, Sulphur dioxide gas, Sodium Hydro-sulphide.	17.86	580
2.	M/s. The Aska Co-op. Sugar Industries (P) Ltd. Nuagaon Aska	Nuagaon Aska	Sugar, Recti-fied spirit, Carbon oil, Oxide gas	23.35	855
3.	M/s. Aska Spinning Mill (P) Ltd. Aska.	Aska	Cotton yarn and Synthetic Synthetic yarn.	8.89	599
4.	Indian Rare Earths Ltd.	Matikhdal Chatrapur	Aluminite, siliminite zircon.	144	1114

Source : Mohapatro, P.K., (General Manager, DIC, Ganjam), "Industrial Development in Ganjam district", Ganjam-90.

By December 1989, 2469 small scale industries have been established.[46] The average daily employment in factories per lakh persons in 1974 in Ganjam district was 147 while it was 338 and 1,0570 for Orissa and India respectively. The employment in household industries per lakh persons in 1981 for Ganjam district was 1148, while it was 1,081 for Orissa and 1,125 for India.[47]

Conclusion

Ganjam which means the Granary of the world is rich agricultural resources but is industrially backward. It has 86%. of its population in the rural sector, 24% of the population belong to scheduled castes and scheduled tribes. The working force of the district constitutes 34.75% of the total population as per 1981 census. The district has more female population than male population. It has eight sub-divisions, fourteen tahasils and twenty nine blocks administered by S.D.O.s, Tahasildars and B.D.O.s respectively. As per 1981 census the percentage of literacy of the district was 30.78 of the total population. Agriculturists constitute 42.14% of the working force. The agricultural labourers were 32.46%, the household sector constitute 3.39% and other sectors constitute 22% of the total work - force of the district. As per 1991 census, only 4.76% of the total workforce is engaged in the organised sector. It was estimated that 1.40 lakh persons were either underemployed or unemployed in the organised sector. The district has good potentialities in fishery and in animal husbandry. It has a lower percentage of net area sown compared to the state and slightly below the national average. The percentage of net area irrigated to net area sown at the district level by 1980-81 was 54.17 percent and the same has been steadily increasing year after year. The district has 11,655 hectares of canals, 81,235 hectares of tanks, 12,487 hectares of wells and 19,827 hectares of irrigation from other sources. The district has good scope for horticulture and sericulture development. The fertiliser consumption was 57 kgs per hectare during 1991-92 in the district. The district has a total stretch of 3366 kms of roads maintained by different organisations. The total length of broad gauge railway line is 79 kms and the narrow gauge railway line is 45 kms and there is a small port at Gopalpur and one small airstrip at Rangeilunda. So far 3055 villages are electrified. There are a few important large industries found in the district. They are shown in table 2.11 and 2.12. The Jayashree Chemicals Pvt. Ltd., Ganjam and M/s. the Aska Co.operative Industries, Aska are the prominent private sector industries of the district.

By December 1989, there were 2469 small scale industries. By 1974, for lakh persons the employment factories were 147 in comparison to the State figure of 338 and 1,057 for National figures. The employment in household industries per lakh persons in 1981 for Ganjam district was 1,148 , while it was 1,081 for Orissa and 1,125 for India. However, the recent employment figures are found in table 2.12.

As on March 31st 1992, there were 143 branches of Commercial Banks, 75 branches of RGB in 27 blocks out of 29 blocks of the district, 27 branches of Central Co-operative Banks and five Land Development banks in the district. The C.D Ratio for the Commercial Banks was 52%, while for RGB and Co-operatives it was 102% and 105% respectively during the same period. The population per branch of a bank is regularly improving with the spread of branches of Banks and the role of banks positively increased in the district. The role of Banks especially in rural development and to the weaker section has been emphasised by the adoption of the principle of anticipated income by the Banks.

An examination of the broad features of the rural economy of Ganjam district faithfully reflects the main characteristics of the state as well as the national economy. Majority of land holdings are small and marginal and bulk of the rural population consists of small farmers, landless agricultural labourers and artisans. High irrigation potential, better prospects of multiple cropping and possibilities of high fertiliser in-take by land spellout the crucial need for credit to the capital starved-farmers for a meaningful transformation of the rural economy. Credit can also help to provide subsidiary income so that farm families can profitably employ themselves. The sources of finance, both institutional and non-institutional, as existed before the creation of RGB were grossly inadequate and the present emphasis on institutional finance means greater responsibility for commercial banks and co-operatives who cannot cope up with it. Therefore, there is need for the RGB to play a big role in the transformation of the rural economy of the district through provision of the right type of credit at the right time to the right people. After all, the RRBs are created specifically to serve this purpose.

Thus a study of the various features of the rural economy of Ganjam provides ample justification for induction of this innovative financial institution the RGB to provide the much needed credit support for development. The success of poverty alleviation programmes hinges on the provisions of institutional credit as it will help to generate income for the rural poor and provide them meaningful employment.

References

1. District Statistical Office, Berhampur, Ganjam, (Enquiry)

2. District Statistical Hand Book, Bureau of Statistics and Economics, Govt of Orissa, Bhubaneswar, (1980-1981), p.1.

3. District Credit Plan, 1990-91, Regional Office, Andhra Bank, Berhampur, Ganjam, p.5.

4. Action Plan, (1988-89 to 1992-93), Dist Industries Centre, Ganjam, Berhampur, p.1.

5. From October 1992 the Paralakhemundi Sub-division was separated from the Ganjam District and has been given the status of a district called Gajapati district. As a result, at present the Ganjam district has come to have only three sub-divisions. However the present work is a study of Rushikulya Gramya Bank for the period 1981 to 1991, the period when the district was not divided. Even after the division of the district the Rushikulya Gramya Bank is functioning as the RRB and of both the districts.

6. DDM, (NABARD), district office of Ganjam and Gajapati, Berhampur (Ganjam), Interview on 31.3.93.

7. Annual Credit Plan (1991-92), Ganjam Regional Office, Andhra Bank, Berhampur, Ganjam, p. 8.

8. Ibid p.7.

9. Action Plan (DIC), *Op.cit* p. 5.

10. PLCP, Ganjam District (NABARD), Regional Office, Bhubaneswar, 1993-94, p. 24.

11. Ibid.

12. District Statistical Hand Book , Ganjam, 1980-81, Bureau of Statistics and Economy, Govt of Orissa . p. 1.

13. Annual Credit Plan, Ganjam (1990-91) Regional Office Andhra Bank, Berhampur, Ganjam, P. 6. 1990-91, p. 6.

14. ACP (1991-92), *Op-cit* p. 6.

15. Rural Development Officer, Regional Office, Andhra Bank, Berhampur, (Enquiry)

16. Action Plan, (D.I.C), *Op.cit*, p. 18.

17. Annual Credit Plan, (1991-92), *Op.cit*, p. 9.

18. PLCP, (NABARD), *Op.cit*, p.20.

19. Misra, S.N, "Brackish Water Fisheries Development in Ganjam district : A projection", *Ganjam-90*, (Samarnika published on occasion of Industries Exhibition - May, Berhampur)

20. Action Plan, (DIC) *Op.cit*, p.16.

21. Annual Credit Plan, (1990-91), *Op.cit*, p.9.

22. Action Plan, (DIC), *Op.cit*, p.13.

23. Annual Action Plan for 1987-88, (IRDP), District Rural Development Agency, Ganjam, Chatrapur, p. 3.

24. PLCP, *Op.cit*, p. 40.

25. DRDA Office, Chatrapur, Ganjam, (Records and Reports - Enquiry).

26. Action Plan, (DIC), *Op.cit*, p. 9.

27. District Statistical Hand Book, *Op.cit*, p. 19.

28. Patra, K.C, "Construction of Harabhangi Irrigation Project - A step in Economic Development of Ganjam", Ganjam - 90, Publish during the Industrial Exhibition, May 1990, Berhampur.

29. PLCP, *Op.cit*, p. 12.

30. Ibid. p. 15

31. Ibid. p. 40

32. District Statistical Hand Book, *Op.cit*, p. 10.

33. "Orissa, Ganjam", (Annexure) *Manual of Lead Bank Scheme*, Central Office - Andhra Bank, Hyderabad, 1987.

34. PLCP, *Op.cit*, p. 30.

35. Deputy Registrar, Co.operatives, Berhampur, Ganjam (Enquiry)

36. PLCP. *Op.cit*, p.29

37. Pradhan, Gourahari, "A Decade D.R.D.A., Ganjam, Chatrapur", *Ganjam-90*, Published during May 1990, Industrial Exhibition, Berhampur, Ganjam.

38. District Statistical Hand Book, Op.cit, p. 2.

39. Action Plan, (DIC), *Op.cit*, p.21.

40. Ibid.

41. Ibid. pp. 22, 23.

42. Ibid, p. 24.

43. Rural Development Officer, Regional Office, Andhra Bank, Berhampur (Enquiry).

44. Ibid.

45. District Credit Plan, Ganjam, (1983-85), Regional Office, Andhra Bank, Berhampur, p. 26.

46. ACP, (1990-91), *Op.cit*, p. 13.

47. Manual of Lead Bank Scheme, *Op.cit*.

3

Credit Agencies and Rural Credit Needs of Ganjam District

Proper assessment of the performance of a financial institution can be made only in the context of the situation in which it is made to work. In this connection it is important to ascertain the total credit requirements of the rural sector of the district economy and the extent to which other institutional sources can meet the requirement. In balance, it would then become possible to find out the kind of role that a particular institution is supposed to play.

The present chapter deals with the difference credit agencies in the rural sector of Ganjam district and the methods followed to estimate the rural credit. In this respect, the role played by the lead bank (Andhra Bank) in projecting the credit targets through District Credit Plan and later by following the Service Area Approaches will be discussed with findings and conclusions.

Estimating credit demand for various activities in the priority sector constitutes an important element of rural lending. Such an estimation helps the financial institutions and Government departments functioning in the district to understand the pattern and dimensions of credit demand pertaining to the activities covered under District Credit Plan. It facilitates the preparation of realistic targets by financial institutions for various priority sector activities in the district.

Accurate estimate of the credit requirements of agricultural or rural sector in India is a very difficult affair. The credit requirements of the farmers vary from region to region, season to season and from crop to crop. There is no definite agency to provide adequate statistical information regarding the credit needs of rural farmers, the rural artisans and other of the rural sector. It is not at all possible to contact all the cultivators and artisans spread over all the parts of the country and to know their various financial needs and purposes. The Majority of the rural people are illiterate and do not keep regular accounts of their family expenditure or of their productive activities and, therefore, they themselves have no clear idea regarding their own financial requirements. On the other hand, with the introduction of agro-industrial technology, the credit needs have increased by varying degrees from person to person, and crop to crop.

The farmers and the other rural people need both consumption and production or occupational and non-occupational loans. To be more specific, the credit needs are broadly of two types i.e. non-recurring and recurring, both occupational and non-occupational. The non-recurring occupational needs of credit relate to purchase of land, construction of irrigational facilities, purchase of farm equipements or their repairs and other long-term assets such as buffaloes, pigs, birds, transport, etc. As regards non-recurring non occupational needs, these are mainly for the purpose of social functions associated with birth, death, marriage and religious ceremonies and buying of gold and silver ornaments, purchase and/or construction of dwelling units including its repairs or extension.

The recurring occupational credit needs are in the nature of acquisition of agricultural inputs such as seeds, fertilisers, etc., payment of wages, land revenues, hire charges for using some agricultural machinery, repayment of instalments of borrowed funds and interest thereon. So far as the recurring needs for non-occupational purchases are concerned, these relate to purchase of food, clothes, utensils, medical and educational items, litigation expenses, transportation and other day to day domestic expenses.

As regards the time for which credit is needed its range is very wide. It stretches to as long a period as 20 years and it is as short as a week. In fact, the recurring needs are so immediate that funds are needed even for day to day operations.

The rural households have a wide variety of needs which relate to almost every activity of life i.e., from basic necessities of life like food and clothing to financing of social functions on the one hand and from acquiring agricultural inputs such as seeds and fertilizers to the purchase of land on the other.

The credit needs of the rural economy in Ganjam district are met by the following institutional agencies.

(1) Co-operative Credit Institutions.

(2) Commercial Banks.

(3) Rushikulya Gramya Bank.

(4) NABARD (Refinancing agency).

Credit support is a crucial factor in any rural developmental programme. In the early stages of rural lending the state Governments have been providing loans to agriculturists in the form of "taccavi" loans in times of floods, famines and such emergencies under the Land Improvement Loan Act, 1883 and the Agriculturist Loan Act, 1884.[1] The availability of funds for those loans depends upon the budgetory provisions from year to year.

These types of loans had many defects like (a) inproper budgetory provision (b) inequality in the matter of distribution (c) bias towards affluent farmers (d) inappropriateness of the basis of security - immovable property as security is generally insisted upon, (e) delays in sanctions and disbursements involving elements of corruption (f) inefficient supervision of end use (g) and lack of co-ordination amongst various departments.

The taccavi loans were supplemented by the Co-operative loans, which started with the advent of the co.operative movement in 1906 in the Ganjam district.

The Cooperatives of Ganjam District

In Ganjam district there are two District Central Co-operative Banks with headquarters at Berhampur and Aska. The Central Co-operative Banks are Berhampur Co-operative Central Bank Ltd., Berhampur and Aska Co-operative Central Bank Ltd., Aska. The Berhampur Central Co-operative Bank has sixteen branches operating at Paralakhemundi, Kasinagar, R.Udayagiri, Khallikote, Beguniapada, Purusottampur, Rambha, Digapahandi, Chikti, Kukudakhandi, Chatrapur, Patrapur, Hinjilicut, Rangeilunda, Goilundi (Berhampur) and at Berhampur (Head Office).

The Aska Co-operative Central Bank has eleven branches operating at Suroda, Dharakote, Buguda, Bhanjanagar, Jaganathprasad, Bellaguntha, Pattapur, Polosora, Kabisuryanagar, Seragada and Aska (Head Office).

Thus in Ganjam district the Co.operative structure is as follows :

(1) District Co-operative Central Bank

(a) Berhampur Co.operative Central Bank (Sixteen branches)

(b) Aska Co.operative Central Bank (Eleven Branches)

(2) Five Nos. of Land Development Banks

(3) 824 different types of Co-operative Societies.[2] (This include Co.operative Urban Bank of Berhampur and the consumer co.operative stores, co.operative marketing societies etc.)

The Berhampur Co-operative Central Bank has mobilised Rs. 1006.09 lakhs of deposits and advanced Rs. 1475.52 lakhs of advances with the C.D. ratio 147 percent by 31.3.91. The Aska Central Co.operative Bank has mobilised Rs. 562.10 lakhs of deposits and advanced Rs. 1164.45 lakhs of loans with the C.D. ratio of 207 percent by March 91 in Ganjam district.[3]

Investment under agricultural sector through co.operative for 1989 to 1991 are as follows :

Table - 3.1

Investment in Agricultural Sector by Co-operative

(Rupees in Lakhs)

Year	*No. of Hects.*	*Amount*
Khariff Programme :		
1989	31314	641.86
1990	14315	214.12
1991	4881	103.69
Rabi Programme :		
1988-1989	11909	185.84
1989-1990	700	14.58
1990-1991	4628	77.83

Source : Deputy Registrar, Co-operative Societies, Berhampur Division, Berhampur, (Enquiry).

The investment programme received a serious set back on account of implementation of the debt relief schemes during 1990. The financing agencies like NABARD, and Orissa State Co-operative Bank restricted their flow of refinance due to debt reliefs and the low recoveries of loans during 1990-91.

The primary Agriculture societies have enrolled 3.02 lakh agricultural families comprising 0.35 lakhs of scheduled caste families. The coverage of agricultural families under Co-operative fold works out to 76%.[4] To supplement the long-term credit requirement of farmers, five co-operative Land Development Banks are functioning in the district which finance like dugwell-energisation, farm machineries, orchards, cashew, coconut plantation and the like. The debt reliefs have equally adversely affected the long term credit structure in the district. The finance provided under long sector during 1988-89 to 1990-91 are shown in table 3.2.

Table - 3.2

The finance provided by five Land Development Banks

(Rupees in Lakhs)

Year	*Amounts*
1988-89	88.09
1989-90	13.05
1990-91	32.01

Source : Deputy Registrar, Cooperative Societies, Berhampur (Enquiry)

To cater to the credit requirement of nonfarm sector in the district five co-operative Urban Banks are functioning. These five co-operative urban banks provide finance for small business, traders, self employment and repair/remodelling of houses, etc. The finances made available by these banks during 1989 to 1991-92 (upto 31.12.91) are as follows.

Table - 3.3

The finance provided by five e Co-operative Urban Banks

(Rupees in Lakhs)

Year	*Amounts*
1989-90	191.55
1990-91	218.28
1991-92	292.50

Source : Deputy Registrar, Cooperative Societies, Berhampur, (Enquiry)

The Berhampur Co-operative Urban Banks which is at the level of a primary co.operative society is one of the oldest co-operative banks of India as it was established on 13.11.1906. It has made an advance of Rs. 346.46 lakhs during March 1992 out of which 66.88 percent is advanced to the priority sector. The percentage of weaker section advance to the priority sector is 66.04 percent and its recovery percentage is 27.45. However, this bank and other urban co.operative banks have no role in the rural sector as they confine their operations to urban localities. To tap deposits, especially from rural areas, the Aska Co-operative Central Bank and Berhampur co-operative Central Bank have opened 22 mini banks at the level of PACs besides one Mahila Branch exclusively at Berhampur.

The co-operative banks and their societies provide short term, medium term and long-term loans to the rural people mainly for agricultural, agrobased and allied sectors. They also provide consumption loans to a limited extent.

To ameliorate the economic condition of tribals and to meet the special requirements of other people belonging to the weaker sections residing in the forest and hill tracts of the district, six LAMPs have been organised which are working for the last one and a half decades. The main objective of LAMPs is to wean away tribals from PODU cultivation i.e., shifting cultivation and to save the tribals from the clutches of the middleman by encouraging them to take up agricultural operations on a permanent basis. The objectives of LAMPS are to motivate the tribals to take up improved agricultural practices, offering them reasonable prices for their agricultural products and keeping this in view, the LAMPs give agriculture loans.

Besides these Co-operative Credit agencies, there is a multipurpose cold storage at Berhampur, Utkal Ayurbedic Co-operative Pharmacy which was established in the year 1937 has 23 branches including a branch in Andhra Pradesh and in West Bengal. A sugar factory at Aska established in 1956 on cooperative basis has influenced the economy of Ganjam district by encouraging the farmers to cultivate sugar-cane in the district. There are 318 outlets functioning under the co-operative sector during the year 1990-91 to provide essential controlled goods especially to the rural population of Ganjam. There are four marketing co-operative societies in the district.[5]

There is a housebuilding consumer's society which advanced Rs. 8.16 lakhs for the construction of 21 houses during 1990-91 and Rs.

13.68 lakhs for the construction of 33 houses in 1991-92. So far 176 houses have been completed and 110 are under construction.[6]

The distribution of chemical fertilizers is also made through some co-operative societies in the district. During December 1991 for Khariff 12351 mts of fertilizers were distributed and for Rabi 3733 mts of fertilizers were distributed by March 1991 through such co-operative societies.[7] For storage, 202 Godowns have been constructed under IDA assistance with total capacity of 16950 mts.[8]

The co-operatives at each stage of the three tier have demonstrated marked dependence on external sources of finance, among which the more important are borrowings. Further, a sizable proportion of even the share capital of the co-operatives comes from the Government. Thus, in the case of resources, co-operatives mainly depend on the Government, Government co-operative funding agencies and the NABARD. The landowners and large farmers get benefits more than the poor farmers/artisan as they have greater influence in the management of co-operatives. Further, the non-productive use of loans is very common. The PACs have suffered from incompetent, ignorant and non-performing managements. Most of the PACs are weak both financially and managerially and suffer from inadequate business, heavy overdues and faulty and inefficient management. Due to the entry of RRBs and commercial Banks in the rural sector, the Co-operative banks have significantly lost their business.[9]

Scheduled Commercial Banks

As on 30.9.1992, there were 143 branches of 17 commercial banks. From the table 3.4 it is seen that, the total deposits mobilised were an amount of Rs. 28693.11 lakhs and advanced Rs. 14540.72 lakhs. The C.D. ratio of all the commercial banks of the district constitute 51%. Amount the Commercial banks of the district the State Bank of Hyderabad has the lowest C.D. ratio of 16% followed by Vijaya Bank Ltd. at 20%. The highest C.D. ratio is found with Bank of India at 125 percent followed by UCO bank at 91 percent.

Table - 3.4

The Commercial Banks in Ganjam District (As on 30.9.92)

(Amount in Lakhs)

Name of Banks	*Deposits*	*Advances*	*Direct Agri-cultural Advances*	*Priority Sector Advances*	*C.D Ratio*
1	2	3	4	5	6
Allahabad Bank (Two Branches)	389.04	193.03	82.30	155.33	50
Andhra Bank (Thirty two Branches)	5868.75	2061.70	189.67	1355.99	35
Bank of Baroda (Two Branches)	324.70	230.12	32.17	97.38	71
Canara Bank (Five Branches)	1485.59	687.48	300.04	547.35	46
Bank of India (Seven Branches)	600.92	753.39	549.79	671.30	125
Central Bank of India (Two Branches)	589.60	197.30	20.03	126.10	33
Indian Overseas Bank (Ten Branches)	1678.25	971.66	363.75	684.89	58
Punjab National Bank (Three Branches)	148.11	94.31	15.25	56.00	63
S B of Hyderabad (One Branch)	189.35	29.53	0.08	16.93	16
S B I (Fortyone Branches)	11834.04	6071.14	1848.75	3922.95	51
Syndicate Bank (Five Branches)	872.26	469.91	123.86	309.00	54
UCO Bank (Six Branches)	844.39	764.30	309.36	673.47	91
Union Bank (Two Branches)	351.44	171.80	48.45	111.48	49
United Bank (Ten Branches)	1116.71	569.30	140.70	400.26	51

Contd.

Table 3.4 (Contd.)

1	2	3	4	5	6
Vijoya Bank (One Branch)	284.02	164.43	17.06	87.66	58
Vysya Bank (One Branch)	281.14	57.46	0.10	14.12	20
Indian Bank (13 Branches)	1834.80	053.86	402.15	671.59	57
Total (143 Branches)	28693.11	14540.72	4743.51	9901.80	51

Source : Agenda Note : District Level Review Committee, 23 Dec. 1992.

Out of 17 commercial banks six of them viz., Andhra Bank, Canara Bank, Central Bank of India, State Bank Hyderabad, Vysya Bank, Union Bank have the C.D. ratio of less than 50% as on 30.9.1992. The total direct loans to the agricultural sector by all the 17 commercial banks comes to Rs. 4743.51 lakhs which constitute 33% of the total deposits. Similarly the total priority sector advances of the 17 commercial banks comes to Rs. 9901.80 lakhs which constitute 68 percent of the total advances. The UCO bank has lent the maximum of its advances to the priority sector, followed by Allahabad Bank and Canara Bank. While 88 percent of the advances of Allahabad Bank has gone to the Priority sector, for the other two banks it was 80 per cent. The State Bank of India advanced 65 percent to the priority sector and Andhra Bank (the lead Bank of the district) advanced 66 percent to the priority sector out of their respective total advances.

All the 17 banks have advanced Rs. 156.32 lakhs towards the DRI advance which constituted 1.08 percent of the total advances of all the banks during the reporting period.[10]

The Rushikulya Gramya Bank (RGB)

The Rushikulya Gramya Bank was established on 14th February 1981 under an act of parliament entitled "Regional rural bank Act 1976". Its area of operation is limited to Ganjam district of State (at present the Ganjam district and Gajapati district). It has now 75 branches with Rs. 2091.85 lakhs of deposits and Rs. 1912.04 lakhs of advances with C.D.

ratio of 91 percent as on 30.9.1992. It has advanced Rs. 816.59 lakhs to the priority sector. The DRI loan of RGB for the said period was Rs. 156.32 lakhs which constitutes 0.44 percent of its total advance for the said period. The Bank has launched a massive expansion programme and opened 7 branches in 1981, 18 branches in 1982, 11 branches in 1983, 16 branches in 1984, 16 branches in 1985, one branch in 1987 and 6 branches as well as one Area office at Aska during the year 1988-89. The credit needs of the rural mass are mostly met through IRDP, IRRP, ITDP, SC and ST Action Plan, SFDP, etc. (Government sponsored Development Oriented Programmes)

The details of the staff as on 30.9.1992 working in the bank are as follows :

(a) Officers	:	142
(b) Clerks	:	114
(c) Other staff	:	86
Total Staff		342

Besides the above staff, Chairman, General Manager, Chief Vigilance Officer and Rural Development Officer are deputed from Andhra Bank, the Lead Bank and the sponsor bank. Their expenditure pertaining to salaries is fully born by the sponsor Bank viz., Andhra Bank.[11]

By and large, the RGB has worked in fostering good public relations and projected itself as a friend and guide of the common man. How far the bank is successful in accelerating the rural development and meeting the economic needs of the target people will have to be seen in the further discussions of the work.

National Bank For Agriculture And Rural Development (NABARD)

With a view to promote integrated rural development to secure the prosperity of rural areas and for matters connected therewith or incidental thereto, the Government of India set up NABARD and it came into operation from 12th July 1982. The NABARD acts not only as a sole refinancing agency, but also acts as a leader of the entire rural credit system in the country.

NABARD, as an apex institution for financing agricultural and rural sectors, provides, by way of refinance, loans and advances, repayable on demand or on the expiry of a fixed period not exceeding 18 months, to commercial banks, Regional Rural Banks, State Co-operative banks and other financial institutions, which are approved by RBI.

There is a district NABARD office functioning in Ganjam district. The District Development Manager (DDM) Nabard has to play a crucial role in co-ordinating the various departments, developmental organisations and the banks of the district from Block level to the district and to help them in estimating the credit needs yearwise. He has to prepare the 'Potential Linked Credit Plan' (PLCPs) for the district. "The PLCPs represent a major contribution as a methodology for realistic assessment of credit feasibility, with due emphasis on viable activities. Very rightly, the National Bank has decided to keep on reviewing, updating and continually improving the quality of PLCPs. The PLCPs should thus prove useful reference documents not only for the district and block credit plans but also for the micro-level service area plan."[12]

The PLCP of Ganjam district prepared by DDM of NABARD presents the requirements of refinances for each year, based on the available potential under each sector, realisable ground level credit projections under term loans and production credit together. The Regional Office of NABARD, Bhubaneswar, with the help of the DDMs has prepared the potential linked credit plans from 1989-90 to 1994-95 and since the 8th five year plan commenced from 1st April 1992, the P.L.C.P. has also extended the projections upto 1996-97.[13]

The DDM office of the district is being equipped with personal computers and has arrangements to provide technical and professional advice locally. Lead Bank Offices, development departments of the district administration and Panchayats will find these district offices of NABARD a source of strength in facilitating their task in many ways.[14]

The PLCPs of 1993-94 has made an estimation of credit disbursements in the district for Rs. 54.58 crores for 1,18,150 beneficiaries.[15] The full refinance support scheme for Ganjam district for the year 1992-93, bankwise allocation of NABARD refinance is presented in table 3.5.

It is to be seen from table 3.5 that out of 17 banks as given in the said table, the refinance allocation estimated for the year 1992-93 for RGB stands as Rs. 270.51 lakhs which is the highest refinance allocation among the Banks. It constitutes 32.85% of the total allocation as per the reference in the table. However the refinance assistance from NABARD is Rs. 20.73 lakhs which is 9.24% of the total refinance assistance of all the Banks in the year under report.

Table - 3.5

Refinance Allocations 1992-93 (Ganjam)

(Rupees in lakhs)

Sl.	*Name of Banks allocation*	*Part-A under ARF Assistance*	*Part-B Refinance*
1.	Allahabad Bank	0.09	03.14
2.	Andhra Bank	87.53	13.64
3.	Bank of Baroda	04.50	01.69
4.	Bank of India	14.13	01.92
5.	Canara Bank	23.17	01.23
6.	Central Bank of India	02.56	00.30
7.	Indian Bank	39.06	07.76
8.	I O B	31.65	12.34
9.	Punjab National Bank	02.97	00.16
10.	S B I	119.77	32.84
11.	Syndicate Bank	15.42	01.18
12.	UCO Bank	08.30	02.08
13.	United Bank of India	21.41	07.04
14.	Union Bank of India	02.40	00.00
15.	R G B	270.51	20.73
16.	O S C B	41.92	44.16
17.	O S C L D	135.35	74.04
	Grand Total	823.55	224.28

Source : Agenda Note : District level Review Committee and District Consultative Committee, Ganjam, Andhra Bank Dt. 23.12.1992.

Estimates of the Credit in the Rural Sector

Credit estimation in the rural sector is not an easy task. There is no agency, which can provide adequate statistical information regarding individual credit needs. This makes it difficult to estimate the aggregate requirements of the agriculture sector.[16] However, with the introduction of the lead Bank schems after nationalisation in the year 1969, efforts were made to make credit estimates through the 'District Credit Plans and Annual Action Plans', periodically and yearwise.

Some economists have attempted to formulate models applicable at the micro level to estimate the credit requirements of a farmer. But the model is not suitable for estimating total credit requirements for the rural sector as a whole. To estimate the rural credit as a whole for the district, the District Credit Plan formulated by the lead Bank at present is the only trusted method as it is a plan of estimation of credit prepared by the technical personel of developmental organisations and the banks of the district. They are to collect the socio-economic data through quick and impressionistic surveys. The main objective of the survey was to assess the resource-potential of the district, to understand the industrial base, the marketing structure of the agricultural economy, the infrastructure for rural development and to establish a liasion with the Government and various department agencies.

The system of credit planning which has become an integral part of credit policy and rural development is to be studied in the following ways :

1. Estimating credit by microlevel model.
2. The lead Bank Scheme and the District Credit Plans.
3. The Service Area Approach and the District Credit Plans.

The field level studies at microlevel can be made to estimate credit in a particular region. But statistical errors cannot be avoided and the study will differ from time to time, place to place, person to person and from one stage to the other stage of development.

a) Microlevel credit estimate model

An individual farmer's/artisan's credit needs can be estimated by assessing the credit needs on the basis of planned activities and the available resources for the process of production.

According to Singh and Gupta, short term credit requirements of a farmer can be estimated by taking the area under cultivation and capital input in a given farm into consideration.[17]

According to their model $Y_i = R_{ij} = 1 P_{ij} X_{ij}$

Where P_{ij} = Capital inputs per acre in the ith farm ;

R_i = Proportion of Credit to capital inputs on ith farm;

X_{ij} = Area under ith crop on jth farm, and

Y_i = Credit requirements.

Singh and Gupta have taken the value of :

R_i = 0.05 small farms.

R_i = 0.45 medium farms.

R_i = 0.40 large farms.

Credit requirements for a block would therefore, be determined as :

$$C = \frac{A_{tk}}{A_{si} = 1} \text{niyi}$$

Where A_t = Total cultivated area in a block

A_s = Sampling holdings

n = Number of holdings.

Since Credit requirement of a farmer, we know, in functionally related to the cost of exogenous inputs like fertilizers, irrigation, other agricultural inputs, net operated area, etc. its requirement can be calculated by using the regression equations of the following type :

$$Y = AX_1^{b_1} X_2^{b_2} X_3^{b_3} X_4^{b_4}$$

$$C = B_1 X_1 \; B_2 X_2 \; B_3 X_3 \; B_4 X_4$$

Where Y = Total returns from crop.

X_1 = Investment on irrigation

X_2 = Invest on draft cattle

X_3 = Expenditure on fertilizer

X_4 = Area cultivated

C = Amount of Credit required.

and b_1 — b_n and B_1 — B_n are respective regression co-efficients.

This model is not suitable for estimating total credit requirement for agricultural sector as a whole since the regression co-efficients vary from region to region. The model has been presented here as a micro-level estimation of credit. The banks are to play the role of a leader of the locality to improve the socio-economic pattern in a general way which needs is met through macro analysis.

After nationalisation, the responsibility of the lead bank (important bank of the locality) has gone up and the designated bank as the leader of socio-economic development of the region has to play a key role in estimating credit and by planning to meet the needs.

b) Lead bank and the DCP

The Reserve Bank of India finalised the lead Bank scheme in 1970 giving a concrete shape to the area development approach. The number of districts allotted to an individual bank was decided on the basis of its size, resources and its regional orientation.[18]

The Lead Bank is expected to assume the major role in the development of banking and credit in the lead districts and it acts as consortium leader by providing leadership in initiating and accelerating the process of development. In order to gain familiarity with the salient features of the district economy, the lead banks were asked to collect basic socio-economic data through quick and impressionistic surveys.

Andhra Bank is assigned the lead bank responsibility in five districts. Four of these districts are in Andhra Pradesh and the remaining one is in Orissa i.e., Ganjam. During 1971 the first round of survey was made by the Andhra Bank. Since then, the Andhra Bank has played a pivotal role as lead Bank of the district and formulated the district Credit Plans. The branch expansion in the rural areas for different banks was given much weightage after the Lead Bank scheme operated in the district "Lead banks, as it was expected under the lead bank scheme, would perform a very significant role in developing banking services in their respective lead districts. It was observed that they have carried out their responsibility in most of their lead districts very successfully, and by and large, their involvement is, obviously increasing either in development of banking services or in the economic activities in their area of operation".[19]

c) The District Credit Plan (DCP)

The District Credit Plan (DCP), which estimates the credit and fixes up the targets for a financial year is the macro-level estimate at the targets for a financial year is the macro-level estimate at the district level. It is an aggregate of unit plans and processed through the decentralised plan or the plan from the villages level to the Block level and then to the district level. As such it is a bottom-up-planning or planning from below. "The aim of the Credit' Planning is to identify the credit gaps and give a direction to the financial institutions to deploy their resources as per plan priorities. The credit plan has to indicate the scope for development of various activities in the district. It should contain all bankable schemes. It is also expected to take care of all the developmental programmes in the district."[20]

The district credit plan was initially prepared and launched in 1978. The district credit plan is more a supply - oriented, than demand-related one. The DCPs were prepared without being related to the scope of lending or absorptive capacity of the area. The target of credit plans of each bank is basically fixed on the basis of the lendable capacity of the branches on the strength of avaiaible lendable resources of the bank. The branches while preparing the plan have taken the following points into consideration :

(a) Incremental deposit

(b) Expected recoveries.

(c) Refinances from refinance organisations.

For explaining the estimated resource position of Ganjam district we may take 1985 as the sample year.

The expected deposit growth in 1985 was estimated at Rs. 2500.00 lakhs and 60% of the same Rs. 1500.00 lakhs was available for lending.

As such the lendable resources from the financial institutions were estimated as :

Deposits	:	Rs. 1500.00 lakhs
Expected recoveries	:	Rs. 1000.00 lakhs
Refinance (from NABARD and others)	:	Rs. 0650.00 lakhs
		Rs. 3150.00 lakhs

Thus the target for 1985 was to lend Rs. 3150.00 lakhs. This was the credit estimated. The table 3.6 provides the sectorwise-plan (targets) and achievements for the said year.

Table - 3.6

Annual Action Plan - 1985
(upto 31.21.1985)

(Rupees in lakhs)

Sl.	*Sectors*	*Target*	*Achievements*	*% of achievement*
1.	Agriculture			
	(a) Croploan	1500.00	1475.22	98.34
	(b) Termloan	824.59	705.05	85.06
2.	Industries	449.32	413.39	92.00
3.	Service Sector	361.25	779.88	215.88
	Total	3135.16	3373.54	107.63

Source : Andhra Bank, Berhampur, Ganjam.

The total outlays which were estimated on the basis of lendable resources available worked out to Rs 3150 lakhs and the targets for the year was fixed Rs. 3135.16 lakhs. The available resources are more than the targets. Against the target, the lending took place for the said year for Rs. 3374.54 lakhs. Thus the percentage of achievement for the year was 107.63. The lending achievement for service sector was more than double the target while in other sectors, the lending remained below the target and the achievement was less than 100 percent.

In the same way the percentage of achievement of AAP, 86, AAP-87, AAP-88, and AAP-(89-90) were 102.31 percent, 111.53 percent, 113.47 percent, 109.5 percent respectively.

The DCPs suffered from the following short-comings.[21]

(1) The DCPs remained a banker's plan where the main concern was aggregation of credit requirements and their apportionment. They were instrumental in developing a credit subsidy linkage for the weaker sections of the society.

(2) The DCPs were mostly prepared without being related to the scope of lending or absorptive capacity of the area. There was not much of analysis of available resource potential,

infrastructure support and the complementary activities which have a bearing on the economic viability of the programmes. As a consequence, credit flow has been more supply oriented than demand related.

(3) Not much attention was paid to the inter-sectoral linkages and hence the DCPs could not serve the purpose of area development plans.

(4) Further, as DCPs were prepared for a short span, mostly 2 years, from the point of view of the grassroot units, DCPs remained only indicative in nature. Grassroot units were unable to use the DCP exercise for understanding and preparing plans for the exploitation of potential in their operational areas.

The DCPs, thus, became documents for the allocation of resources among the banks rather than being articulated with district development plans. Another draw-back of DCP is that, there is lack of effective co-ordination and co-operation between the credit institutions on the one hand and the concerned Government and other development agencies on the other. However, if there is a lack of involvement of the branch manager in the preparation of DCPs, then the plan becomes meaningless to the area. Thus to avoid these defects, the plans are made more and more decentralised through the introduction of Service Area Approach (SAP).

From 1988, potential linked Credit Plans have been prepared by the Zonal Offices and the district offices of NABARD. It is prepared by the co-ordinated efforts of local bankers and state Government department officials and the DDM of NABARD. By June 1990, PLCPs have been prepared in respect of almost all districts of the country.[22]

By the introduction of PLCPs, NABARD, RBI and Credit institutions with well defined responsibility and instructions from the top levels will contribute to better quality of decentralised credit planning. The PLCPs by their very nature have to be reviewed and updated frequently taking into account fresh data becoming available, new developments and changing situations and new insights gained during implementation including acceptance by people of the schemes and the preparedness of Governmental machinery to provide support.[23]

(c) Service Area Approach and District Credit Plan.

For the effective grassroot level implementation of development schemes, the DCP has to be translated into micro plans for similar units. In this regard the experience of earlier DCPs has not been encouraging and the new PLCPs are yet to evolve a mechanism for this purpose.[24] The recent development of SAP was introduced by RBI with effect from 1st April 1989.[25]

The service Area Approach of bank branches for rural lending has brought in a new dimension in relation to micro-level credit planning. This represents another effort towards decentralisation of credit planning for the rural sector. The approach aims at planning from below i.e., the village level.

The service Area Approach has five stages in its implementation.

(i) Identification of Service Area for each bank branch of the rural and semi-urban areas including the Regional Rural banks.

(ii) A systematic survey of the villages allocated to such bank branch to identify the scope for lending and determine the areas of development on the basis of potential.

(iii) Preparation of village and branch credit plans aggregation thereof at block and district levels.

(iv) Co-ordination between different agencies concerned with development including the banking sector in ensuring the timely provision of credit and non-credit inputs, and

(v) A continuous system of monitoring the performance under the credit planning branch-wise and bank-wise. The Co-operative have been also included in the scheme.

The allocation system of specific service areas is made on the basis of the cluster approach. In selecting the village for a particular bank, generally, as far as possible, a particular Gram panchayat is allotted. If a particular Grama Panchayat has more than one branch, the allotment may be made to the branch, which has the dominant share in financing in that Grama Panchayat in terms of number of accounts. Subject to the above criteria, the existence allocation of villages to different branches for the purpose of implementation of IRDP may also be kept in view. The non-target group beneficiaries, in the service area of a RRB branch, will be financed by the branch of the concerned sponsor bank or by the nearest branch of any other commercial bank.

A Committee headed by the lead District Officer of the RBI with the lead Bank Officer of the concerned district and concerned District Officer from NABARD as member would allocate service areas to each branch at a block level meeting in consultation with the concerned bank branches and the B.D.O. this committee would also designate the commercial bank branches, that will finance the non-target group beneficiaries in the service areas of RRB branches.

According to the Approach each rural bank and RRB has been allocated a specific service area generally of 15 to 25 villages.

After fixation of the services area, each branch is to undertake a survey of the specific village and prepare village profiles. Such survey will cover different aspects such as existing status of various economic activities and potentialities foe their expansion and also for undertaking new activities; available infrastructure in the area, existing skills of the villages and coverage of rural families by the credit institutions, etc.

Each branch would prepare annual credit plans for its own service area on an ongoing basis. The credit plan should reflect both the needs and the potentialities of the area, on the basis of the information gained through the survey as also other available information from local development agencies.

Programmes such as integrated Rural Development (IRDP) Self Employment for Educated Unemployed Youth (SEEUY), Self Employment for Educated Unemployed Programme for Urban Poor will continue to be handled as hitherto but will form part of each branch's credit plan.

The annual credit plan prepared by all the branches in a block, together with the lending programmes of the co-operative would be consolidated into the block credit plan at the block level Bankers

Committee. All the banks operating in the block including the branches of District Co-operative Banks, Co-operative Land Development Banks and RRB are the members of the Committee. In addition, the BDO and the technical officers of the concerned Block/District are also the members of the committee. The Lead Bank Officer of the concerned district in the ex-officio chairman of the committee and in his absence, the convenor, bank's branch manager will preside over the meeting.

The block level committee is expected to meet atleast once in a quarter to perform the following functions :

(1) to discuss the credit plans and to finalise them.

(2) to review the progress the DCPS.

(3) to discuss the operational problems of DCPs.

(4) to review the progress of Government sponsored programmes like IRDP, SEEUY etc.

(5) to allocate service areas to new branches opened in the block.

The determination of credit requirements is an integral part of the production plan and has to be linked with production requiring external resources. The production requirement may have to be determined with references to various factors such as the area of the farm, the type of the soil, the nature of the crops, the type of farming, the cropping pattern, the methods of cultivation the scale of finance infrastructural facilities required and available.

Where the NABARD DDMs are posted at district level, he prepares the PLCP based background paper and ensures that the same is circulated by the lead Bank officer to all the bank branches. This will form the basis for the preparation of the Annual Credit Plan of a bank of the block.

All the various inputs required to achieve a feasible target of production has then to be converted into monetary terms at current prices. Hence a dynamic approach is essential for proper estimation of demand through appropriate agencies.[26]

Therefore, the DCPs prepared by the Lead Bank have to play a dynamic role in the credit planning of the district economy.

The broad steps involved in estimating the credit demand for activities covered in the DCP can be stated as follows :

(a) Confirmation of the technical feasibility of the activity.

(b) Establishing economic viability of the activity.

(c) Establishing the potential number of technically feasible and economically viable units.

(d) Estimating the number of units which would demand credit.

The potential size of an activity would depend upon the supply of resources needed to carry it on and the demand for its output, (Product/ services). Either of them, supply or demand factor, can act as constraint in determining the potential level of operation.

For the purpose of the District Credit Plan, the term "resources" can be extended beyond the physical materials and man power resources. It would encompass man - made resources viz., infrastructural facilities (including ancillary services like veterinary services and marketing facilities supply of critical inputs (i.e. fertilizers, seeds, raw materials) technical and extension services and even subsidy aids.

On the other hand services and industries which have to depend upon local demand, the size of local market could be the constraining factor.

The discussion on estimating potential number of units technically feasible and economically viable is stated below :

S ⟵ N ⟶ D

S = Supply constraints (these includes, infrastructural and critical inputs, extension manpower skills and subsidy).

D = Demand for the product (estimation of demand may require compilation of data and economic analysis).

N = Number of units technically feasible and economically viable.

Interplay of S and D gives N which is important to identify constraining factor in S or D for arriving at N.

Similarly the units which are actually in need of credit during the financial year under report have to be identified correctly for the D.C.P.

Presently officers of RBI and NABARD are involved in various aspects of co-ordination and monitoring at the district level with the single objective and improving the quality of credit planning and its dispensation under Service Area Approach. From 1.4.91 Service Area Monitoring and Information systems (SAMIS) has come into operation in the District Credit Planning. Under this system the DCP provided information on Rural areas and Urban areas of the district collectively and separately. The DDM of Ganjam district appointed by the NABARD at the district level has a lot of responsibility in guiding, and preparing the District Credit Plans on the basis of the potential linked credit plans of NABARD.

Thus the estimation of credit of different banks are undertaken by fixing the targets of lending on the basis of available financial resources for a year from different sources. When the lending exceeds the target, it is said that the particular bank has exceeded 100% of its target, and when it remains below the target, the performance of the bank is considered unsatisfactory. Taking into account the district credit plan, the target fixed for credit by the different banks are the credit estimates. Table 3.7, diagram 3.1 and 3.2 provide a comparative picture of district credit estimates and achievements in relation to RGB from year 1985 onwards. The comparisons for DCP and RGB are made from the year 1985 as said year was chosen as the base year in the earlier part of this chapter. In the diagram 3.1, the trend of percentage of achievement of RGB and the percentage of achievement of DCP are shown upto 1989-90. In the year 1990-91 the figures of achievement for DCP was available only upto Sept. 1991 and for 1991-92 the figures of achievement for both RGB and DCP was not available. Thus the last two periods cited in the table. 3.7 were excluded from the diagram 3.1. The increasing role of RGB in terms of credit estimation and achievement can be understood from the analysis of the data of the table 3.7 and from the diagram 3.1 and 3.2.

Table - 3.7.

Estimation of Credit and Achievement of DCP and RGB from 1985 onwards

(Rupees in Lakhs)

Year	*Target (Estimated Credit)*		*Achievements*		*Percentage of RGB credit estimates in the district credit estimation*
	RGB	*DCP*	*RGB*	*DCP*	
1985 (Jan-Dec)	240.00	3135.16	265.89 (110.78%)	3373.54 (107.6%)	7.65
1986 (Jan-Dec)	272.60	3328.90	328.30 (120.43%)	3405.90 (102.31%)	8.18
1987 (Jan-Dec)	310.00	3528.16	505.57 (163%)	3934.28 (112%)	8.78
1988 (Jan-Dec)	368.50	3791.87	647.11 (175.61%)	4302.88 (113.51%)	9.71
1989-90 (Apr-Mar)	580.28	4345.66	740.73 (128%)	4758.76 (109.5%)	13.35
1990-91 (Apr-Mar)	812.84	4332.33	725.73 (89.25%)	1577.98*	18.76
1991-92 (Apr-Mar)	944.27	5930.96	NA	NA	15.92

* Achievement of DCP of 1990-91 are upto September 91.

(Figs. in bracket show the percentage of achievements in respect of their concern target).

Source : Compiled from data of RGB Head Office and Regional Office, Andhra Bank, Berhampur, Ganjam.

The table 3.7. in the last column provides the information on the increasing trend of RGB's contribution in the district credit estimations. The RGB's contribution has increased from 7.65% in the year 1985 to 18.76% in the year 1990-91. But there is a fall of 2.84% in the estimation of the credit in the year 1991-92 in comparison to the year 1990-91 The diagram 3.2 clearly shows the increment in the RGB

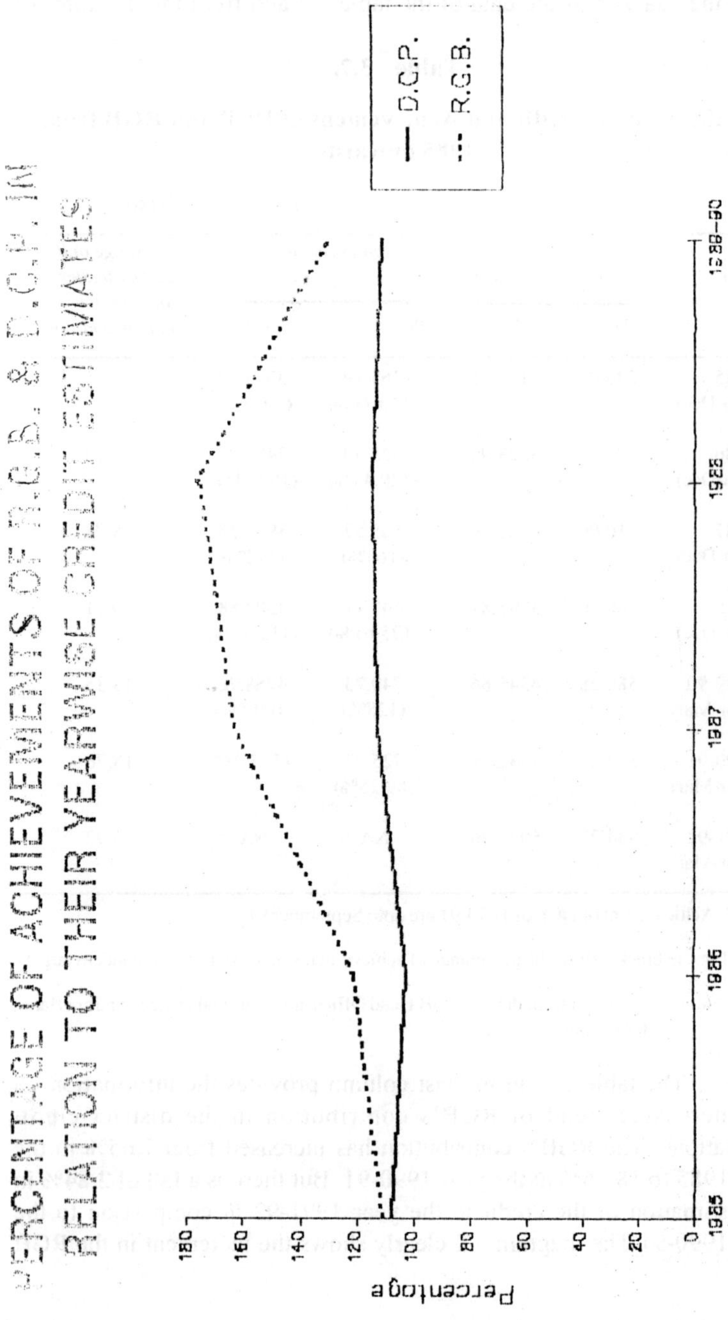

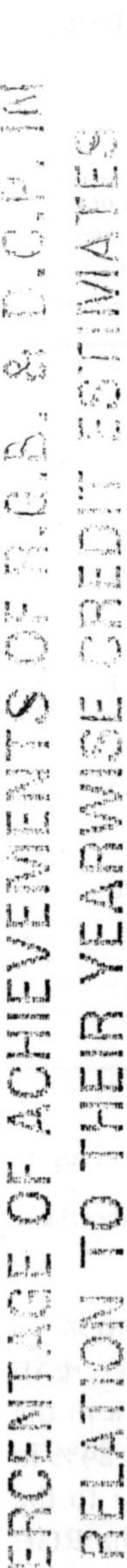

Diagram 3.1 (Source Tab. 3.7)

YEARWISE CREDIT ESTIMATES OF R.G.B. & D.C.P.

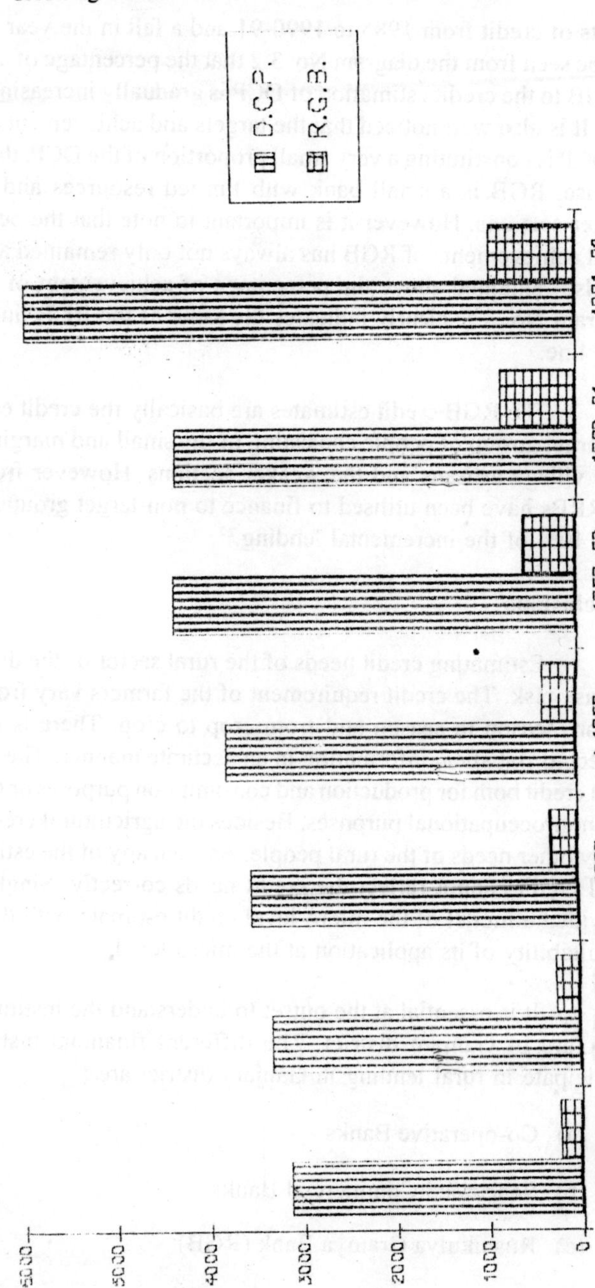

Diagram 3.2 (Source Tab 3.7)

targets of credit from 1985 to 1990-91 and a fall in the year 1991-92. It is to be seen from the diagram No. 3.2 that the percentage of contribution of RGB to the credit estimation of DCP is gradually increasing year after year. It is also well noticed that the targets and achievements of RGB in the DCP is constituting a very small proportion of the DCP. this is mainly because, RGB is a small bank with limited resources and to specific weaker sections. However it is important to note that the percentage of credit achievements of RGB has always not only remained above 100% but also remained above the percentage of achievement of the district. Diagram No. 3.1. clearly indicates the same as the RGB line above the DCP line.

The RGB credit estimates are basically the credit estimates for the target group of people consisting of the small and marginal farmers, poor village artisans and the weaker sections. However from 12.9.92, the RRBs have been utilised to finance to non-target groups in order of their 40% of the incremental lending.[27]

Conclusions

Estimating credit needs of the rural sector of the districts is not an easy task. The credit requirement of the farmers vary from region to region, season to season and from crop to crop. There is no media to collect to statistical information in an accurate manner. The rural people need credit both for production and consumption purposes or occupational and non-occupational purposes. Besides the agricultural credit, there are many other needs of the rural people. As such any of the estimates of the rural credit cannot reflect the credit needs correctly. Singh and Gupta provided a model of the micro-level credit estimate with the remark of unsuitability of its application at the micro-level.

It is essential at the outset to understand the institutional credit structure of Ganjam district. The different financial institutions that participate in rural lending in Ganjam district are :

(a) Co-operative Banks

(b) Scheduled Commercial Banks

(c) Rushikulya Gramya Bank (RGB)

NABARD being the apex body in refinancing the rural sector through its District Officer plays also an important role in the rural credit structures of the district indirectly. The Andhra Bank is the lead Bank of the district and sponsored Bank of RGB has a pivotal role in estimating the credit needs of the district.

The district credit plans adopted by Lead Bank constitutes the mosy realistic method of preparation of credit targets (estimates) for different banks of the district. Thus to ascertain the rural credit needs of the Ganjam district of Orissa, it is essential to study the DCPs prepared by Andhra Bank (lead Bank). The DCPs become a major source of statistical information for the study of RGB in this work. The targets of different credit plans are fixed on the basis of the available resources. The scale of finances fixed for different purposes of loan play their role too in determining the targets for sectorwise lending. The scale of finance is also subject to change from time to time and from plan to plan.

The credit estimates of DCP for the sample year 1985 was discussed for understanding the credit targets of the district for the said year. The achievements for the said year and the percentage of achievement in respect of the targets of the year after 1985 were discussed for the district. The Service Area Approach adopted through the lead Bank Scheme from April 1989 is one of the effective methods of estimating the credit targets. The estimates are made at the village level not only on the basis of available lendable resources but by the field level micro study of availability of potentials in infrastructure, agriculture, irrigation power, transport and manpower etc. The District Officer of NABARD and Lead Bank Officer of RBI are playing an important role in guiding and attending the block level bankers meeting and the District level meetings. The potential linked credit plan prepared by NABARD is a background paper not only to the District Credit Plan but to the Block Credit Plans also. The present DCPs under Service Area Approach (SAA) is a decentralised Credit Plan from the bottom. The villages are surveyed in all aspects and then the credit estimated are made. The villages and Grama Panchayat Surveys are discussed at the block level and block credit plans are prepared. After the Block Credit Plans are added up at macro-level and DCPs, are prepared. The DCPs from 1991 onwards became a major source of statical information of yearwise credit estimations of Ganjam district in the present work.

Thus on the basis of the credit estimation in the D.C.P. it is seen that the percentage of credit estimation of R.G.B. has continuously increased from the year 1985 to 1990-91. But in 1991-92, it has decreased to the extent of 2.84 per cent from the previous year. However the percentage of achievement of credit of RGB has always remained above the percentage of achievement of the district credit plan (DCP) upto 1990-91.

The RGB has to play an increasingly important role in relation to the poorer sections of the rural masses of Ganjam by year-marking more and more credit in its yearwise estimates. Proper and adequate credit estimation is an essential factor for meeting the credit needs of the rural people and for rural development of the district. The allocation of credit of RGB being less than 16% of DCP as in financial year 1991-92, is rather inadequate to meet the growing needs of the rural poor of the district.

References

1. Lall, G.S., (Edited) "Rural Finance : The Multi - Agency Approach", *The Journal of Banking Studies*, Vol. X No. 3 July September 1987, P. 180.

2. Patnaik, P.C., (Deputy Registrar, Co.operative societies, Berhampur Division), "Glimpses of Co-operative activities in Ganjam Dist", *Swakhyar Ganjam Sundar Ganjam Smaranika*, 1992, Chatrapur.

3. Rural Development Section, Lead Bank, Regional Office, (Andhra Bank), Berhampur, (Enquiry - February '92).

4. Ibid.

5. Deputy Registrar, Co.operative Societies, Berhampur Ganjam, (Facts collected - Enquiry).

6. Ibid.

7. Ibid.

8. Ibid.

9. Lall, G.S., (Edited), *Op.cit*, P. 165.

10. Lead Bank Sources - Enquiry.

11. Annonymous, "Rushikulya Gramya Bank in the service of the Rural poor". *Sakhyara Ganjam Sundar Ganjam Smaranika*, 1992.

12. Malhotra, R.N., (Governor, RBI), "Service Area Approach", *Reserve of India Bulletin*, Vol. XLIV No. 9, September, 1990, P. 415.

13. Annonymous, Chapter-1, "Introduction", *Potential Linked Credit Plan of Ganjam District of Orissa*, NABARD, Regional Office, Bhubaneswar (1993-94), P. 6.

14. Malhotra, R.N., *Op.cit*, P. 719.

15. PLCP, *Op.cit*, P. 2.

16. Sadhu, A.N. and Singh, Amarjeet, "Agricultural Credit", *Fundamentals of Agricultural Economics*, Bombay Himalaya Publishing House, (3rd Ed.), 1989, P. 297.

17. Ibid, P. 298.

18. Annonymous, "Introduction", *Credit Plan - 1980-82*, Ganjam district, Orissa, Central Office (Lead Bank Dept.), Hyderabad, 1980.

19. Kulshrestha, U.C. "Role of Lead Bank in branch expansion - a case study", *The Indian Economic Journal*, Vol. 34 No. 1, July - September, 1986, P. 56.

20. Annonymous, "Bankable schemes and assessment of credit demand", *Annual Action Plan 1984*, Regional Office, Andhra Bank, Berhampur, Ganjam, P. 143.

21. Annonymous, "District Credit Plans", *Hend Book on Service Area Approach*, Central Office, (Lead Bank Dept.), Andhra Bank, Hyderabad, P. 44.

22. Ibid. P. 46.

23. Ibid, P. 47.

24. Ibid, P. 47, 48.

25. Ojha, P.D., "Service Area Approach - a new challenge Banks", *The Journal of the Indian Institute of Bankers*, Vol. 61, No. 1, January - March, 1990, P. 35.

26. Srivastava, Lalima, "Role of Institutional finance in Agricultural Development of Uttar Pradesh", (Research Work), Allahabad University, (Mimeograph), 1982, P. 75.

27. DDM, NABARD, Ganjam Interview on 26.3.93.

4

Rushikulya Gramya Bank : Its Lending Techniques and Operation

Regional Rural Banks are powerful primary instruments for redistributing of income in rural areas[1]. They have been identified as the agencies meant to provide finance on an increasing scale to the needy and deserving sections of the population, particularly those belonging to the weaker sections of the society. As such, the main objective of the Regional Rural Bank is the "Provision of credit and other facilities especially to the small and marginal farmers, agricultural labourers, artisans and small entrepreneurs in rural areas[2]. By Sept. 1991, the number of RRBs in the Country as a whole was 196 and the number of districts covered by RRBs was 385 with 14,531 branches. The aggregate out-standing advances of RRBs at the end of Sept. 1991 stand at Rs. 3,804 crores as compared with Rs 3,555 crores as at the end of Sept. 1990, registered a growth of 7.0 percent. During the said period the RRBs of Orissa advanced Rs. 20265.00 lakhs which is only 5.32 percent of the advances of all RRBs of the country. The C.D. ratio of RRBs of the country has declined by 9 per cent i.e. from 83 per cent as at the end of Sept. 1990 to 74 per cent as at the end of Sept. 1993.[3]

In rural credit in recent years there has been a rapid increase in the share of institutional agencies as distinguished from non-institutional sources. According to All India Rural Debt and Investment Surveys, the dependence of rural house holds for cash debt on non-institutional agencies had come down from about 93 per cent in 1950-51 to 83 per cent in 1961 to 71 per cent in 1971 an to as low as 39 per cent by 1981. There has been a major thrust in channeling institutional credit to the weaker sections in 1980s. The credit outstanding under agricultural and allied activities from all agencies increased from Rs, 10,200 crores to Rs. 35,300 crores between 1980-81 and 1988-89, showing an annual growth rate of 16.8%. This strongly supports the presumption that there is evidence to show that the share of institutional credit in total rural credit has increased considerably in the 1980s."[4]

The main objective of any financial institution in an underdeveloped rural economy is to strengthen the financial infrastructure and to generate new income with the expansion of productivity employment. With more than 85% of the people of Ganjam district of Orissa remaining in the rural and semi-urban areas the importance of credit supplied by the financial institutions for rural development hardly needs any emphasis.

The Rushikulya Gramya Bank being the RRB in Ganjam district has appeared in the field of rural lending in the year 1981. It aimed to facilitate the provision of credit to the poorest of the poor in rural areas as it was felt that the commercial banks continued to have an urban - bias, while co-operatives were illequipped for the task. In this background, the main objective behind the establishment of RGB in Ganjam district was to "make available institutional credit to weaker sections of the society, who had by for little or no access to cheaper loans."[5]

The specially designed monetary institution has to protect the economic interest of the target group from the exploitation of money lenders and the middle men in the rural areas of the district. This chapter will examine the techniques of credit policies and lending operations on the assumption that more credit flow will help rural development of the district. The present chapter is divided into the following three sections.

Section (A) : RGB lending to Agriculture and Allied sectors.

Section (B) : RGB lending to Industries and service sectors.

Section (C) : RGB lending to Government sponsored programmes and to the priority sector.

However, the chapter started with the introduction of RRBs in India and the importance of rural credit. Before the above sectionwise discussions it is essential to differentiate the RRB's lending from that of the commercial banks and co-operatives of the district.

The RGB in Ganjam district being the RRB in the district is different from the commercial bank in its organisation, in its policy and functions. In this chapter we are concerned with the lending policies of the RGB. The RGB is lending to the specific target groups on the basis of India, RBI NABARD. The RGB is empowered to mobilise deposits and grant loans directly to small and marginal farmers, agricultural labourers, rural artisans, small entrepreneurs and persons of small means engaged in any productive activity and also to all types of co-operative societies including FSS operating within its area of operation. RGB can provide loans for production as well as consumption purposes within Ganjam district and later within Ganjam and Gajapati district of Orissa (After the division of Ganjam district).

While lending in Government sponsored programmes, the RGB has to follow the scale of finances prepared by DRDA and has to take up the co-operation of the Block Development Officer and other development agencies in agriculture, animal husbandry, horticulture, etc. the Andhra Bank, being the parent bank of RGB, has an important role to play in guiding the lending operation through their officers on deputation for its day-to-day functioning.

The RGB in Ganjam district gets refinance facilities from Andhra Bank (Sponsor bank) and from NABARD. The RGB is scheduled bank as per the RBI Act, 1934 and in terms of section 42 (I) of the Act, the RGB is required to maintain with RBI an average daily balance the amount which shall not be less than 3 per cent of its net demand and time liabilities. While working out net liabilities, for the purpose of maintaining CRR (Cash Reserve Ratio) and SLR (Statutory Liquidity Ratio) under section 24 of Banking Regulation Act, 1949, RRBs are allowed to exclude borrowings from apex refinance institutions and from the sponsor bank.[6]

Since, the RGB deals only with small borrowers, the level of business of RGB branches compared to that of a rural branch of commercial bank is much lower. The RGB branches are found in the remote, interior parts of the district viz., at Adava, Birikote, Luhagudi,

Kainpur, Ramagiri and Chelliguda. These areas have less potentialities for bank business and communication and other infrastructural facilities are inadequate. Those RGB branches have no easy access to the sponsor commercial bank and to the head-office and suffer from administrative disturbances. For the said reason, the branches maintain a higher cash reserve which results in losses for them.

The RBI provides the concessions to RRBs in reducing cash reserve ratio to 3%. In the same way the statutory liquidity ratio to 25%, which is less than the SLR and CRR of the Commercial Bank.[7]

The RGB being a bank to finance primarily persons living below the poverty line for which the norm accepted till recently was the earning income of Rs 6000/- per annum. It has further raised to Rs. 6400/- per annum.[8] The average norms for identifying the small farmers at 1981-82 prices with effect from 1st July 1984 was 5 Acres of irrigated and 9.5 acres of non-irrigated lands were fixed in Ganjam district of Orissa, excepting the Paralakhemundi Sub-division (Gajapati district at present), the Digapahandi and Sanakhemundi blocks. For those areas the norms were 6.75 acres of irrigated and 12.75 acres of non-irrigated lands.[9]

The Dantwalla Committee suggested that the RRBs have to be instrumental in filling up the quantitative and qualitative credit gap at a low cost operation. The RRB (RGB) is not to aim at profit, but to provide loans to the target group, most of whom could not avail themselves of institutional credit even for their genuine productive requirements for one reason or the other from commercial banks. Neverthless, in accordance with the new policy of Government of India, the credit facilities by RRBs are extended to some extent to the big farmers as well under the land improvement scheme Agricultural refinance corporation."[10]

With a view to facilitating their operations in the context of their catering exclusively to the weaker sections, the Reserve Bank has granted many concessions to the Regional Rural Banks. For instance, these banks are included in the second schedule to the Reserve Bank of India Act immediately on their establishment, giving them direct access to the Reserve Bank's refinance assistance.[11] Since the establishment of

NABARD in 1982, the paternal role has been shifted from the RBI to the newly formed apex organisation. It provides short term refinance upto 50% of the outstanding eligible loans of RRBs at 3% below the bank rate.[12]

A steering committee on RRBs has been constituted by NABARD to act as an advisory body. Its functions among others relate to framing and reviewing policies in respect of lending policies and lending rate. It sponsored the lending schemes for RRBs, extended refinance facilities monitored and administered the credit expansion activities and above all patronised the RRBs (RGB in Ganjam district). The NABARD could step in to the shoes of the RBI in respect of the Banking Regulation Act 1949.[13]

At the time of processing the loan application, the RGB considers the following points.

(a) The scheme under which advances are sanctioned should be suitable to prevailing local conditions.

(b) The application should provide the evidence of some experience in the activity for which loan asked by the applicant.

(c) The scheme should be productive and sound, resulting in creation of employment and incremental income.

(d) The proposed project should feasible and practical.

(e) It should have a potential perpetuality of the activity.

(f) The applicant should bear a good moral character.

(g) The recovery of principal amount with interest should be ensured.[14]

The table 4.1 and 4.2 provides information on agriculture lending of RGB and the district respectively. On the other hand in Annexure -3 and 4 the lendings of RGB and other financial institutions of the district in industry and Services sector are given comparatively.

The RGB so far has not provided any advance to the following sectors.

(i) The waste land development/farm forestry.

(ii) World Bank project (Except IDA, IFP, Assisted inland fishery).

(iii) Area Development.

(iv) In trade and services :

(a) Education (b) Housing finance (it has no refinance facility)[15]

The basic policy of RGB is to finance agricultural and allied activities, trade, transport, industry, service and to professional activities taken on a modest scale in rural areas at a low rate of interest as compared with other commercial banks. Thus the maxim of profitability peculiar to banking industry is made secondary to the objective of service for economic uplift of the rural masses of the district. The RGB has to play a role more as an agent of economic development of the district rather than a banking institution seeking profit.

SECTION- A

RGB Lending to Agricultural and Allied Sectors.

Agricultural and rural development are continuing process and banks have to commit themselves to rural financing on a long-term basis.[16] the role of rural credit and rural credit institutions, as pacesetter for economic development, reducing regional inbalances within states/ districts and as an instrument of bringing socio-economic changes in backward areas, during post-green revolution period has acquired new dynamism.[17] Thus RGB being a rural credit agency in Ganjam district has a major role to play in the agricultural sector of the district. In Ganjam district 80% of the farmers belong to the categories of small and marginal farmers. They live in the rural areas. The various crops they produce are paddy, sugarcane, Ragi, Groundnut, Chilly and varieties of vegetables. In some parts of the district land is cultivated for both Khariff and Rabi crops. Hence, for the proper utilisation of land the poor farmers need credit as an important and crucial input for achieving the desired output.

The establishment of RGB in the unbanked rural areas has created an awareness of banking among the inhabitants of the district. The bank advances direct loans to farmers in the form of crop loans and term loans. The crop-loans are the short term loans, which provide the working capital to the farmers. The term loans are medium term and long term loans. Under the scheme of short term loans, credit is provided for seeds, fertilizers, insecticides, agricultural tools and implements. Generally such loans are advanced on the condition of their repayment immediately after the harvest of the crop. The term loans are given for the purchase of agricultural implements like iron ploughs, land-levellers, hand tools, sprayers, hay-press, sugar-can crushers etc. The agricultural term loan are given for minor irrigation,, horticulture crops, agricultural activities, fisheries (marine, inland and brackish water prawn) animal husbandry, construction of bullock sheds, implement sheds, farm sectors etc.

Before Sept. 1990, The RGB was charging concessional interest rates and it was less than the interest rates charged by the commercial banks in the district. But afterwards, as per the RBI direction interest rates are directly made related to the quantum of loans.[18]

The Rushikulya Gramya Bank charges interest in the following way from 9.10.1991.

(a) 11.5% upto Rs. 750/-

(b) 12.5% from Rs. 750/- to Rs. 1500/-

(c) 14% to above Rs 1500/-

The interest mentioned above are fixed for the priority sector advances. For non-priority sector the interest rate is 19.5% upto Rs. 7500/- and 22.5 % to the amounts above the amount of Rs. 7500/-.[19]

The advances of RGB are being made mainly to the priority sector. The priority sector includes the weaker sections of the society.

"Ideally the weaker sections, whatever be the legal or constitutional interpretations, should include those unfortunate members of a society who by virtue of their birth, sexual status material possessions and for various other sociological or historical reasons, happen to be poor, ignorant, illiterate, unpriviledged and under priviledged.[20] The credit requirements of farmers, small scale industries and self employed professional groups have been covered under the priority sector lending.[21] The concept of priority sector is mainly intended to ensure that the assistance from the banking system flows in an increasing measure to those sectors of the economy, which, through contributing significant proportion of national product have not received adequate support of institutional finance in the past. This inter-alia, implied below of required credit to various sectors in accordance with the national plan priorities.[22]

The performance of RGB in agricultural sector and allied activities will be judged in the following ways :

(a) By comparing the AAP targets and achievements of its own from 1981 Dec. to 1990 - 91 March.

(b) The percentage of achievement of RGB (achievement in percentage of its own target) will be compared with the percentage of achievement of the district credit plan (All the financial institutions including RGB).

(c) The achievement of RGB is a part of the achievement of the DCP. Thus the part of contribution of RGB in leading to the agricultural sector will be examined by percentage.

(d) The average loan of a branch of RGB will be compared with the average loan of the branch of commercial banks of the district.

(e) The lending operation of RGB in agricultural sector will be compared with the nine RRBs of Orissa. (to know about the percentage of contribution of RGB in Orissa).

(f) The RRB lending of Orissa in agriculture will be compared with the RRB lending of the nation.

Table 4.1 gives the details of the agriculture lending of RGB in Ganjam district from the year 1981 (Jan.- Dec.) to 1991-92 (Apr. - Mar.).

TABLE- 4.1

RGB lending in Agriculture sector of Ganjam District

(Rs. in lakhs)

Years	Crop Loan		Term Loan		Total Loan	
	T	A	T	A	T	A
1981	-	4.00	-	5.00	-	9.00
1982	29.25	32.00 (109.4)	15.41	24.16 (156.78)	44.66	56.16 (125.75)
1983	89.00	49.83 (55.98)	49.83	44.60 (89.50)	138.83	94.43 (68.01)
1984	90.00	99.73 (103.03)	39.76	89.46 (225)	129.76	182.19 (140.40)
1985	130.00	99.95 (76.88)	71.00	100.18 (41.09)	201.00	200.13 (99.56)
1986	130.00	128.29 (98.68)	94.70	38.00 (40.12)	224.70	166.29 (74.00)
1987	145.00	179.18 (123.57)	70.00	62.17 (88.81)	215.00	241.35 (112.85)
1988	200.00	160.48 (80.24)	67.40	126.36 (187.47)	267.40	286.84 (107.27)
1989-90	204.29	143.96 (70.46)	193.20	130.68 (67.63)	397.49	274.64 (69.09)
1990-91	249.05	108.36 (43.50)	241.70	122.70 (50.76)	490.75	231.06 (47.08)
1991-92	382.28	163.45 (42.75)	94.70	40.71 (42.98)	476.98	204.16 (42.98)

Note : From 1981 to 1988 calender years thereafter the financial years i.e. April to March.

T. represent to Targets (Estimates)
A. represent to Achievements.

Figures in the brackets represent the percentage of achievement inrespect of concern targets.

Source : Annual Reports from 1981 to 1991-92, Rushikulya Gramya Bank, Berhampur (Ganjam) Orissa.

As the bank came into operation in Ganjam district in the year 1981, there was no target figures pertaining to the crop-loan and term loan for that year. The reason for not having the targets for the year is due to non-availability of time to the bank authorities for planning the credit. As 1981 was the year of establishment for RGB in the district, emphasis was laid on the recruitment of staff and opening up of branches. In the agricultural sector it has lent only 9 lakhs which forms a very negligible part of the total lending in the district.

In the second year the achievement of RGB in terms of target was satisfactory being 10% in the crop loan and 156% in the term loan. The total achievement of these two sectors, which represent the agricultural sector of RGB was 125.75%.

In the crop-loan sector the achievement of RGB was better i.e. more than 100% in the years 1982, 1984 and 1987, while all other years it was below 100% of achievements. The achievement of the crop loan upto 1984 was not upto the mark. The reasons are "Firstly, due to natural calamities, secondly, due to the low performance of banks thirdly, there was lack of co-ordination between the Agricultural Dept. and finance institutions".[23]

The District Credit Plan of 89-90 points out that in the year 1987 the co-operative bank and RGB have contributed 505 of the achievement under the crop-plan of the district.[24] The RGB has achieved good results in the year 1987 in the crop-loan sector. The percentage of achievement was 123.57. In 1986 and 1987, the achievement under the crop loan was not only unsatisfactory to RGB but also in the total district. Similarly for the year 1989-90. 1990-91 and 1991-92 the performance of crop loan was not satisfactory both in the RGB and in the district. The District credit plan of 1991-92 passes the remarks that "The performance of the commercial banks was quite satisfactory, but non-achievement of target was due to shortfall in the co-operative and Rushikulya Gramya Bank."[25]

Thus the RGB during the first eleven years of its working had achieved success only in the years 1982, 1984 and in 1987 in the crop-loan sector and its inefficiency in meeting its own targets in the crop loan is causing even a low performance for the district achievement in Agricultural sector.

In the year 1990, the low performance in crop-loan is mainly influenced by Agricultural Rural Debt Relief Scheme (ARDRS) which was implemented in June 1990.[26]

In case of term loan the RGB performance crossed 100% in the year 1982, 1984 and 1988 only. In all other years the performance remained below its own target. In the year 1982, it was 156.78%, in 1984 it was 225% and in the year 1988 it was 187.47%. During the years of natural calamities, some of the crop-loans were converted into term loans for the defaulters.[27] The reasons of un-satisfactory performances of RGB in these two sectors as well as in the whole of agricultural sector is due to the following grounds :

The target group farmers are uneducated, illiterate and economically poor. They do not understand the value of cheap credit in the process of production. There is lack of timely availability of inputs like fertilisers, pesticides and seeds from the government organisation of from co-operatives. The available ground water irrigation potential is not utilised to the maximum extent. It is under utilised. The ground water survey reported that Ganjam district has quite satisfactory potentiality in ground water.[28] On the other hand, the reasons for not reaching the target under agricultural term loans are mainly :

(i) lack of power.

(ii) delay in processing the applications for loan.

(iii) non-availability of animals for cultivation purposes as well as for animal husbandry programmes.

(iv) non-recycling of loans due to heavy overdues.

(v) lack of extension services and training.

(vi) disposal of assets by the beneficiaries.

(vii) no proper maintenance of the land records etc.[29]

It is witnessed from the diagram 4.1. that the achievement curve lies above the targets during 1982, 1984, 1987 and in 1988 in case

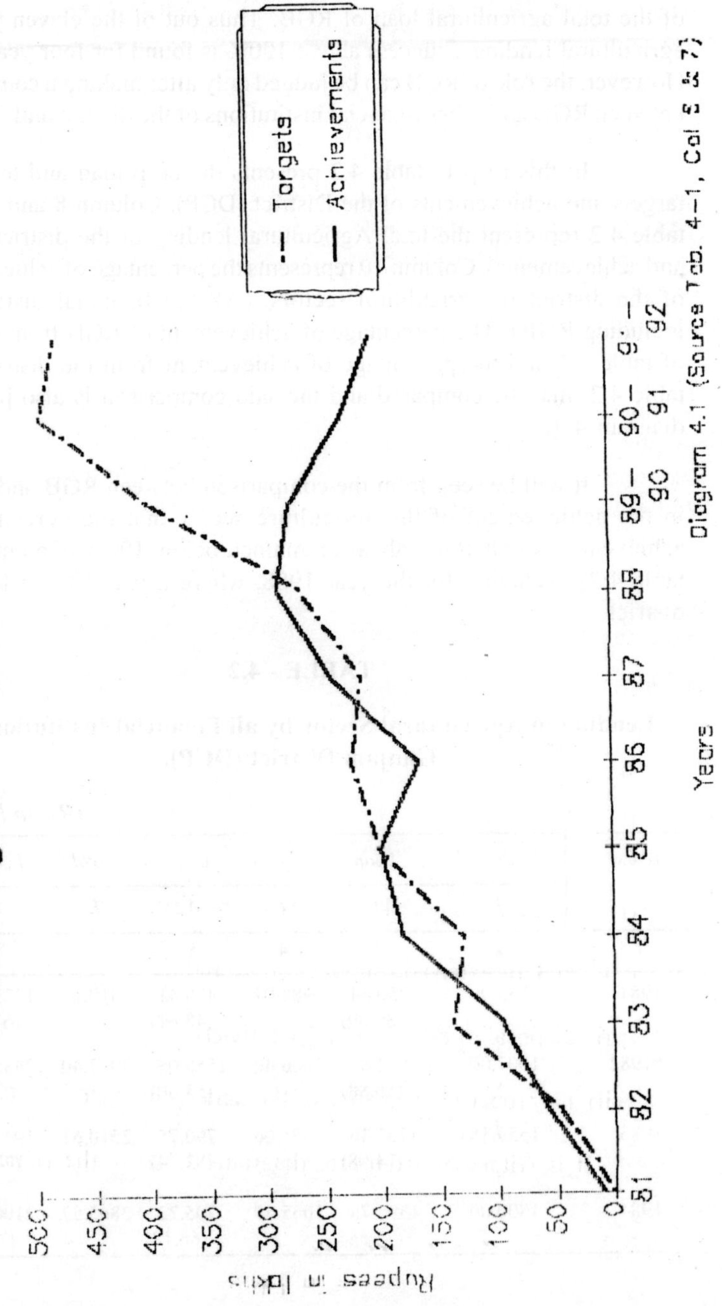

Diagram 4.1 (Source Tab. 4—1, Col 5 & 7)

of the total agricultural loan of RGB. Thus out of the eleven years of agricultural lendings, success above 100% is found for four years only. However, the role of RGB can be judged only after making a comparison between RGB and other financial institutions of the district and the state.

In this respect table 4.2 presents the crop loan and term loan targets and achievements of the District (DCP). Column 8 and 9 of the table 4.2 represent the total Agricultural lending of the district (target and achievements). Column 10 represents the percentage of achievements of the district in agricultural sectors. (All the financial institutions, including RGB). The percentage of achievement of RGB from the data of table 4.1 and the percentage of achievement from the district from table 4.2. may be compared and the said comparison is also ploted in diagram 4.2.

It will be seen from the comparison between RGB and district in the achievement of the agriculture sector that the percentage of achievement of DCP has always remained below 100% (Column 10 of table 4.2) excluding for the year 1988, where it was 101.29% for the district.

TABLE - 4.2

Lending in Agricultural Sector by all Financial Institutions of Ganjam District (DCP).

(Rs. in lakhs)

Years	*Crop*	*Loan*	*Term*	*Loan*	*Total*	*Loan*
	T	*A*	*T*	*A*	*T*	*A*
1	2	3	4	5	6	7
1981	835.00	750.64 (89.89)	984.07	478.41 (48.61)	1819.07	1229.05 (67.56)
*1982	1007.00	872.88 (86.88)	2906.40	1558.05 (53.60)	3913.40	2430.93 (62.11)
1983	1559.55	1155.46 (74.08)	951.06	790.75 (83.14)	2510.61	1946.21 (77.51)
1984	1800.00	1395.75 (77.54)	1065.57	705.22 (66.18)	2865.57	2100.97 (73.31)

Contd.

TABLE 4.2 (Contd.)

1	2	3	4	5	6	7
1985	1500.00	1497.17 (99.81)	824.59	727.31 (88.20)	2324.59	224.48 (95.69)
1986	1509.00	1466.94 (97.21)	863.00	507.13 (58.76)	2372.00	1974.07 (83.22)
1987	1700.00	1442.11 (84.83)	581.02	600.00 (103.26)	2281.02	2042.11 (89.52)
1988	1915.00	1612.55 (84.20)	609.08	944.18 (155.01)	2524.08	2556.73 (101.21)
1989-90	2078.78	1680.85 (80.85)	860.95	918.04 (106.63)	2939.73	2598.89 (88.40)
1990-91	1846.85	937.95 (50.78)	990.37	659.08 (66.54)	2837.22	1597.03 (56.28)
1991-92	1555.03	762.28 (49.02)	1102.84	369.66 (33.51)	2657.87	1131.94 (42.58)

Note : From 1981 to 1988 calender years, thereafter the financial years i.e. April to March.

T. represent to Targets (Estimates)
A. represent to Achievements.

Figures in the brackets represent the percentage of achievement inrespect of concern targets.

* In the year 1982, targets are upto Dec. only.

Sources: District Credit Plans and Annual Action Plans from 1981 to 1991-92, Ld. Bank, (Andhra Bank), Berhampur (Ganjam) Orissa.

It is an interesting observation that, in the year 1988 the RGB and the district, both have exceed their targets in agricultural lending. In the said year the percentage of achievement of RGB was 107.27% while the district has 101.29%.

The diagram 4.2 has made comparison between the percentage of achievement of RGB and the percentage of achievement of the district. The RGB achievement curve has remained above the District achievement curve for the period 1984, 1985, 1987 and in 1988. But in all other periods the district agricultural credit has remained above the percentage

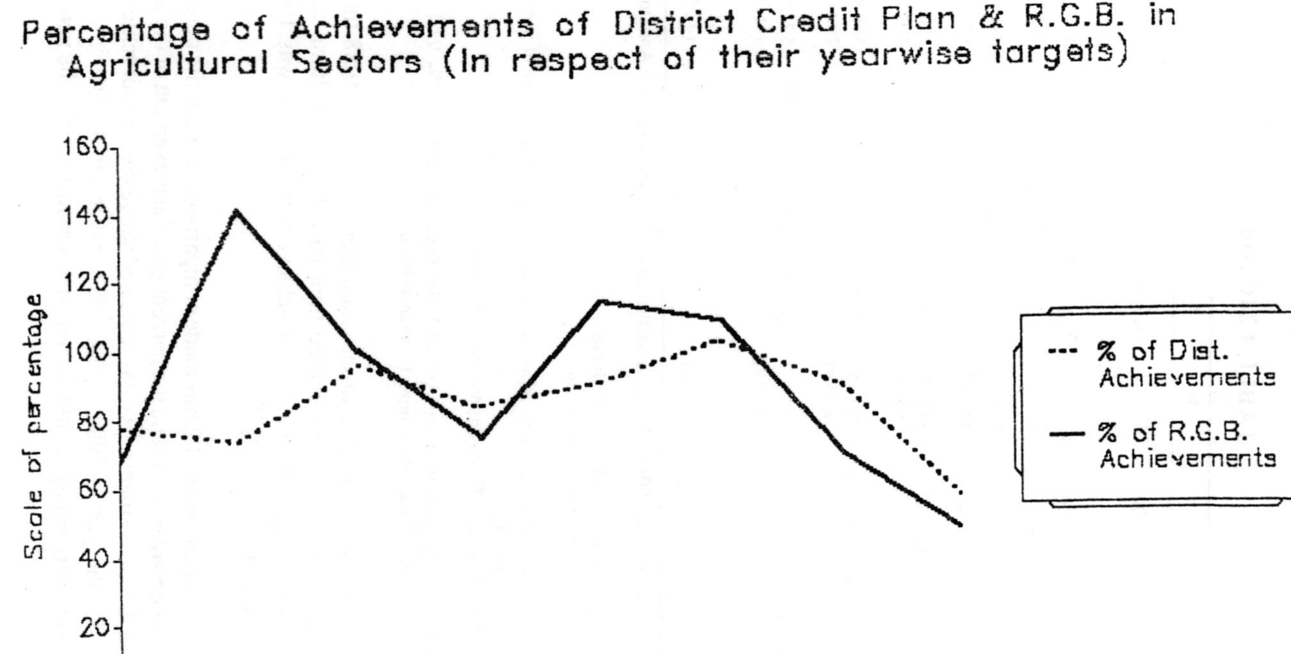
Percentage of Achievements of District Credit Plan & R.G.B. in
Agricultural Sectors (In respect of their yearwise targets)
Scale of percentage
160
140
120
100
80
60
40
20
% of Dist. Achievements
% of R.G.B. Achievements

of achievement of RGB. The achievement of RGB has suffered from big fluctuations in the years. This definitely not a healthy sympto.n of the credit practice of any financial institution. The credit curve should show more or less stable progress, which is not found in case of RGB.

TABLE - 4.3

Percentage of contribution of RGB in the District Credit Plan from 1983 to 1991-92

(By Percentage)

Year	*% of RGB contribution*	*District*
1983	4.85	100
1985	8.67	100
1986	8.99	100
1987	8.42	100
1988	11.21	100
1989-90	10.56	100
1990-91	14.46	100

Source : Data of the table 4.1 and 4.2

Table 4.3 on page 138, provides the information on the percentage of contribution of RGB lending to the total agricultural sectors of the district from 1983 to 1990-91. Periods of 1981, 1982 and 1991-92 were avoided as the detailed informations on Target achievements were not available. The percentage of contribution of RGB in the agricultural sector of the District fluctuated from 4.85% to 14.46% during 1983 to 1990-91. (Table. 4.3) The percentage went on increasing from year to year slowly and this has slightly declined in the years 1986, 1988, and 1989-90. However the contribution of RGB in the district agricultural credit is very negligible being below 15%. The RGB being a special organisation for the specified class of people has to play an important role in the agricultural sector of Ganjam district. The RGB has yet to play a major and more effective role in the rural sector as an institution meant to provide finance, mainly to agriculture, which is the heart of rural development of the district.

The role of RGB in the agricultural sector of Ganjam district may be compared by taking the average lending of an average branch of RGB and an average branch of the 17 commercial banks operating in the district. Table 4.4 and diagram 4.3 present the said comparison.

Column '4' of the Table 4.4 in page provides information on average advance of a branch of commercial banks and column '7' provides the same with regard to branch of RGB.

TABLE - 4.4

Comparative Average Advances of RGB and the Commercial Banks of Ganjam District in agriculture sector

(Amount in lakhs)

Year	*Commercial Banks* No. of Branch	Total Lending	Average Lending	*RGB* Branch	*RGB* Total Lending	Average Lending
1983	110/15 Banks	584.13	5.31	36	94.43	2.62
1984	112/15 Banks	726.19	6.48	32	182.19	3.50
1985	117/16 Banks	943.58	8.06	68	200.13	2.94
1986	117/16 Banks	739.82	6.32	68	116.29	2.44
1987	123/16 Banks	836.88	6.80	69	214.35	3.10
1988	123/16 Banks	1232.02	10.01	70	286.84	4.09
1989-90 (Apr-Mar)	141/17 Banks	1519.89	10.77	75	274.64	3.66
1990-91 (Apr-Mar)	141/17 Banks	696.64	4.94	75	162.77	2.17

Source : District Credit Plan and RGB Annual Action Plan

It is seen that in every year the average advance of a branch of commercial bank remained above the advance of a branch of RGB. In the year 1983 an average advance of a commercial bank branch was Rs. 5.31 lakhs, while the average advance of a branch of RGB was Rs. 2.62 lakhs.

It is to be seen from diagram, 4.3 and table 4.4 that the per branch advances of commercial banks are much higher than the per branch advances of RGB in all the years under consideration.

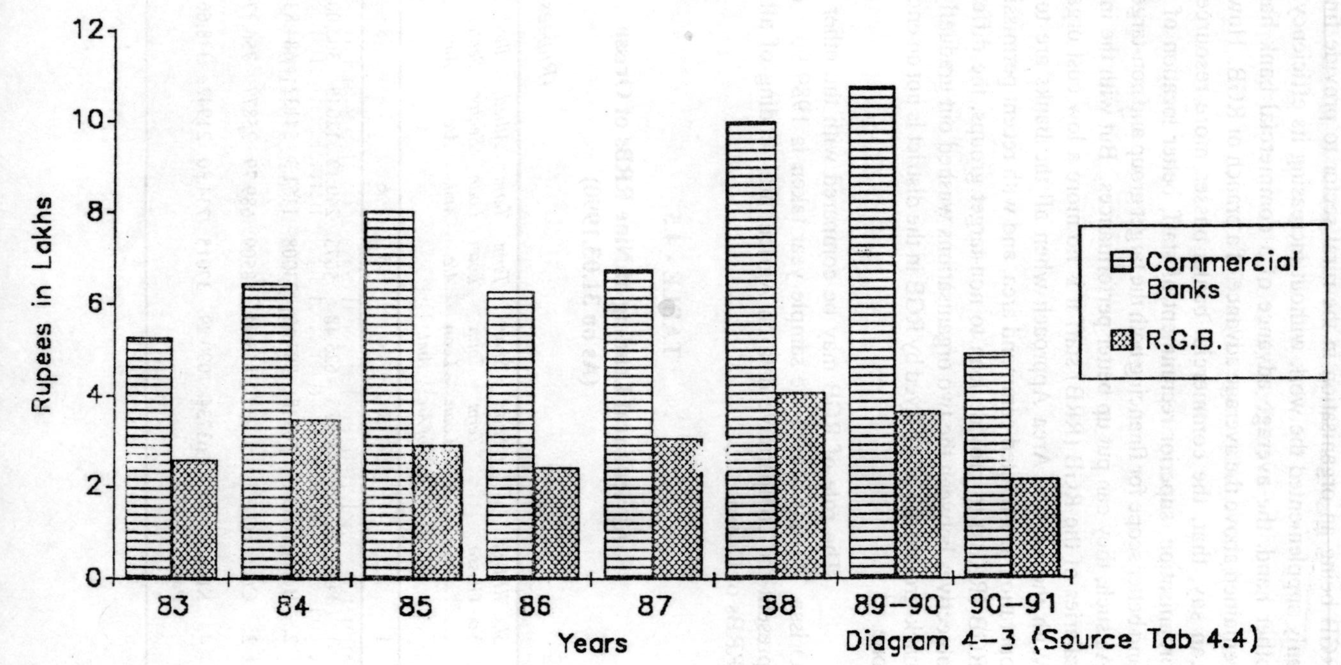

Diagram 4–3 (Source Tab 4.4)

It is seen from the facts of the table 4.4 and diagram 4.3 that RGB being an organisation in the rural sector to provide finance has only supplemented the work without increasing its efficiency. On the other hand, the average advance of a commercial bank has always remained above the average advance of a branch of RGB. However one can say, that, the commercial banks passes more resources, batter organisation, superior recruitment of staff, better location of branches and better scope for financing both the target group and non-target groups. As such, they can put up better performances. But with the increase of salaries of the RGB (RRB) staff it is no more a low cost organisation. With the Service Area Approach when all the banks are to do their operation in a limited command area, and with recent permission to the RGB (RRBs) to provide loan to non-target groups, the differences in objectives between the two organisations washed out gradually. In this back-ground the role played by RGB in the district is not an encouraging one.

The role of RGB may be compared with the other RRBs in Orissa. In this regard the sample year taken is 1989-90. Table 4.5 present the comparative data on Agricultural lending of all the nine RRBs of Orissa.

TABLE - 4.5

Agricultural Lending of Nine RRBs of Orissa (As on 31.03.1990)

(Rupees in lakhs)

Sl. No.	*RRB of Orissa*	*Short Term Loan of A/c.*	*Short Term Loan Amt.*	*Term Loan A/c.*	*Term Loan Amt.*	*Allied Sector A/c.*	*Allied Sector Amt.*	*Total Amount of Agriculture loan*
1	2	3	4	5	6	7	8	9
1.	Puri G.B.	25633	625.48	5073	240.12	12045	302.00	1167.60
2.	Bolangir G.B.	70948	887.10	73008	1151.3	54132	684.83	2723.46
3.	Cuttack G.B.	51935	855.94	18509	689.79	25877	756.37	2302.10
4.	Koraput Panchbati G.B.	63734	1090.29	37015	734.30	21942	348.66	2175.25

(Contd.)

TABLE - 4.5 (Contd.)

1	2	3	4	5	6	7	8	9
5.	Kalahandi Anchal G.B.	25799	499.38	11591	271.34	11903	266.05	1036.77
6.	Baitarani G.B.	12971	185.48	18699	286.93	14655	254.16	726.57
7.	Balesore G.B.	8096	185.19	2905	113.36	4385	116.35	414.90
8.	RGB, Ganjam	10413	249.45	8985	223.84	6010	130.51	603.80
9.	Dhenkanal G.B.	10714	215.95	4280	109.00	4023	63.06	388.01
	Total (Orissa)	260243	4794.26	180065	3820.21	154972	2921.99	11536.46

Source : RRB statistics (1989-90), Bombay, NABARD.

Out of Rs. 11536.46 lakhs of advances in agricultural sector, the RGB has advanced Rs. 603.80 lakhs only which constitutes 5.23% of the total RRB agricultural advances of Orissa during March 90. The Bolangir Gramya Bank advanced 23.60% of the RRB agricultural loans of Orissa and is in the highest position. The Dhenkanal Gramya Bank reveals the lowest performance i.e., only 3.36% of the total RRB agricultural lending of the state. The RGB is in 7th position out of the total nine RRBs of Orissa, while lending to agricultural sector during March 1990. (As per the data of the table 4.5)

The total beneficiaries of Orissa in the agricultural sector in RRB lending was 595280 during 1989-90. Thus the average Orissa RRB loan in agriculture per a beneficiary constitute Rs. 193/- only. On the other hand, the total number of beneficiaries in the district was 25408 and thus the average agricultural loan for a beneficiary in the district comes to Rs. 237/-. In a comparison of these two averages, it is found that the district average loan per beneficiary is better than the State average. The beneficiaries of RGB in agricultural sector constitute only 4.26% of the total. (As per the data of table 4.5).

Out of Rs. 20265/- lakhs of total RRB advances of Orissa during Sept. 1991. The total agricultural lending is Rs. 9119.75 lakhs which constitute 45 per cent of the total lending. On the other hand, at the all India level during September 1991 the total lending constitute Rs. 380360.16 lakhs and the total agricultural lending of the nation is Rs.

185013.73 lakhs, which constitute 48.64% of the total lending. The total agricultural lending of the nation is Rs. 185013.73 lakhs, which constitute 48.64% of the total lending. The total agricultural lending of the state constitutes only 4.92% of the RRB lending of the country during Sept. 1991.[30]

Thus, the RGB has advanced 5.23% of the total RRB lending to agricultural sector in Orissa by March 1990 and the RRBs of Orissa on the other hand advanced 4.92% of the total RRB agriculture lending of the country as on Sept. 1991.

The Findings of the Analysis

After the comparative analysis of the date and facts regarding the role of RGB in agriculture sector the following findings emerge.

The percentage of achievement of RGB to the achievement of the district in agricultural sector is very insignificant. It has however improved from the year 1984 onwards. By 1990 March the percentage of contribution of RGB to the district agricultural lending is only 10.56% and by March 1991 it has increased to 14.46%. During December 1987 and Dec. 1988, the percentage were 11.81% and 1121% respectively. In other years it has remained below 10% (Table 4.3)

In the croploans the RGB achievements exceeded the targets in the year 1982, 1984, and in 1987. As such during these periods the performance of the RGB is the best one. RGB and Cooperative Banks has contributed more than 50% in croploan sector of the district during 1987. Afterwards, due to the natural calamities and with introduction of ARDRS the croploan achievements were disturbed. On the otherhand the non-cordination of the agricultural Department and the Bank personals as the non-involvement of other developmental organisations in execution of policies and practices became the main reason of the low performance of RGB.

In case of term loans, the RGB has performed better in the years 1982, 1984, and 1988 by crossing 100% of achievements. The reason of the unsatisfactory performance of RGB is due to the undeveloped behaviour of farmers in agricultural sector. The farmers are illiterate.

Agricultural inputs were not provided at the right time to the farmers and the ground water potentialities were not fully utilised. Lack of power, delay in processing the loan applications, continuous overdues, disposal of assets by beneficiaries, malpractices followed by the officials and beneficiaries, non-availability of raw materials, plough animal and cows etc. were the main reason of poor performance.

In a comparison between the croploan and term loan of RGB in the years 1984, 1985, 1986, 1988, 1990-91, and 1991-92 the percentage of achievements of crop loan remained below the percentage of achievement of term loans of RGB.

The target and achievement of the total agricultural sector were fluctuating in a narrow range upto 1988. But after 1988, the target were neverachieved and the gap between them increased (Diagram 4.1) This is not a good symptom of a credit policy of RGB.

The performance of RGB has suffered from big fluctuations when compared to the performances of the district in this sector in percentage. (Diagram 4.2). The performance in term of achievement can be treated as a good one only when the same is more or less stable in progress, which is not seen in case of RGB.

The average agricultural loan of a branch of RGB has always remained below the achievements of an average branch of commercial banks. With the increase in the salaries of RGB staff, with the introduction of SAA to all the banks including RGB and allowing the RGB to advance loans to non-target groups, the differences in functioning and lending has been minimised and the special objective of RRB has been lost to a great extent. As such, the efficiency of the branches of RGB has to be increased by merging them either with the sponsor bank or by setting a new national level rural banking organisation or striking an innovation in the structure of RGB.

In lending to agriculture the RGB has been placed in the 7th position among the RRBs of the State. (By lending only 5.23% of the total agricultural loans of all RRBs) and in the same way the RRBs of Orissa has lent only 4.92% of the total RRB agricultural RRB loans of the country by Sept. 1991.

RGB, even now is essentially a bank for target groups and more than 96% of its lending is diverted to the target groups. Thus the scope of making profit is very limited for RGB. As such, the Dantwala Committee in 1977 has passed the remark - "as district level organisation, the RRBs can be trusted to take banking closer to the rural households and ensure effective supervision over the end use of credit."[31] As such a class of people say that the problem cannot be solved either by abolition of RRBs or merging them with commercial banks/co-operative banks. When it is accepted that, RRBs should retain their separate identity, the policy regarding their coverage, size and client etc. has to be checked out."[32] The contradictory view of continuing the RRBs in their separate identity or merging them with other banks all the two extreme concepts.

The Rushikulya Gramya Bank is now passing through strains no doubt, but it has to persist in accepting the challenge of agricultural and rural development as a whole in the district. The scope of lending and business is necessarily to be extended for increasing the efficiency by changing the organisational pattern of RRBs. Top priority in the objectives for rural development and the development for the neglected rural people of the district is an essential need, which the RGB has to perform.

Agricultural credit is to manifest as a key instrument of economic development in rural sectors of India and since the mid fifties the rural banks have been the most important channels for the same. In this regard, the RGB in Ganjam district has also played a role in agricultural sector by directing much-needed credit to the neglected area on priority basis. The RGB deployed quite a substantial amount of finance for the improvement of economic standard of different categories of rural farmers and persons involved in the allied activities in the villages and semi-urban areas of the district. It has lent under well-defined schemes and with clearly laid down, predetermined repayment schedule for croploans, term loans and loans for allied activities, which constitute the whole of agricultural sector of RGB.

The important suggestions for the improvement of the RGB in agriculture sector are mainly :

(1) Loans to be sanctioned to the proper beneficiaries through an easy way.

(2) Recoveries on overdues of agricultural loan has to be conducted with the coordination of bank officials and district/block administration.

(3) Timely supply of credit imputs to the farmers and artisans (Capital goods, essential articles, seeds fertilizers and animals) by the concerned authority of the district.

(4) Increasing the irrigation potentialities with the extension of the ground water use through lift irrigation and by energisation of such irrigation projects.

(5) Providing cement to such irrigation plants in convenient - and concessional manner.

(6) Increasing the use of biogass, incr⸗sing hor⸗cultural activities, animal hasbandry fishery, etc. as allied activities.

(7) Providing training to the beneficiaries.

(8) Improving the pattern of working and getting desirable changes in the organisation of the RRBs (RGB in Ganjam). The rural development and easy cheap credit to the neglected rural population must be primary and the only objectives of RRBs.

In the existing multi-agency system of rural credit, the RGB is yet to play a pivotal role in the lending to agricultural and rural sector of Ganjam district. The agriculture is the key of economic development and providing cheap loan to target group farmers and agricultural labourers is the fundamental objectives of RGB. The objectives yet to be fulfilled.

SECTION - B

RGB Lending to the Industrial Sector & Service Tertiary Sector

This section of study on RGB lending is sub-divided into : (a) Lending to industrial sector (b) Lending to the service/tertiary sector and follows the same methods of analysis in explaining the role and position of RGB in Industry and service sector as explained in agricultural sector.

(a) Lending to the Industrial Sector

Financial input is an important factor for development of small, tiny, cottage and village industries. If proper financial capital is not available, the economic progress of village India is not possible. Most of the target class of people waiting for loans are found in the rural areas. In those areas Bank cannot-hope to make profits due to the prevailing poverty. However, RGB being a special kind of banking organisation oriented towards financing the target group has to play a key role in providing institutional finance to such small entrepreneurs, otherwise, it will be difficult for the industries to grow by borrowing money at exhorbitant rates of interest from other sources.

The economy of Ganjam district is predominantly an agricultural one and small scale industrial activities are usually undertaken as an activity of leisure time and to supplement income. Industry as the main occupation is a new concept for the inhabitants of Ganjam district.

The small scale village and cottage industries obtain financial assistance from Orissa State Financial Corporation (OSFC), nationalised commercial banks, non-nationalised scheduled commercial banks, Rushikulya Gramya Bank and the Co-operative Banks in the district. In pursuance of the orgnisational goals to provide institutional credit to the rural poor, RGB (RRB) has come up as an arm of the government to implement government sponsored, poverty-alleviation programmes. Consequently, RGB (RRB) has drawn and evolved diverse and multifarious schemes in consonance with the loan programmes of the government. The lending schemes of RGB (RRB) is tailor-cut not only to supplement but also to implement the lending schemes sponsored by the government.[33] But in Ganjam district the RGB has not-received the co-operation and co-ordination of the District Industries Centre (DIC) and with DRDA for the implementation of the lending programmes of the industry sector.

The Rushikulya Gramya Bank 's restricted by the objective in providing loan to the target groups consisting of rural artisans, and small traders in rural area, which considerably limits the operation of RGB in this sector. Usually, commercial banks finance the working capital requirements of small scale industries (SSI). With the introduction of liberalised refinance scheme of Industrial Development Bank of India (IDBI) commercial banks have come forward to provide block capital finance also. The Reserve Bank of India (RBI) has already urged the commercial banks for quick disposal of cases upto Rs. 25,000/- at the branch level under special employment scheme[34].

Table - 4.6 in next page presents the targets and achievements of RGB in lending to the industrial sector from 1983 to 1991-92. The Initial two years were not taken into account, considering them as periods of establishment and branch extension. In the industry and service sector the analysis started from the year 1983 onwards.

TABLE - 4.6

RGB Lending Industry Sector

(Rupees in Lakhs)

S. No.	*Years*	*Targets*	*Achievement*	*Percentage of Achievement*
1.	1983	28.32	4.8	16.94
2.	1984	3.46	44.53	333.23
3.	1985	4.00	7.33	183.25
4.	1986	5.00	6.95	139.00
5.	1987	15.00	9.07	60.46
6.	1988	16.00	10.68	66.75
7.	1989-90	33.44	3.85	11.51
8.	1990-91	34.30	4.14	12.06
9.	1991-92	98.57	34.04	34.53

Note : From 1983 to 1988 are calender years and thereafter the periods are financial years.

Source : RGB Annual Action Plans/District Credit Plans.

It is seen from the table 4.6 that, the role played by RGB in the provision of credit to the industrial sector is not encouraging. The

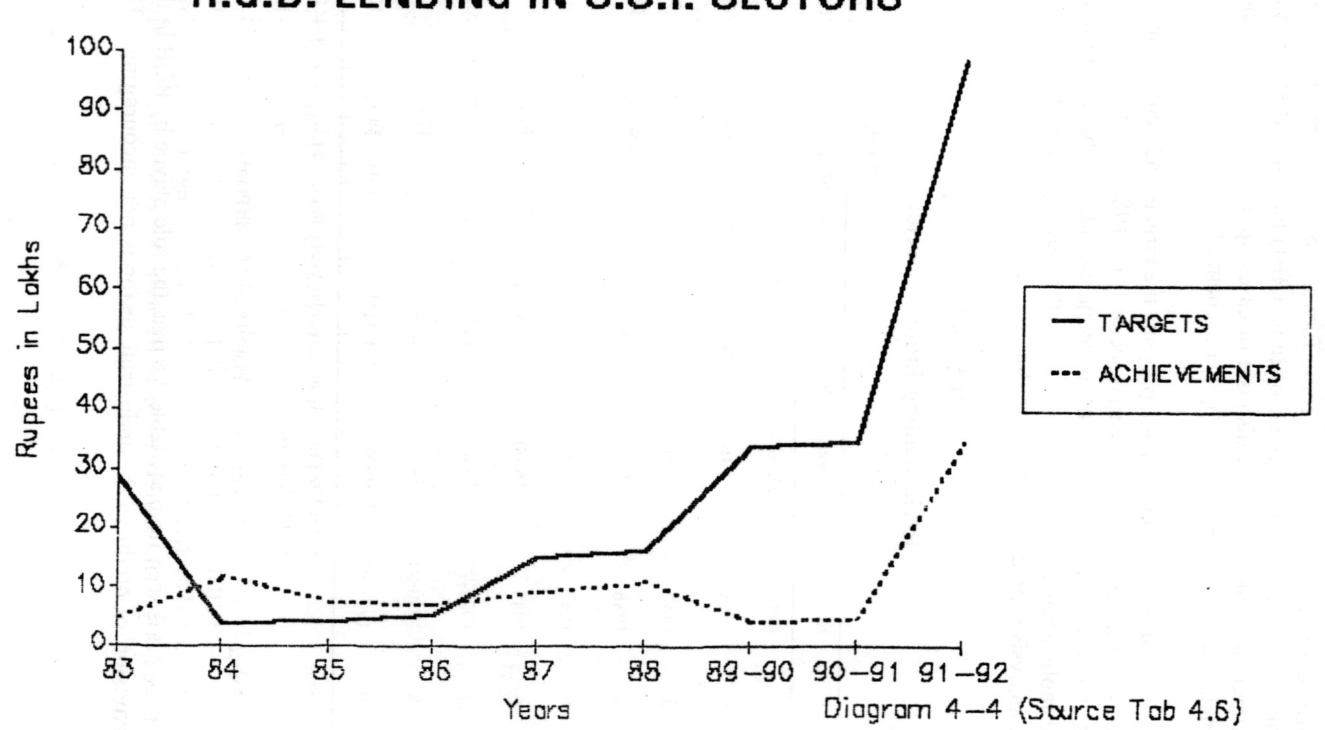

Diagram 4—4 (Source Tab 4.6)

percentage of achievements for the year 1984, 1985 and 1986 are quite satisfactory. But this cannot be regarded as much of an achievement, when, the smaller targets of those years are seen. For such a big district the amounts of targets were only Rs. 3.46 lakhs, Rs. 4 lakhs and Rs. 5 lakhs for the year 1984, 1985, 1986 respectively.

It is seen from the table 4.6 and the diagram 4.4 that there is a big fluctuation between the targets and achievements. The diagram 4.4 has been drawn with the data of the target and achievements of S.S.I sector of RGB (Table 4.6).

In the year 1981, there was no target for RGB. In the said year it has lent Rs. 0.79 lakhs. In the next year i.e., by 1982 the target for SSI sector was Rs. 2 lakh and it has lent Rs. 1.15 lakhs. The percentage of success was 75.55%. These two years were not mentioned in the table 4.6 or in the diagram 4.4.

In the year 1987, and 1988 the percentage of achievements were 60.46% and 66.75% respectively, but the amounts of loan in this sector have increased. While in the year 1986 the amounts of loan were Rs. 6.95 lakhs it has increased to Rs. 9.07 lakhs in the year 1987 and to Rs. 10.68 lakhs in the year 1988. In the financial years of 1989-90, 1990-91 and in 1991-92, the targets were more than the double the targets of the previous years for the RGB. But it is very much surprising to see the low achievements of these periods. While the bank has made provision for lending, there is no demand for such loans. This is mainly because the target group are not industrial oriented in their profession. They do not have the skill, training, and encouragement to undertake industrial activities. They are illiterate, ignorant and economically poor. As such the percentage of achievements of those three financial years were 11.51%, 12.06% and 34.53%, which is not satisfactory. However, during the period 1991-92 the maximum amounts of loan were made available to the beneficiaries, i.e. Rs. 34.04 lakhs out of the target of Rs. 98.57 lakhs. Quantitatively, there is an improvement in the said year in the lending of SSI sector of RRG. It is seen from the diagram 4 that the Gap between target and achievements of RGB has negetively widened from 1986 on wards.

For a comparative analysis of the role of RGB in relation to the other financial institutions providing finance to S.S.I. sector in the district, the data provided in Annexure-3 may be studied. On the basis of the same data the table 4.7 provides the percentage of achievement in relation to their respective targets of RGB, commercial Banks,Co-operatives and OSFC below.

In the comparison of the achievements the year 1991-92 has not been included as the relevant data for the year could not be collected. Thus the comparison of the respective institutions were made for the period 1983 (Jan.-Dec.) to 1990-91 (Apr. -March)

The table 4.7 in next page shows that except in the three years i.e. 1984, 1985, and 1986, the RGB has not fared well in its performance in comparison to other financial institutions. But the percentage of achievement may not be treated as a sufficient reason to judge the comparative position of RGB. The percentage of achievement may be found better if the targets are fixed at a lower level.

TABLE - 4.7
Industrial Sector Lending in Ganjam district
(All financial institutions)

(Percentage of Achievments)

Year	*RGB*	*Com. Banks*	*Co.op. Banks*	*OSFC*	*District as a whole*
1983	16.94	86.15	357.75	79.22	95.62
1984	333.23	72.40	391.67	22.67	104.22
1985	183.25	110.38	64.91	88.76	92.39
1986	139.00	75.1	214.85	93.15	118.26
1987	60.46	117.24	33.92	205.85	131.86
1988	66.75	149.84	74.13	40.72	82.10
1989-90	11.51	127.88	-	66.80	125.03
1990-91	12.06	43.38	-	90.75	56.76

Note : From 1983 to 1988 are that calender years and thereafter the financial years are taken.

Source : Annexure 3

It is seen from the table 4.6 that the RGB during the year 1991-92 has a target for Rs. 98.57 lakhs and the achievement was Rs. 34.04 lakhs. The amounts advanced were the highest. But the percentage of achievement was only 34.04 percent. While advancing Rs. 11.53 lakhs in the year 1984, the percentage of success becomes 333.23% as the target was very low i.e. only Rs. 3.46 lakhs. As such, the comparison may be more effective if the relative contributions of different financial institutions to be seen from the district lending in industrial sector.

The achievements of the district may be assumed as 100% and then, the relative contributions of financial institutions to the district may be found as in table 4.8.

TABLE - 4.8

Percentage of contribution of the financial institutions in industrial sector of Ganjam district.

(By Percentage)

S. No.	*Years*	*RGB*	*Com. Banks*	*Co-op. Banks*	*OSFC*	*District*
1	2	3	4	5	6	7
1.	1983	1.62	42.39	25.31	30.66	100
2.	1984	3.05	36.80	21.80	38.33	100
3.	1985	1.76	32.89	9.31	56.01	100
4.	1986	1.17	20.32	45.41	33.08	100
5.	1987	1.27	25.57	6.65	66.49	100
6.	1988	2.50	59.78	13.05	24.65	100
7.	1989-90	0.49	64.64	18.07	16.78	100
8.	1990-91	1.19	47.87	-	50.93	100

Source : Worked out from the data of Annexure - 3

The size of contributions of RGB, commercial banks and co-operatives to the district lending can be seen from the diagram No. 4.5 in next page, which has been worked out by utilising the data of the table 4.8.

It is seen from table 4.8 and diagram No. 4.5 that the contribution of RGB to the industrial sector in the district is the lowest when compared to other financial institutions participating in all the years under

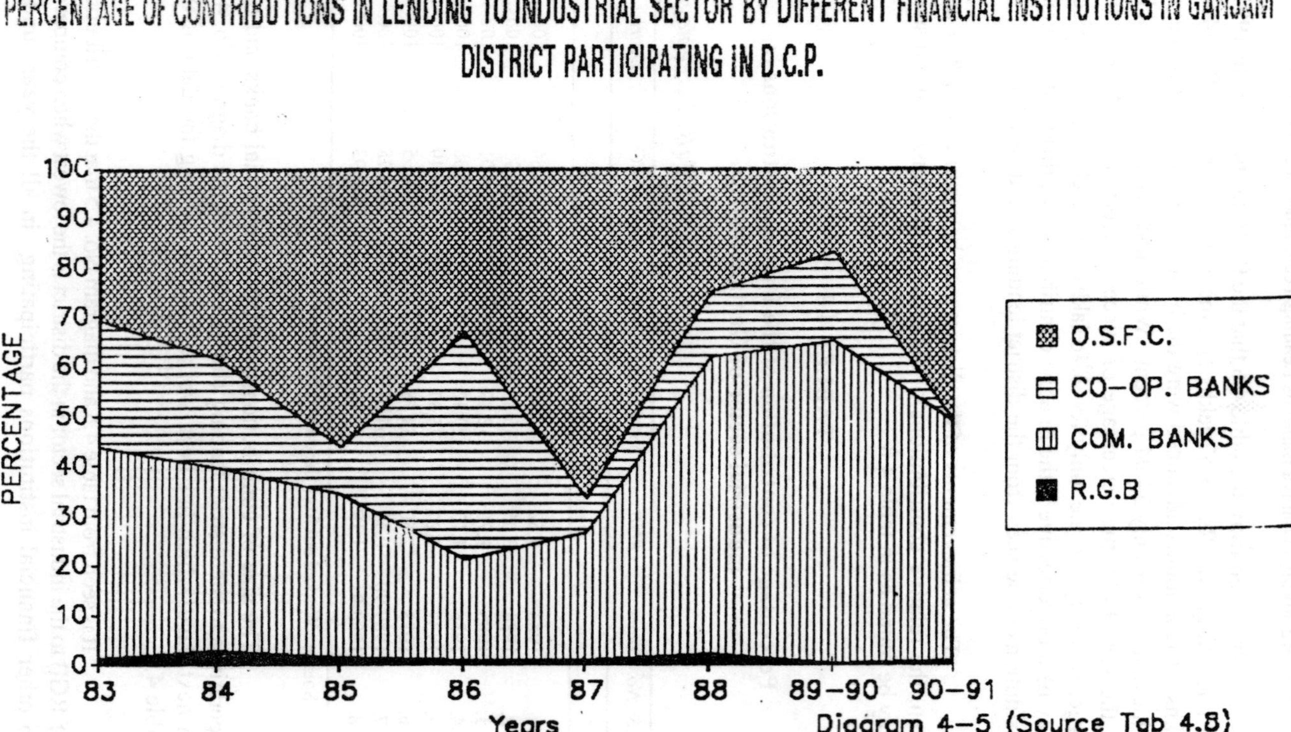

Diagram 4–5 (Source Tab 4.8)

consideration. It has lent 3.05% in the year 1984 and 2.5% in the year 1988 but thereafter in all other years the contribution of RGb is less than 2%. The shaded area at the bottom of diagram No. 4.5 is the yearwise total contributions of RGB. The portion of area shown for RGB is a negligible proportion of the total area and it is a negligible percentage of contribution in the district. Even the Co-operative banks, except for the year 1990-91, have contributed better percentage than the RGB in the district. The co-operatives reduced their role in 1989-90 not fixing any target for the industrial sector. In 1990-91, they neither fixed the target nor did they lend to this sector. The target and achievement of Co-opratives for the year 1991-92 (upto Dec.) as shown in Annexure - 3 was found from the Berhampur Co-operative Central Banks Ltd. only.

The Orissa State Financial Corporation (OSFC) is a specialised organisation for providing loans to the industrial sector of the district. Hence, there is no need for making a comparison of achievement of RGB with the said institutions. But in a comparison with the commercial banks, the performance of OSFC has remained below the performance of commercial banks in the years 1983, 1988 and in 1989-90.

By 31.3.91 the RGB with its 75 branches has advanced Rs. 4.14 lakhs. Its average loan for a branch of RGB in the district comes to Rs. 552/- only. In the same way the commercial banks with their 141 branches during March 1991 have advanced Rs. 166.36 lakhs. The average loan per branches of commercial bank in the industrial sector of Ganjam district comes to Rs. 1.18 lakhs.

The table 4.9 provides the information on the lending of all the nine RRBs of Orissa by the end of March 1990.

Table 4.9 reveals that the RGB in Ganjam district has contributed only 0.78% of the total S.S.I. lendings by RRBs of Orissa during 1989-90 (March), RGBs rank in sharing in the field of lending to the industries during the said period in the state of Orissa is the lowest in the list (Column 6 of table 4.9). In the same way, the per branch average lending of RGB (column 5 of table 4.9) is also the lowest. It has lent only Rs. 0.2 lakhs, which is a negligible amount, and it is much less than the state average of Rs. 2.42 lakhs. The Kalahandi Anchala Gramya Bank is at the top by lending Rs. 7.24 lakhs per branch and sharing 28.02% of the total RRB lending of the state during 1989-90 (March). At the all India level the RRBs have outstanding advances of Rs. 321 crores to the rural artisans, village and cottage industries during Sept. 1991.[35]

TABLE - 4.9

Lending to the industries by RRBs of Orissa As on 31.3.1990

(Rupees in Lakhs)

Sl. No.	*Name of the RRBs of Orissa*	*No. of Branches*	*Amounts advance (Rs.)*	*Per branch average advance*	*Individual % of share to the State*
1.	Puri Gramya Bank	100	122.54	1.22	6.15
2.	Bolangir Anchal Gramya Bank	155	483.52	3.2	24.3
3.	Cuttack Gramya Bank	121	292.80	2.42	14.71
4.	Koraput Panchabati Gramya Bank	90	363.52	4.04	18.27
5.	Kalahandi Anchal Gramya Bank	77	557.51	7.24	28.02
6.	Boitarani Gramya Bank	90	97.00	1.07	4.87
7.	Balesore Gramya Bank	63	18.98	0.30	0.95
8.	Rushikulya Gramya Bank	75	15.61	0.20	0.78
9.	Dhenkanala G.B.	48	38.13	0.80	1.91
	Total (Orissa)	819	1989.63	2.42	100

Source : RRB Statistics (NABARD) 1989-90 Statement No. 6 Column - 11.

The reasons for the of low performance of RGB in Industry Sector

The most important reasons for the low performance of RGB in Ganjam district are as follows :

(i) It has to advance to the target group only, they are poor, and illiterate and have no background of industrial activities.

(ii) The branches of commercial banks, Co.operatives and the OSFC have more resources to lend in this sector and the District Industry Centre has a systematic link with commercial Bank and OSFC only. It is learnt in an interview with the Rural Development Officer of RGB that the bank has no link with the sponsored programmes of the District Industries Centre (D.I.C.). It lends to the target group on its own.[36]

(iii) The branches of commercial Banks advance loans to the target group as well as to the non-target groups. The position of RGB can be improved if the target group artisans, without taking loans from other sources, are dependant on RGB only. Among the RRBs of Orissa, the RGB has been placed at the lowest position in achievements of lending in industrial sector. It shows a very low performance of RGB in the State.

(iv) However as a whole the achievements of the DCP in industry sector is also not satisfactory. The district is industrially backward and the scope of modern industrial activities are limited. From time to time it is observed in the District Credit Plan that the performance is not satisfactory. As such, an industrial sub-committee was constituted during the credit plan of 1982-85 period to study the reasons for low performance.[37] It was seen that the industrial activities in Ganjam district are only confined to a few categories i.e., mainly traditional activities like carpentry, Bamboo works and Handloom. Thus the committee recommended for spread of modern industrial activities over rural Ganjam.

For providing encouragement, the developmental organisation, the Government agencies from the block level has to educate the people and should arrange training. The lack of power, shortage of raw materials and quick process of loans are essential for stimulating the industrial activities in Ganjam district.

On the otherhand the market for the village products should also be extended on the basis of advertisement, exhibitions, by providing transportation facilities and through Government help, otherwise, this adverse performances of RGB in the industrial sector cannot be improved.

(b) RGB Lending in Service and Tertiary Sector

The Service Sector advances constitute a major part of the priority sector advances. It is the activity of the bank, where advances of several types for increasing the production and providing employment can be made for economic development.

In this sector, the bank provides, loans to retail traders, small business men, transport operators, professionals and self employed persons. The consumption loans for medical expenses, educational needs, loans to meet the cermonial expenses are also given in this sector.

The performance of RGB in this sector is most satisfactory. The achievements of RGB in providing loans has always exceeded the targets in this sector.

RBI and the Government of India are attaching a lot of importance to the category of professional and self-employed persons. Loans to professional and self employed include loans for the purpose of purchasing equipment, repairing or renovating existing equipment and/or acquiring and repairing business premises or for purchasing tools and/or for working capital requirements to medical practitioners including dentists, chartered accountants, cost accountants, lawyers, or solicitors engineers, architects surveyors, construction contractors or management consultants or to a person trained in any other art or craft who holds either a degree or a diploma from any institution established, aided or recognised by Government or to a person who is considered by the bank as technically qualified or skilled in the field in which he is employed. Preferance is given by banks to finance professionals like doctors etc., who are carrying on their profession in rural or semi-urban areas. The term also includes firm and joint ventures of such professional and self-employed persons. The limit of borrowing to such persons is Rs. 2 lakhs out of which one lakh should be the working capital.[38]

Advance granted to private retail traders dealing with essential commodities and consumer co-operative stores and other private retail traders with credit limits not exceeding Rs. 25,000/-

Small business includes individuals and firms managing a business enterprise established mainly for the purpose of promoting any services whose original cost price of equipment used for the purpose of business does not exceed Rs. 2 lakhs. Advance for acquisition, construction, renovation of house boats and other tourist accomodation are included here.[39]

Table 4.10 provides the yearwise date of the Services and tertiary sector lending of RGB from 1983 (Jan. to Dec.) to 1991-92 (Apr. to Mar.).

TABLE - 4.10

RGB Lending in Tertiary and Service Sector

(Rupees in Lakhs)

Year	*Targets*	*Achievements*	*% of achievement*
1983	2.39	21.4	895.39
1984	29.24	59.36	203.00
1985	35.00	58.43	166.94
1986	42.9	155.06	361.44
1987	80.00	255.15	318.93
1988	85.00	349.59	411.28
1989-90	93.48	456.02	487.82
1990-91	115.85	489.31	422.36
1991-92	111.54	96.84	86.82

Note : From 1983 to 1988 are the calender years and thereafter the financial years.

Source : RGB Annual Reports from 1983 onwards.

It is seen from the table 4.10 that only in 1991-92 the achievement is below 100%. But in all other years the percentage of achievements of RGB in this sector is above 100%. In the first year i.e., in 1981 during the period of establishment and in the next year i.e. in 1982 (both the periods are not shown in the table) the lendings were Rs. 2.30 lakhs and Rs. 23.40 lakhs respectively. The first year has no targets while for the second year the target was 10 lakhs. As such the percentage of success in 1982 was 234%.

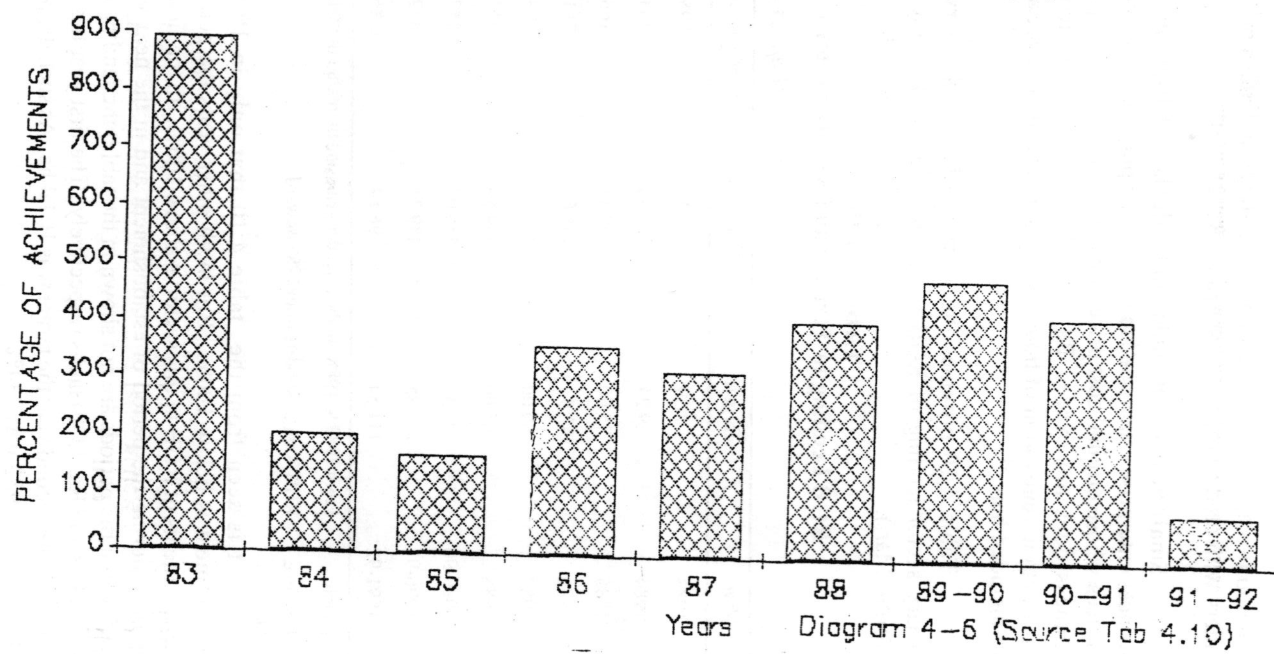

Diagram 4-6 (Source Tab 4.10)

It is seen from the diagram 4.6 that the highest achievement is found in the year 1983. The percentage of achievement was 895.39%. On the other hand during the year 1991-92, the percentage of achievement was the lowest one and remained below 100%. The percentage of achievement was only 86.82%.

The Diagram 4.7 presents the target and achievement curves of RGB in quantitative terms. The target curve always remained below the achievement curve upto 1990-91. Only in the year 1991-92 the target curve remained above the achievement curve.

In the year 1983, the percentage of achievements of RGB is better than that of any other financial institutions of the district. The commercial banks have also crossed their targets and got 143% of achievements. But the Co.operatives and OSFC have a very low percentage of achievements.

On the other hand, during 1984, the RGB, commercial banks and co-operative banks have exceeded 100%. RGB has the achievements of 203%, commercial banks 195.83% and Co-operative Banks by 483.5%. The OSFC has only 44.55% of success.

In 1985 RGB has an achievement of 166.94% Commercial banks have 295.27% of success over the targets.

In 1986 and 1987 only Co-operative Banks could not exceed their targets, while in 1988 the OSFC has not crossed the targets. During 1989-90, Co-operatives have not fixed their targets and OSFC remained below the target. The RGB and Commercial banks remained above their targets, achieveing 487.82% for RGB and 118.83% for Commercial Banks.

In the year 1991-92 RGB has 422.36 percentage of success, Co-operatives have the success of 1705.98% and OSFC has 152.2% of success while Commercial Banks remained below the target, achieving only 79.42 per cent.

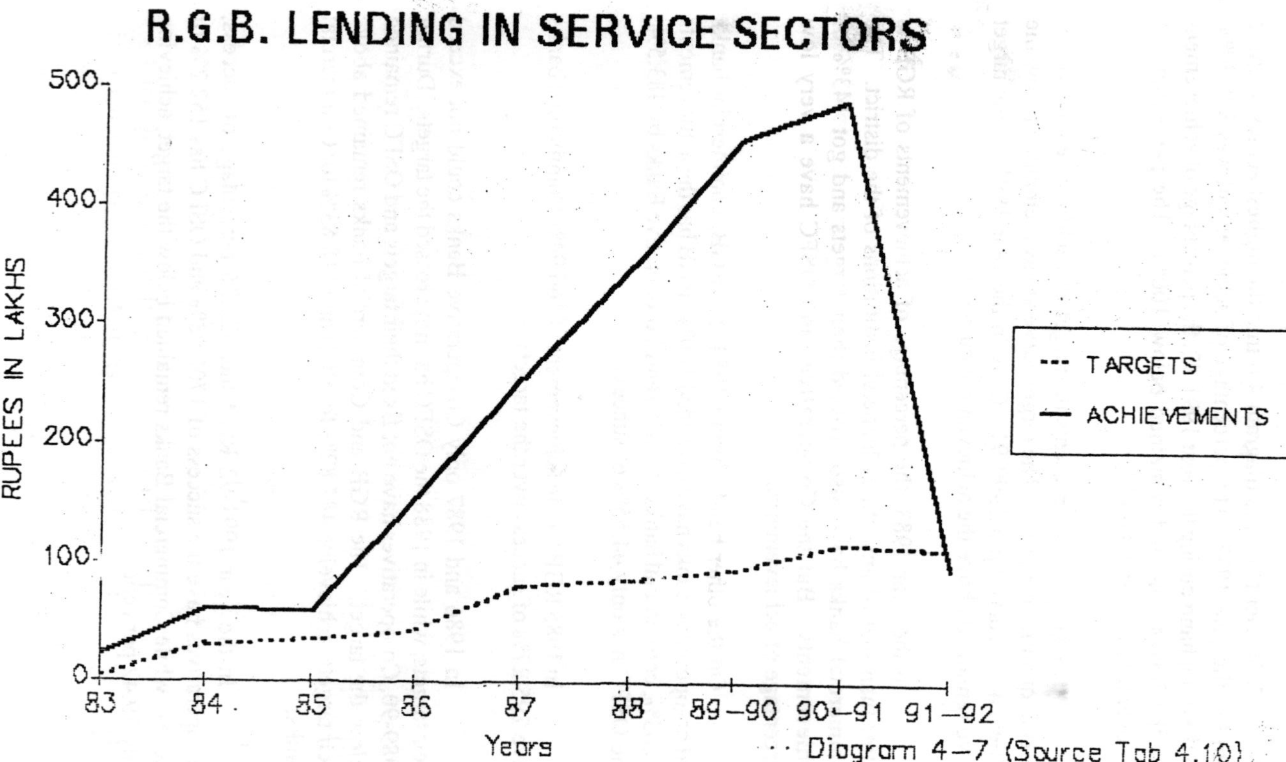

Diagram 4—7 (Source Tab 4.10)

TABLE - 4.11

Percentage of Achievement of all Financial Institutions in Ganjam District (Tertiary/Service Sector).

(By percentage)

Year	*RGB*	*Com. Banks*	*Co.op. Banks*	*OFC*	*District*
1983	895.39	143.03	18.53	22.39	117.52
1984	203.00	195.83	486.5	44.55	187.51
1985	166.94	295.27	78.03	138.61	220.74
1986	361.44	196.18	83.36	150.2	183.93
1987	318.93	154.82	91.42	155.14	166.79
1988	411.28	181.55	155.84	47.8	176.47
1989-90	487.82	118.83	-	68.35	176.23
1990-91	422.36	79.42	1705.98	152.2	148.09

Note : 1983 to 1988 calender years, thereafter financial years.

Source : Annexure - 4.

From the above analysis it is clearly seen that the achievement of RGB is always above 100% and was quite satisfactory. The Commercial banks, the Co-operatives and OSFC have some time crossed the targets and at other times remained below the targets. However the district level achievement has shown a consistent improvement in crossing the targets. One important observation is found from the table-4.11 that, the percentage of achivement of RGB always remained above the percentage of achievements of the district excluding for the year 1985 where the RGB has the achievement of 166.94 and the district has an achievement of 220.74%.

The table 4.12 presents the data on percentage of contributions of RGB, Commercial Banks, Co-operatives Banks and OSFC in the Tertiary and Service Sector of the district from 1983 to 1990-91.

The data of the table 4.12 has been plotted in the diagram 4.8. It is seen from the table 4.12 and diagram 4.8 that the percentage of contribution of RGB in the district lending in this sector is continuously increasing from 6.66% in 1983 to 37.44% in 1990-91.

TABLE - 4.12

Percentage of Contributions of different financial institutions of Ganjam district in Service/Tertiary Sector.

District = 100%

Year	*RGB*	*Com. Banks*	*Co-op. Banks*	*OSFC (Ganjam)*	*District*
1983	6.66	88.47	0.82	4.04	100
1984	11.86	67.84	16.05	4.24	100
1985	7.32	76.37	5.84	10.42	100
1986	18.44	57.95	7.51	16.08	100
1987	21.66	53.11	5.78	19.43	100
1988	26.47	58.90	8.82	5.79	100
1989-90	32.95	50.81	11.28	7.93	100
1990-91	37.44	39.99	10.90	11.64	100

Note : 1983 to 1988 calender years, thereafter financial years.

Source : Annexure - 4.

The commercial banks have always shared a major percentage and upto 1989-90, these were above 50%. In 1990-91, when RGB contributed 37.44% of the total lending of the district, the Commercial banks were slightly above the RGB in contributing 39.99 percent of the total lending of the district in this sector. The share of the Co-operatives and OSFC always fluctuated and remained below 20%. During 1990-91, the Co-operatives lent 10.90% and OSFC contributed 11.64% of the total lending of the district in Service/Tertiary sector. The diagram No. 4.8 in the next page has clearly market the total lending of the district and the percentage of lending of RGB in the concerned sector.

In the comparison of average loan per branch of RGB and a branch of commercial banks of the district; an branch of RGB was advancing an average amounts of Rs. 6.52 lakhs while a branch of the commercial bank has an average of Rs. 3.70 lakhs of advances as on period 31.3.1991.

It shows that the RGB as an agent of rural development and as a stimulator of income generation has played an effective role in comparison to other financial institutions of the district.

PERCENTAGE OF YEARWISE CONTRIBUTION OF DIFFERENT FINANCIAL INSTITUTIONS OF GANJAM DIST. IN LENDING TO SERVICE & TERTIARY SECTORS (IN D.C.P.)

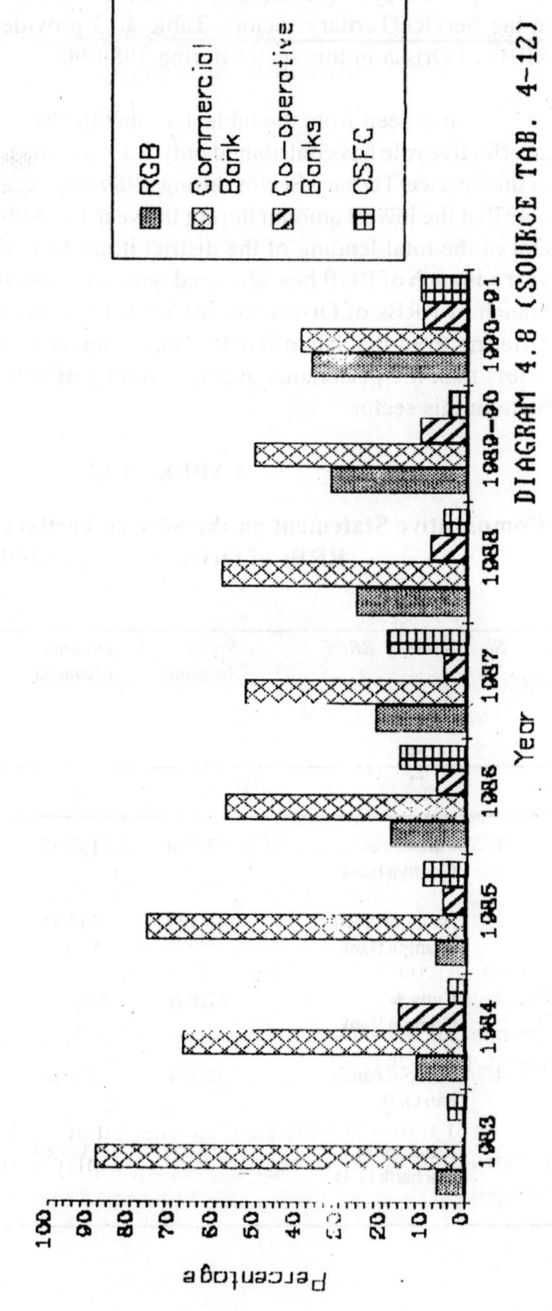

We may now compare the role of RGB with other RRBs of Orissa in the Service/Tertiary sector. Table 4.13 provides the date on all the RRBs of Orissa in this sector during 1989-90.

It is seen from the table 4.13 that the RGB entrusted with such an effective role has contributed only 5.39% of the total lending of Orissa in the Service/Tertiary Sector during 1989-90. Again, it is interesting to note that the lowest amount during the year 1989-90 (the reporting year). Out of the total lending of the district it has lent only 5.39 During this year a branch of RGB has advanced only Rs. 4.99 lakhs while an average branch of RRBs of Orissa haslent Rs. 8.47 lakhs. (The data of RGB is differing from the date of DCP). Thus, the per branch lending of RGB is less than the per branch average lending of a branch of RRBs of the State in this sector.

TABLE - 4.13

Comparative Statement on the Service/Tertiary Sector Lending of RRBs of Orissa as on 31.3.1990

(Amounts in lakhs)

Sl. No.	*Name of RRBs*	*No. of Accounts*	*Amounts Advanced*	*Percentage of contribution by individual RRBs to the Service Sector advances of the State*
1	2	3	4	5
1.	Puri Gramya Bank	58,950	137.55	19.8%
2.	Balasore Anch. Gramya Bank	44,324	547.44	7.88%
3.	Cuttack Gramya Bank	82,809	2247.55	32.36%
4.	Koraput Panch-bati G. B.	35,334	450.26	6.48%
5.	Kalahandi Anchalik G. B.	29,048	383.69	5.52%

(Contd.)

TABLE - 4.13 (Contd.)

1	2	3	4	5
6.	Baitarani Gramya Bank	41,139	603.50	8.69%
7.	Balasore Gramya Bank	27,211	492.79	7.09%
8.	Rushikulya Gramya Bank	23,799	374.88	5.39%
9.	Dhenkanal	23,000	462.66	6.66%
	Orissa	3,65,614	6943.32	99.88 =100

Source : NABARD Statistics on RRB 1989-90 Statement No. 6, p. 25.

Consumption and Other Loans.

As on March 1990 the RGB lent Rs. 0.01 lakh in consumption loans, for other purposes it has lent Rs. 456.49 lakhs which in total constituted Rs. 456.5 lakhs while the total of these two advances for the state comes to (Rs. 123.51 + Rs. 1596.65) Rs. 1720.16 lakhs. The percentage of RGB in these loans constitute 26.53% of the total lendings of this sector of the state.[40]

At the all India level the RRBs of the Nation i.e. 196 RRBs of the country have advanced Rs. 4,143 crores towards the service sector, Rs. 44 crores were advanced towards consumption loans and Rs. 411 crores were advanced for other purpose during Sept. 1991.[41]

In this way, the RRBs of the district (RGB) and of the state and at the national level, are playing an effective role in the development of service and tertiary sector.

However, at the end it is to be concluded that while the role of RGB in the industrial sector is not satisfactory it is quite satisfactory in the Service/Tertiary Sector. The RGB's involvement in the service sector has a steady rise. The percentage of achievement and the percentage of contribution to the lending of the district in Service sector has shown its relative success over the years and over other financial institutions of the district.

It is remarked that not only the RGB, but also other financial institutions of Ganjam district have done well in this sector. The main reason is that, the Govt. sponsored poverty alleviation programmes are more in number and they suit the services sector to a greater extent.

The RGB, operating in a relatively more developed and coastal district like Ganjam has yet to play an effective role in the process of development of the state in contributing more and more in lending to all the sectors and by minimising the overdues.

SECTION - C

The Priority Sector Advances of RGB

The main objective of nationalisation of commercial banks and thereafter the establishment of RRBs was to ensure the desired credit flows to the neglected sectors of the economy on a priority basis. Economic growth with social justice has been accepted as the major objective of our Planning process. The RGB in Ganjam district has continued its endeavour to assist the weaker sections of the district through various programmes involved under priority sector.

Provision of proper bank finance to the rural poor is an important ingredient of anti-poverty rural development strategy. So far in the priority sector lending the role played by RGB is satisfactory.

It can be seen from the table 4.14, the RGB has always earmarked a larger part of its advances for the priority sector. In the year 1982, (the second year of its establishment) the priority sector advances were 64.9% of its total advances. In the year 1988, and in 1989 the bank has advanced only to the priority sector and not to any other purposes. By the year end 1990 and 1991 the priority sector advances constituted 92.29% and 92.43% respectively.

The diagram 4.9 presents the data on priority sector percentage to total advances of RGB. The curve has a upward movement from 1982 to 1983. In the year 1984 and in 1985 it has fallen slightly. In 1986, it has again gone up to 94.23%. But in the year 1987 it has fallen down to 75.01%. During the year 1988 and 1989 the achievements were 100%. On the other hand in the years 1990 and 1991 (Dec.) it was above 92%.

Table 4.14 presents the total advances and the total priority sector advances with the percentage of priority sector advances made by RGB from 1982 onwards.

TABLE - 4.14

Priority Sector Advances and the Total Advances of RGB

Year	*Total advance in lakhs of Rupees*	*Outstanding P.S. advancing in lakhs of Rupees*	*Percentage of P.S.advance to total advance*
1982	93.07	60.41	64.90
1983	193.67	189.40	97.79
1984	318.63	308.52	96.82
1985	430.36	346.62	82.54
1986	582.32	548.77	94.23
1987	794.90	596.26	75.01
1988	1125.01	1125.01	100.00
1989	1331.63	1331.63	100.00
1990	1565.58	1444.98	92.29
1991	1848.05	1708.21	92.43

Source : Annual Credit Plans, Lead Bank (Andhra Bank), Berhampur, Ganjam.

It is seen from the table 4.14 and will be seen from diagram 4.9, that after 1982, the priority sector advances of RGB always remained above 75% by considering the table 4.14 and table 4.15, it is seen that after 1983, the percentage of advance made by RGB has always remained above the percentage of achievement of the district.

TABLE - 4.15

The Priority Sector Advances of District (All Financial Institutions including RGB).

Year	*Total Advances (Rs. in lakhs)*	*Outstanding P.S. advances (Rs. in lakhs)*	*Percentage of P.S. advances to the total advances*
1	2	3	4
1982	N/A	N/A	N/A
1983	6941.48	5426.83	78.17
1984	8412.21	6950.41	82.62
1985	8331.71	6091.75	73.11

(Contd.)

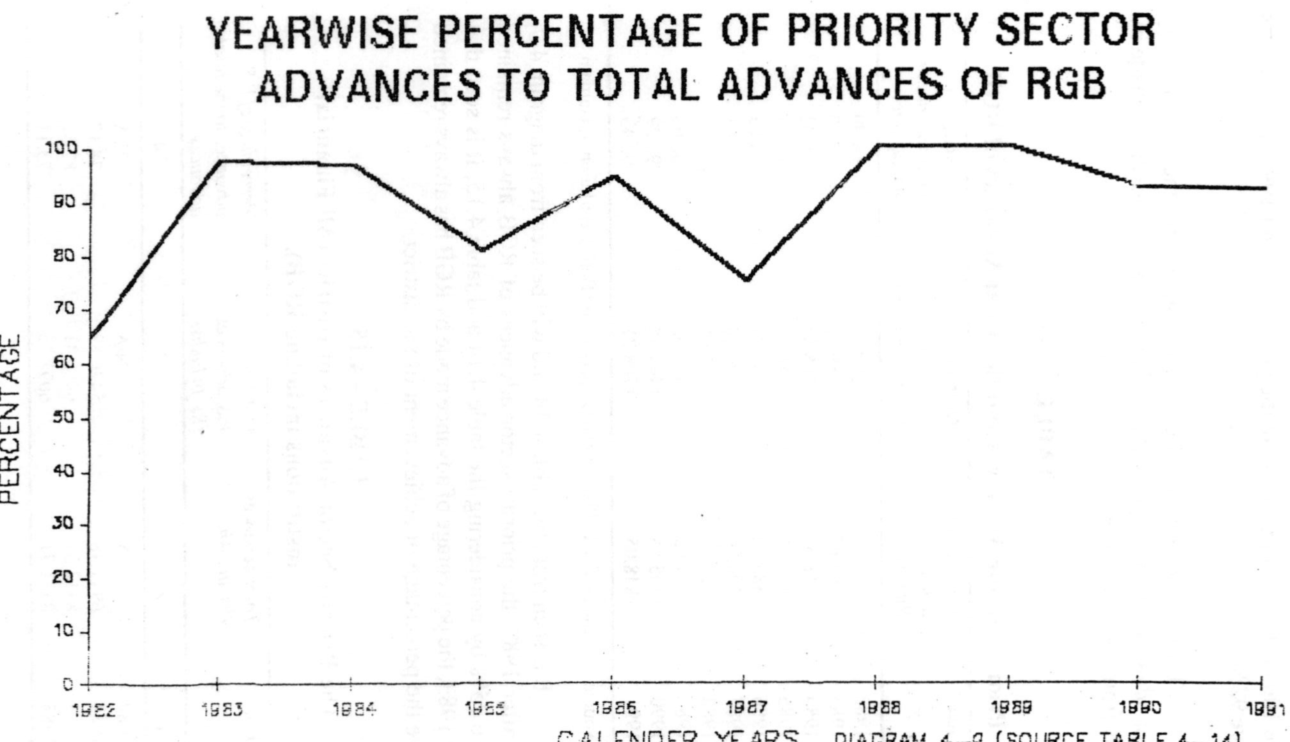
YEARWISE PERCENTAGE OF PRIORITY SECTOR
ADVANCES TO TOTAL ADVANCES OF RGB
PERCENTAGE
100
90
80
70
60
50
40
30
20
10
0
1982
1983
1984
1985
1986
1987
1988
1989
1990
1991
CALENDER YEARS
DIAGRAM 4—9 (SOURCE TABLE 4—14)

TABLE - 4.15 (Contd.)

1	2	3	4
1986	11023.88	8253.30	77.75
1987	11039.88	8253.30	74.75
1988	13742.67	10681.90	77.72
1989	17105.99	13370.59	78.16
1990 (131.03.90)	18369.35	12327.03	67.10
1991 (upto Dec.)	18554.21	?263.13	66.09

Source : DCPs (Andhra Bank) Ganjam.

Thus in priority sector the role of RGB is quite satisfactory. The diagram 4.10 provides a clear picture of the priority sector advances of the different Banks including RGB and Cooperatives as on Dec.'1991. During the reported period, the Aska Cooperative Central Bank has provided 100% of its advances to priority sector and stood at the top, while RGB is in the second position in the district providing 92% of its advances to the priority sector. The Allahabad Bank and the Bank of India advanced 91% of their total advances to the priority sector. The Lead Bank (Andhra Bank) has advanced 72% of its advance to the priority sector. The State Bank of India has advanced only 42% of the total advances to the priority sector in the said year.

The RGB in Ganjam district by Dec. 1991 has an outstanding advance to the priority sector of Rs. 1708.21 lakhs, which constituted 92% of the total advances by the said time. (Outstanding amount is equal to outstanding amount of previous year plus disbursement made during current year minus the recovery).

The percentage of advances made to the weaker section in relation to the total advances was 74.47% i.e. Rs. 1165.92 lakhs out of the total dvances of Rs. 1565.58 lakhs by December 1990. Out of the total number of beneficiaries of 71233 during December 1990, the beneficiaries of the priority sector were 67840 and the beneficiaries of weaker section out of priority sector were 58605 constituting respectively, 95.23 percent and 82.27 percent.[42]

The priority sector advances of RGB are reaching to the rural people through different programmes of State and Central Governments.

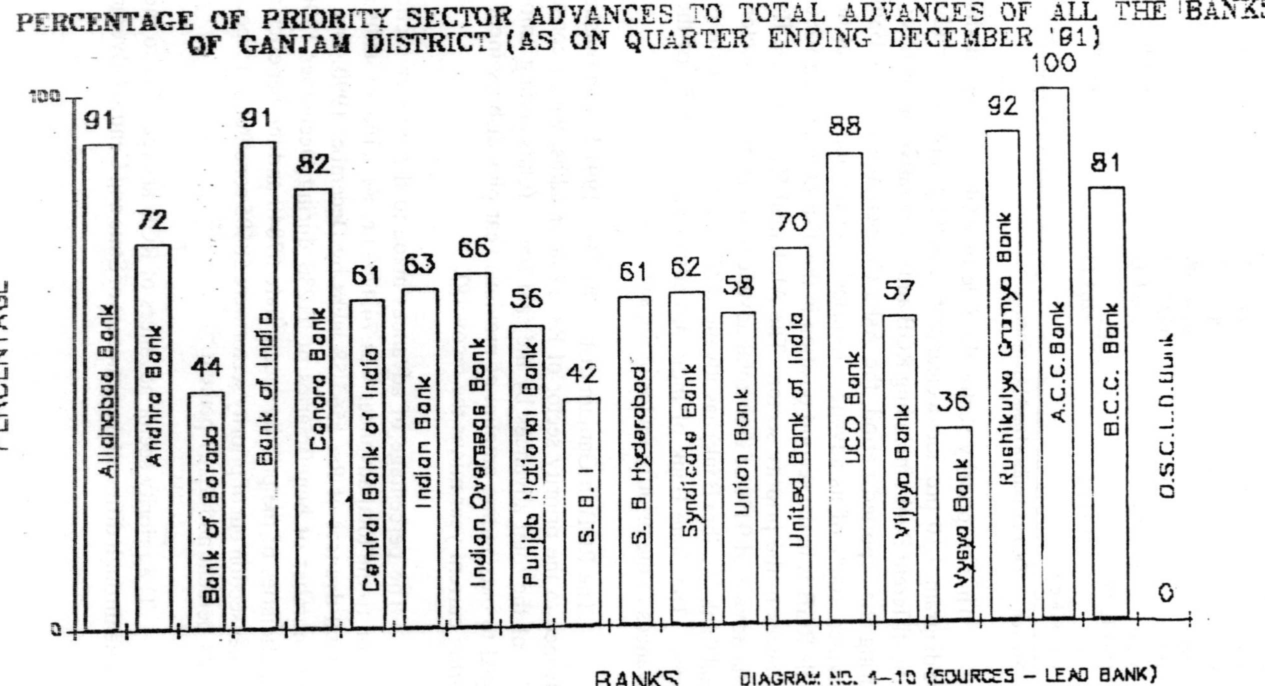
PERCENTAGE OF PRIORITY SECTOR ADVANCES TO TOTAL ADVANCES OF ALL THE BANKS OF GANJAM DISTRICT (AS ON QUARTER ENDING DECEMBER '81)
PERCENTAGE
100
0
Allahabad Bank
91
Andhra Bank
72
Bank of Baroda
44
Bank of India
91
Canara Bank
82
Central Bank of India
61
Indian Bank
63
Indian Overseas Bank
66
Punjab National Bank
56
S. B. I
42
S. B Hyderabad
61
Syndicate Bank
62
Union Bank
58
United Bank of India
70
UCO Bank
88
Vijaya Bank
57
Vysya Bank
36
Rushikulya Gramya Bank
92
A.C.C.Bank
100
B.C.C. Bank
81
0
BANKS
DIAGRAM NO. 4—10 (SOURCES – LEAD BANK)

(a) Twenty Points Programme and the RGB.

The major portion of the priority sector advances of RGB is flowing through this programme. This programme covers a large number of other programmes which aim at poverty eradication in the rural areas of the district.

The basic task of economic planning in India is to bring about a structural transformation of the economy so as to achieve a high and sustained rate of growth, a progressive improvement in the standard of living of the masses leading to the reduction of poverty and unemployment and provide the material base for a self-reliant socialistic economy.

It was seen that, the benefits of the growth had been cornered by the people in the urban and metropolitan areas, denying thereby the due to the people in the rural areas. Even the advantages of those schemes which were intended for the development and uplift of the rural areas, were cornered by the rich and it never reached the poor in the rural areas. Hence, in order to eradicate rural poverty, the late Prime Minister Smt. Indira Gandhi had announced the 20 point economic programme on 1.7.1975.

The same programme again was revised by Smt. Indira Gandhi on 14.1.1982. After her death, when her son, late Rajiv Gandhi became Prime Minister he also revised the programme in 1986.

In the new twenty point programme the various activities, which are undertaken by RGB in Ganjam district are as follows :

(1) Attack on Rural Poverty
- (a) Integrated Rural Development Programme (IRDP)
- (b) Economic Rehabilitation of Rural Poor Programme (ERRP).
- (c) Differential Rate of Interest (DRI) Schemes.
- (d) Village and Cottage Industries.

(2) Better use of Irrigation water.
- (a) Dugwell
- (b) Pumpset.
- (c) Energisation.

(3) Justice to Scheduled Caste and Scheduled Tribes (Orissa Scheduled Caste and Scheduled Tribe Development (OSCSTD)

(4) Concern for the consumers (Government Fair Price Shops).

(5) Energy for the village (Biogas).

The yearwise outstanding amounts for the twenty points programme are as follows :

TABLE - 4.16

Year	*Outstanding Amounts (Rupees in Lakhs)*
1982	32.47
1983	93.74
1984	117.39
1985	132.61
1988-89	616.24
1989-90	791.83

RGB, Head Office, Berhampur (Ganjam).

(b) Integrated Rural Development Programme and RGB in Ganjam District (IRDP)

This programmes was started in the year 1978-79 by the Government of India with the State Governments financing on 50 : 50 basis. The objective of the programme is to assist selected families below the poverty line in rural areas to cross this line by taking up self-employment by providing income-generating assets including working capital, where necessary, to the target group families through package of assistance, comprising subsidy and institutional credit. The target group has been defined as follows :

"Target Group.

The Target group of the programme consists of small farmers, marginal farmers, agricultural labourers, rural artisans, and others whose annul family income is below the cut-off line. The small and marginal farmers and agricultural labourers have been defined as under :

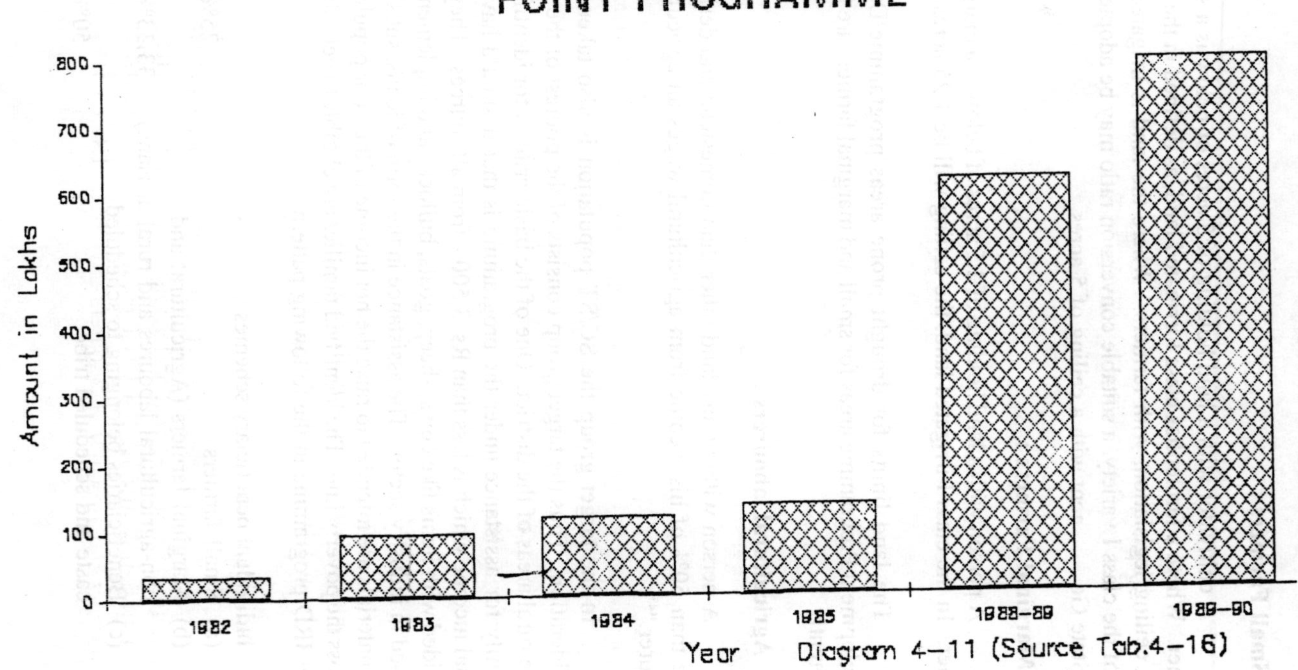
OUTSTANDING ADVANCES OF R.G.B. IN 20
POINT PROGRAMME
Amount in Lakhs
800
700
600
500
400
300
200
100
0
1982
1983
1984
1985
1988-89
1989-90
Year
Diagram 4—11 (Source Tab.4—16)

(i) Small Farmers :

A cultivator with a land holding of 5 acres or below is a small farmer. Where a farmer has class I irrigated land, as defined in the state land ceiling legislation, with farmers. Where the land is irrigated but not of the class I variety, a suitable conversion ratio may be adopted by the State Government with a ceiling of 5 acres.

(ii) Marginal Farmers :

A person with a land holding of 2.5 acres of below is a marginal farmer. In the class I irrigated land, the ceiling will be 1.25 acres.

The land limits for drought prone areas programme/Desert Development Programme areas for small and marginal farmers are fixed differently.

(iii) Agricultural labourers :

A person without any land other than homestead and deriving more than 50% of his income from agricultural wages an agricultural labourer."[43]

In the target group the SC/ST population is also taken into consideration. Thus the target group consists of the poorest of the poor in the rural areas of the district. One of the basic criteria for identifying a family for assistance under the programme is that it should have an annual income which is less than Rs. 3,500/- from all sources. They are provided with items like cows, sheep, goats, bullocks and implements to be used in industry sector. The assistance in the form of loans, subsidies and materials are intended to raise the net income of the poor population to cross the poverty line. The identified families are eligible to get subsidy under IRD programme in the following pattern :

(1) Individual beneficiary schemes :

(a) Small farmers	25%
(b) Marginal farmers (Agricultural and non-agricultural laboures and rural artisans).	33.33%
(c) Beneficiaries belonging to scheduled caste and scheduled tribe.	50%

(2) Community M.I. Works : 50% of the cost apportionable to SF/MF.

(3) Training : Full cost to be met out of IRD funds subject to the pattern prescribed for stipendry etc.

(4) Follow up assistance for setting up units under RIP/RAP. : 33.33% of the capital cost subject to ceiling of Rs. 3000/-

(5) Infrastructure : 100% to set up institutions schemes 50% to Co.operative societies and institutions.

(Source : Andhra Bank, Berhampur)

The programme aims at integration of field programmes reflecting the economic activity of the rural family whose employment and development is the basic objective. This is to be brought about by developing the primary, secondary and the tertiary sectors. In the primary fisheries and forestry development will be intensified. In the secondary programme for villages and cottage industries, skill formation and supporting services will be developed. Tertiary sector will be developed by creating facilities for organised marketing, processing and allied activities so as to absorb increasing number of local people.

In the process of rural development, identification of the real poor, formation of projects and necessary arrangement to provide credit to right persons are the most important steps to be taken by different agencies like DRDA in the district level and blocks at the village level.

IRDP is a comprehensive, multi-dimensional approach to rural development. The success of this programme depends on active effort from beneficiaries, bank officials and administrative agencies.

The G V K Rao committee[44] recommended that the Panchayat Raj bodies have to be activised. The block development officer has become in effective and the credibility of the organisation has been eroded. The observation made by the committee about B.D. Os was in line with the recommendation made by the programme evaluation study. The committee has also observed that Co-operatives have not kept pace with the ever-increasing credit requirements of agriculture and rural development. The entry of the commercial banks into the field of credit has in no way improved matters. In fact, commercial banks are much more security - conscious than co-operatives.

The RRBs seem to be more effective than commercial banks as their objectives are different from those of the commercial banks. The RRBs are to operate in the rural areas for the development of target group people. As such the RGB is playing a very useful role in the priority sector.

The table 4.17 presents the beneficiaries in IRDP, the disbursement of amounts and the outstanding amounts year-wise. It can be seen from the said table that the number of beneficiaries as well as the disbursements and outstanding balance of RGB is increasing year by year. Column '4' of the table presents the percentages of IRDP advance to the outstanding priority sector advances of RGB year-wise.

The data of the table 4.17 reveal that in the year 1982, 37% of the priority sector advances were diverted towards the IRD Programme. Afterwards it has came down upto 1987 and thereafter in 1988-89 financial year has gone up to 16.56% and in other two rest of the years it has flactuated to 11.47% and 13.90%. However, more or less, the yearwise disbursements in this sector went on increasing, representing an increasing involvement of RGB in IRDP of Ganjam district.

TABLE - 4.17
IRDP of RGB

Year	*No. of*	*Amount*	*% of*	*Outstanding*
1	2	3	4	5
1982	1436	22.76	37.67	1659
1983	2676	37.57	19.83	52.09
1984	718	15.08	4.83	54.12
1985	1360	24.35	7.02	65.30
1986	2302	40.75	7.42	90.86
1987	3917	89.59	15.02	150.82
1988-89	8387	220.54	16.56	309.05
1989-90	4928	153.11	11.47	391.36
1990-91	7592	211.15	13.90	539.74
				(cost of 25649 outstanding beneficiaries)

Note : 1982 to 1987 are the calender years, thereafter the financial years.
Source : RGB, Statistics Section. Berhampur, Ganjam

(c) Economic Rehabilitation of Rural Poor (ERRP) and the RGB.

The ERRP scheme was introduced in Orissa in June 1980, as a result of a decision taken at a state level meeting called for making a review of the working of the IRD Programme in the state. The main purpose of the new scheme was to free the programme of Rural Development from the hard financial rates of the commercial banks. It has aimed to remove poverty of the target families who are to poorest of the poor in rural areas. This programme has a high subsidy component, and loan components carry a very low simple interest of 4 percent per year.

The Main Features of the Scheme

(i) The poorest families of the village would be selected by the villagers themselves in a village level meeting to be attended among others by (i) the BDO or his (iv) the local member of the Panchayat Samiti.

(ii) The important schemes would be those where there would be no loan component. Alternatively the loan component of the existing schemes would be reduced to the minimum extent.

(iii) Government would develop their assets until an optimum income level was reached before withdrawing from the project.

(iv) The poorest family for this purpose would be one which has no income yielding assets of any kind and whose principal means of livelihood through wage earnings with an annual income no exceeding Rs. 1200/-

The programme in its objective ensures an annual net income of not less than Rs. 1500/- to each of the identified families. The identified families are to be given assistance not in cash but through the provision of some income generating assets for raising their economic conditions.

At the time of allotment of various assets to these families, their attitude, background, level of skill, etc. have to be taken into consideration as all may not be are provided with the facilities of dairy, piggery, goatery, sheep, poultry, etc., in animal husbandry projects or in fruit plantation or in fishery or in sericulture and in non-agricultural schemes. The ERRP is only a part of the IRD Programme.

The yearwise allotment of funds i.e. the advances made to this scheme by RGB is presented in table 4.18.

TABLE - 4.18

ERRP in RGB

(Amounts in lakhs)

Year	*No. of beneficiaries*	*Amounts disbursed*	*Amounts outstanding*
1982	226	5.35	3.29
1983	916	16.64	10.13
1984	1313	24.83	16.82
1985	1238	26.37	21.53
1986	2235	36.98	39.28
1987	2976	58.10	62.63
1988-89	3182	6016	89.46
1989-90	1893	39.86	102.44
1990-91	180	3.23	88.62

Note : From 1982 to 1987 in calender years, thereafter in financial years.

Source : RGB, Head Office, Berhampur (Gm).

Thus, there was a continuous increase in the sums disbursed as well as in the outstanding advances. However in the year 1990-91 the ERRP achievement was not a good one.

(a) DRI Scheme and RGB

The Differential Rate of Interest (DRI) scheme was introduced in the year 1972 with a view to provide concessional bank finance at the rate of 4% per annum to selected low-income families for acquiring productive assets. The Banks are required to lend under this scheme a minimum of one percent of their total outstanding advances, at the end of the previous year. Banks have to ensure that not less than 2/3rd of such advances are routed through their rural and semi-urban branches and not less than 40% of their total credit under the scheme is given to eligible beneficiaries belonging to SC/Sts.[45] The table 4.19 presents the yearwise advances of RGB under the DRI scheme.

TABLE - 4.19

DRI Loan of RGB

(Rupees in lakhs)

Year	*1982 Dec*	*1983 Dec*	*1984 Dec*	*1985 Dec*	*1986 Dec*	*1987 Dec*	*1988 Dec*	*1989 Dec*	*1990 Dec*	*1991 Dec*
Outstanding loans	11.70	15.90	21.25	26.87	43.33	24.03	29.98	21.89	12.65	12.80
Percentage of DRI loan to total advance.	12.57	8.20	6.66	6.24	7.44	3.02	2.66	1.64	0.87	069

Source : Annual Credit Plane of Ganjam District Lead Bank (Andhra Bank).

The RGB discontinued this scheme ; as such ; the outstanding advances from 1987 onwards has come down lowering the percentage of DRI loan to the total loan of the bank for the beneficiaries.

(e) Better use of Irrigation Water.

In this scheme the RGB is providing loanable funds to the eligible rural farmers for dugwell and pumpsets for better use of irrigation water. NABARD provides subsidy to such schemes.

Ganjam district has vast utilisable water resources to irrigate more and more of its cultivable lands which are yet to be fully utilised. "Out of the total 4,79,725 hect of cultivable area in the district nearly 2,16,372 hect are irrigated area."[46] The Major sources of Irrigation in the district are canals and dugwells. The level of ground water exploitation in the district is yet to reach 65% level.[47]

Considering the importance of agriculture in economy there is a strong need to improve the irrigation potential on a priority basis. As such priority has been given for rapid expansion of irrigation potential in district both in the 7th plan and in the 8th plan period.

The RGB is providing loans as in Table 4.20 towards irrigation. The role of the RGB in providing financial assistance of this loan is seen from 1983 to the financial year 1990-91 in the table 4.20. (Upto 1985, the loans are given in the name of increasing the irrigation potential and power generation. But after 1986 onwards they are given in the name of, loans for dugwell and loans for pumpsets). However the loans for irrigation has got an improvement only after the year 1987 and in the financial year 1988-89. The number of beneficiaries in the particular loan has increased with fluctuations.

TABLE - 4.20

Advances by RGB for Irrigation

Year	*Name of the Schemes*	*No. of Accounts*	*Amounts disbursed Rs. in lakhs*	*Amount outstanding Rs. in lakhs*
1983	Increasing Irrigation potential	296	5.03	-
	Power generation	37	1.32	-
1984	Increasing Irrigation potential	237	6.01	-
	Power generation	117	5.83	-
1985	Increasing Irrigation potential	138	3.81	-
	Power generation	116	5.73	-
1986	Dugwells	53	1.73	8.03
	Pump set	19	1.38	7.18
1987	Dugwells	70	3.00	5.82
	Pump set	60	4.54	13.33
1988-89	Dugwells	230	14.29	19.39
	Pump set	217	16.86	24.34
1989-90	Dugwells	161	10.83	27.28
	Pump set	129	12.92	38.07
1990-91	Dugwells	107	7.43	37.76
	Pumpset	195	14.26	50.81

Note : 1983 to 1987 are the calender years, thereafter the financial years.
Source : R.G.B. (Head Office, Statistics Section) Berhampur (Gm.)

As irrigation is an important infrastructure for agricultural development, the RGB has to increase its lending in this sector without keeping any rigid restrictions.

(b) Small Scale Industries and Village, Cottage Industries.

In the industry sector, the achievements of RGB is not very satisfactory and the matter has been discussed in the earlier part of the chapter. However in the table 4.21 the lending pattern of RGB to village and cottage industries and SSI has been presented again for a clear understanding of the role of RGB in this priority sector.

TABLE - 4.21

Lending to Village and Cottage Industries (SSI Sector) by RGB

(Rs. in lakhs)

Year	*Accounts*	*Amounts*	*Outstanding Amount*
1986	480	6.95	8.99
1987	545	9.07	9.18
1988-89	836	14.26	13.94
1989-90	148	3.85	15.61
1990-91	205	4.14	15.76

Source : Statistics Section RGB, Head Office, Berhampur Ganjam.

It is seen that, the performance in the financial year 1988-89 was a good one as it has lent the maximum amounts to maximum number of persons. The RGB's role in this sector is steadily improving but to perform a meaningful role it has still to cover a lot of ground.

(a) Biogas

The objective of the scheme is to provide financial assistance for setting up Biogas plants in rural and semi urban areas without any recurring expenditure on the part of the farmers for delivering fuel, light and manure. For the construction of such plants assistance to the beneficiaries for bank finance are provided by Orissa Khadi and Village Industries Board and Village Industries Commission. Subsidy is provided by Orissa Khadi and Village Industries.

The RGB has started implementation of the scheme from 1984. As on March 1985, the bank has disbursed loans to 124 beneficiaries to the tune of Rs. 1.73 lakhs. Against this total disbursement of Rs. 1.73 lakhs, the bank has drawn refinance from NABARD to the tune of Rs. 1.56 lakhs which is 90% of the total.[48]

The yearwise accounts, total disbursement in lakhs and the outstanding amounts in lakhs are presented in table 4.22. From the table 4.22, it is found that the RGB is doing well in this sector. Both the accounts and amounts disbursed increased from year to year. But in the year 1990-91 it has lent Rs. 8.96 lakhs in 403 accounts which is less than that for previous year. The outstanding amounts were Rs. 14.98 lakhs by the end of 91 March.

TABLE - 4.22

Lending Towards the Biogas by RGB

(Amounts in lakhs)

Year	*No. of Accounts*	*Amounts Disbursed*	*Outstanding Amounts*
1986	83	2.85	6.21
1987	73	2.17	7.87
1988-89	262	9.23	15.87
1989-90	576	10.81	21.81
1990-91	403	8.96	14.98

Source : Statistics Section, RGB Head Office, Berhampur.

(h) S.C.F.C.C.

For the purpose of stepping up the lending efforts to the weaker sections of the society the RGB has entered into a tieup arrangement with Orissa Scheduled Caste Finance Co-operative Corporation (OCFCC) Limited which was established in 1979-80. Since the establishment of the corporation the margin money loan to the scheduled castes and scheduled tribes was provided by this organisation.

The main objectives of this Corporation is as follows :

(i) To improve the economic condition of the SC/ST farmers or entrepreneurs through the implementation of development oriented schemes like animal husbandry, fishery, business and small scale industry, dairy farming and other schemes of occupational nature.

(ii) To arrange financial assistance for the eligible people through any agency or financial institution.

(iii) To provide 25% of the financial requirements for the scheme as the marginal money loan at 4% rate of interest per annum. The interest will be charged from the second year of the margin money loan given.

(iv) To take necessary steps to provide subsidy to the beneficiaries given by the Government through Banks.

The income criterion for eligibility is that the total annual family income of the SC family should not exceed Rs. 4,300/- in urban and semi-urban areas and Rs. 3,500/- in rural areas. The beneficiaries identified for this scheme will be over and above the beneficiaries under the ERRP and IRD programme.

The Bank is expected *to* bring subsidy money from the Government advance to provide loans for different schemes to these two groups of people.

It is also essential that in order to restrict the misuse of loans, the bank should provide the loans in the form of equipment necessary for the project.

The RGB's yearwise position of SCFCC is presented in table 4.23

TABLE - 4.23
SCFCC of RGB

(Amount in Lakhs)

Year	*Outstanding Accounts*	*Outstanding Amounts*
1986	4092	43.65
1987	6277	75.24
1988-89	11327	144.19
1989-90	14121	195.26
1990-91	17459	267.21

Source : RGB Statistics Section, Head Office, Berhampur (Gm).

From the table 4.23, it is clearly seen that the outstanding accounts and advances continuously increased. By 1991, the outstanding accounts were 17459 while 4109 accounts were the actual accounts of the particular year. Similarly out of the outstanding amounts of Rs. 267.21 lakhs, an amount of Rs. 98.71 lakhs were the net amounts disbursed in the said year.

Thus it is seen that the RGB is actively participating in different sponsored poverty-aleviation programmes. Besides the programmes discussed, the RGB also has undertaken programmes like Bay of Bengal Programme, and inland fishery programmes etc. and performs a specific role to the target people of the district.

Conclusion

The Rushikulya Gramya Bank was established on 14.02.81 and it provided facilities of banking in the rural unbanked parts of the district and to the specific groups called the "target groups". Till now the RGB with its 75 branches has been able to meet the local financial needs and allied problems. The establishment of RGB and its active involvement in the socio-economic programmes of the Government brought about a greater awareness among the villagers in the district regarding the important role of loanable funds.

The RGB being a purpose-oriented financial organisation dealing with small borrowers of the target groups of people cannot make profit the main aim of its working. Its main aim of business is different from that of any other branch of commercial bank in the district. Its main aim is to work as an agent of economic development in the under developed parts of the district.

The RGB has lent only 6.90% of the total lending by all RRBs of Orissa by the end of March 1990 considering the number of rural poor in the district. It is a very small percentage which represents a very poor performance in comparison with the state in general. It occupies the sixth position in lending among different RRBs in Orissa. The main reason for the poor performance of lending by the RGB in comparison to the RRBs of Orissa is due to the prevailing illiteracy and ignorance of the people of Ganjam district.

The RGB has lent 14.46% of loans to the agricultural sector of the district by 31.12.91 (Table 4.3). The RGB branch has lent an average amount Rs. 2.17 lakhs to the agricultural sector by March 1991, while a branch of the commercial bank of the district has lent Rs. 11.94 lakhs in the said period. (Table 4.4)

The percentage of achievement of RGB to the achievement of the district in agricultural sector is very insignificant. The role of RGB is not a negligible one, but not a very satisfactory one in the agricultural sector. The major constraints of lending in agricultural sector is non-repayment of loans under the crop loan and conversion of the same into term loans. The ARDRS programme of the Government imposes financial burden on the bank and the viability of the bank has been jeopardised.

RGB draws schemes and prepares plans, keeping in view the credit needs of the rural population, aiming at increasing productivity in agriculture and allied activities, small scale and cottage industries and in the service sector. The schemes are generally prepared by the officials of the RGB in the remote villages by field visits and discussions with the people. The RGB has adopted the Service Area approach and accordingly the lending activities are also increased.

Generally, the RGB gives loans in kind rather than in cash. This means that the sanctioned loan amount is not directly handed over to the borrowers, but it is provided in the form of assets. The loans are repaid with simple interest if they are returned within the stipulated period and compound interest is charged if the payment is done after the said period.

The economy of Ganjam district is predominantly agricultural and industrial activities are usually undertaken as supplements to their main source of income. The RGB has a low performance in the industrial sector due to the following reasons :

(i) It lends to the target group only, these are illiterate and lack in entreprenual activities.

(ii) Branches are opened in the undeveloped areas of the district, where people donot possess banking knowledge.

(iii) The DIC and RGB have not kept any link with the Government soposored programmes.

The role played by RGB in the industrial sector is not a very significant one. It has lent 1.19% of the total lending of the district during 1990-91 (Table 4.8) and 0.78% of the total RRB lending of the state in the industrial sector during the said period (table 4.9). The industrial activities can be encouraged in the district by opening raw material banks for artisans and by providing training facilities to them. The proper identification of the artisan is a major need for an improvement of this sector. The Andhra Bank being the sponsor bank of RGB has to bring to the notice of the people the benefits of taking finance from RGB.

The lack of adequate marketing facilities and lack of other infrastructural needs like power, road and transport are also the main constraints for the successful lending operations of the RGB in this sector. The DRDA, DIC and other financial as well as the Government organisations relating to the rural development of the district have to mantain active co-operation and proper co-ordination in the field of lending. The poor artisans may be exempted from stamp duties while taking loans from RGB.

The performance of the Services Sector of RGB is a most satisfactory one. The achievement curve of RGB has always remained above the target curve of RGB upto 90-91 (Diagram 4.7). In this sector the RGB has the percentage of contribution of 37.44% by March 1991, while commercial banks have 39.99%, the co-operative sector has 10.9% and OSFC have 11.64% in the total district lending (Table 4.12,). On the other hand the contribution of RGB in the state RRB lending for service sector is 5.39% only by March 1990. Thus, the RGB has played an effective role in Ganjam district by providing loan to the service sector.

The RGB has followed the objectives of social justice in the promotion of economic development and confined its lending to the neglected rural target people and weaker sections on a priority basis.

Provision of bank finance to the rural poor is an important ingredient of anti-poverty rural development strategy. So far in the priority sector the role played by RGB is rather encouraging. But it is very natural to expect the RGB to advance more to the priority sector as it is a bank for priority sector and target group of rural economy. Rural development has been given up greater importance in the five year plans and the uplift of the target people is the ultimate goal of a welfare economy. The RGB in Ganjam district by December 1991 has advanced 92.43% of the total advances to the priority sector. The percentage of advances made to the weaker sections in relation to the total advances by December 1990, was 74.47%. Similarly out of the total number of beneficiaries of 71233 during December 1990, the beneficiaries of the priority sector were 67840 and out of them beneficiaries belonging to weaker section were 58605.

It is revealed that RGB in the district provides loans to the target groups of rural poor mainly on the basis of two schemes such as ERRP and IRDP. The investigation shows that the loans under these schemes have also increased from year to year. Under the schematic loans the service sector has got a bigger share than the agricultural sector.

Under the ERRP scheme the SC / ST borrowers got 50 percent subsidy, while the general borrowers got 33.5 percent subsidy on the loans. Similarly under the IRDP the SC / ST borrowers got 33.5 percent of subsidy while the general borrowers get 25 percent of subsidy on the amounts of loans. The subsidies are mostly provided in kind rather that in Cash.

Besides, under DRI scheme the weakest among the weak are provided loans and for this they are to pay only 4 percent interest per annum. But it is observed that at present the RGB does not adhere strictly to the scheme of DRI.

The rate of interest of RGB loans ranged from 9.5 to 10.5 percent per annum in for of agricultural purposes and ranged from 10.5 to 11.5 percent in for of non-agricultural purposes. The period of repayment ranges from 1 to 5 years or more in case of the loans to service sector. However from 9.10.1991 the rates of interest were linked to the quantity of loans differently to the priority and non-priority sector for maintaining uniformity among all banks.

The RGB in the priority sector has advanced for irrigation water, Biogas, SCFCC scheme, Bay Bengal programmes and inland Fishery programme. In this way the RGB is playing a significant role in the rural development and for the economic uplift of the rural poor of Ganjam district of Orissa. However, in comparison to the branches of commercial banks and other RRBs of State the role of RGB does not appear to be much satisfactory as it clearly falls short of the great expectations with which the institution was launched. In the field of rural finance of the district.

References

1. Venkataratnam, M. *Social lendings (An attack on poverty and unemployment)*, Central Office, Andhra Bank, Hyderabad, September, 1987. P. 1.

2. Desai, S.S.M. "Objectives and Management of RRBs", *Rural Banking in India*, New Delhi, Himalaya Publishing House (2nd Revised Edition), 1986. P. 298.

3. Annonymous, "Regional Rural Banks", *RBI Bulletin (Supplement)*, January 1993, PP. 39, 40.

4. Malhotra, R.N., "India's Monetary Policy and the Role of Banking system in Economic Development." IBA Bulletin, March, 1990, PP. 198, 199.

5. Vyas, M.R. *Financial performances of RRBs*. Jaipur (Rajasthan) Arihant Publishers, 1991, P. 13.

6. Kulkarini, J.R. (Mimeograph), College of Agricultural Banking (RBI), Pune.

7. Vyas, M.R. *Op.cit*, P. 17.

8. Ibid, P. 42.

9. DDM, NABARD, Ganjam, Berhampur, Interview on 26.3.96.

10. Souvenir (75-80) Jaipur Nagaur Anchalika Gramya Bank.

11. Dhingra, I.C. "Regional Rural Banks", Rural Economics New Delhi, Sultan Chand and Sons (8th Revised Edition), 1986, P. 299.

12. DDM, (NABARD), *Op.cit*.

13. Vyas, M.R., *Op.cit*, P. 18.

14. Guide Lines for lending (Office record), RGB Head Office, Berhampur, Ganjam (Enquiry)

15. Rural Development Officer, RGB, Head Office, Berhampur (Interview during October, 1990.)

16. Malhotra, R.N., "The Role of Banking in Rural Development", *RBI Bulletin*, Vol. XL, No. 9, September, 1986, P. 563.

17. Patel, A.R. and Khankhoje, D.P. "Rural Credit", *Rural Economics*, New Delhi, Sultan Chand and Sons (Ist Edition), 1985.

18. DDM, NABARD, *Op.cit*.

19. Pradhan, Lokanath, (BM), RGB Samarjhola, Interview - 5.1.93.

20. Roy, Jyotilak Guha, "Development of weaker sections - Role of social scientist", *Kurukhetra*, Vol. XXVIII, No. 8, May, 1990, P. 27.

21. Madhakar, R.K., "Indian Banking - the next phase", *The Journal of the Indian Institute of Bankers*, Vol. 58, No. 3 July - September, 1987, P. 137.

22. Rao, B. Ramachandra, "Priority Sector Advances - Evolution and Monitoring", *The Journal of Indian Institute of Bankers*, Vol. 58, No. 3, July - September, 1987, P. 132.

23. District Credit Plan (1989-90) and Annual Action Plan - 1988, Regional Office, Andhra Bank, (Ld. Bank), Berhampur, P. 75.

24. D.C.P., (Ld. Bank), 1989-90, P. 90.

25. A.C.P., (Ld. Bank), 1990-91, P. 56. and A.C.P., (Ld. Bank), 1991-92, P. 52.

26. A.C.P., (Ld. Bank), 1991-92, P. 53.

27. Rural Development Officer, Head Office, RGB, Berhampur, (Ganjam), Orissa - Interview, May ' 1991.

28. A.C.P., (Ld. Bank), 1989-90, P. 129.

29. Observation of the scholar from the discussion with the beneficiaries and Bank Officials of RGB - (Samarjhola Br.).

30. Table 11-13, *RBI Bulletin (Supplement)*, January, 1993, P. 40.

31. Jethwaney, Sonika, "Regional Rural Banks : A Review" *Indian Bank's Association Bulletin*, (Rural Development Issue) Vol. X, No. 12, P. 247.

32. Ibid.

33. Vyas. M.R. *Op.cit*, P. 31.

34. Action Plan (1988-89 to 1992-93), DIC, Ganjam Berhampur, P. 86.

35. RBI Bulletin, January 1993 (Supplement), *Op.cit*, P. 41.

36. Rural Development Officer, RGB Head Office. (Enquiry - May 91).

37. DCP, Ganjam, (1982-85), Ld. Bank, *Op.cit.*, P. 88.

38. Ibid.

39. Rural Development Officer, Ld. Bank, (Andhra Bank), Regional Office, Berhampur, Ganjam, (Enquiry).

40. RRB Statistics, (NABARAD), 1989-90. Statement No. 6.

41. RBI Bulletin, Jan. ' 1993, (Supplement), P. 41.

42. Statistics section, RGB Head Office, Berhampur, Ganjam, (Enquiry).

43. "Basic concepts", Integrated Rural Development Programme and Allied Programmes of Training of Rural Youth for Self Employment (TRYSEM) and Development of Women and Children in Rural Area (DWCRA), Manual, Department of Rural Development, Ministry of Agriculture, Government of India, New Delhi, November, 1988, P. 1.

44. Singh, V.S. "An insight into poverty alleviation programmes", *Yojana*, vol. 32, No. 8, 1988 (Apr. 1-15), P. 24.

45. *Hand Book on Service Area Approach*, Central Office, Andhra Bank, Hyderabad, P. 31

46. ACP, (Ld. Bank), 1990-91, *Op.cit.*, P. 70.

47. PLCP, Ganjam, *Op.cit.*, P. 12.

48. Statistics Section, RGB Head Office, Berhampur, Ganjam, (Enquiry).

5

Capital Structure and Sources of Capital of Rushikulya Gramya Bank

The RRBs for their survival and success need a sound capital structure. The lending activities of these banks will be effective and will proceed along desired lines only when these banks themselves are financially strong. The in-flow and out-flow of funds of the banks are to be set into a regular cyclical rhythm. In case of RRBs the overdues has adversely affected recycling of funds and, as a result, for lending they depend more and more on refinance from NABARD and sponsor banks. RRBs like any commercial bank must earn profit and the profits must be reinvested for the expansion of business and to effectively serve the neglected target groups of the rural areas. If the sources of capital for RRBs dry up, overdues keep rising and losses accumulated without end, then their viability is jeopardised.

It therefore, becomes an essential part of this work to examine the different sources of capital that are available to RRBs in general and the RGB in particular.

To study the capital structure and sources of capital of RGB it is necessary to examine the details of the external and internal sources of capital, the growth of deposits, the refinance facilities for lending purposes, the recovery provisions and their implementation. The loss and profit of RGB have to be analysed in detail as continuous losses are a definite sign of deteriorating health of the institution. In this regard the period of study for a comparative analysis has been taken as from 1983 (Jan - Dec) to 1991 (April - March). The comparison of RGB is done with the different financial institutions within the district as also with the other RRBs of the state. The latest available data at national level on RRBs in respect of deposit mobilisation and other related matters are also discussed.

The main sources of capital funds for Rushikulya Gramya Bank are both internal and external. Share capital and reserve funds constitute the main source of internal capital. The share capital comes from the constituents i.e., the central Government, state Government and sponsor Bank in the ratio of 50:15:35 as stated in table 5.1. According to the Banking Regulation Act 1949, which governs the operations of RRBs, 20% of the net profit of the bank is to be transferred annually to the reserve fund. Besides, they have to make provisions for various purposes as necessary under the Act. The reserve fund in case of RGB is a nominal one as the bank has been incurring losses year after year.

External Resources

The external sources of funds for RRB are :

(a) deposits.

(b) loans from sponsor bank.

(c) refinances from NABARD.

The Refinance from NABARD constitute a major source of funds for business for RRBs. All types of loans and advances granted by RRBs for financing agriculture and allied activities as also for financing artisans, cottage and village industries, small entrepreneurs, small traders and others for productive purposes are backed by refinance from NABARD. Advances granted under the head of consumption loans, advances against fixed deposit, receipts and advances to staff are not eligible for refinance.[1]

The recoveries of the past loans are constitute another source of finance for the present business. As such, the RGB procures resources from both internal and external sources as follows :

(1) Share capital

(2) Mobilsation of deposits

(3) Refinance
   (a) from NABARD
   (b) from sponsor bank

(4) Recovery of past loans.

(5) Profits

Share Capital of RGB

The Regional Rural Bank Act, 1976 provides for each RRB to have an authorised capital of one crore which may be divided into one lakh of fully paid up shares of one hundred rupees each and to start with issued capital of Rs. 25/- lakhs subscribed.[2]

The RGB has started with an authorised capital of Rs. one crore and the paid up share capital of the Bank is Rs. 50 lakhs contributed by share holders[3] in the ratio as shown in the table 5.1.

TABLE - 5.1

Share Capital of RGB

S. No.	*Subscriber*	*Share in subscription*	*Amount in Rs.*
1.	Government of India	50%	25 lakhs
2.	Sponsor Bank (Andhra Bank)	35%	17.5 lakhs
3.	Government of Orissa	15%	7.5 lakhs
	Total	100%	50 lakhs

Source : RGB, Head Office, Berhampur.

The Board of directors have the power to increase the issued capital of RRBs after consulting the RBI, the concerned State Government and sponsor bank with the prior approval of the Central Government.[4] The working Group under the chairmanship of S.M. Kelkar recommended ammendments to the RRB Act 1976. The RRB amendment Act of 1987 came into effect from September 28, 1988 and based on this amendment the authorised capital of the RRBs has been raised from Rs. 1 crore to Rs. 5 crores.[5]

The Deposits of RGB

Volume, types and ownership of deposits are the three major yardsticks to measure the success of Banks in respect of resource mobilisation.[6] The deposits of RGB is a major source of capital and the success of bank business depends mostly upon the growth of deposits. Expansion of credit without mobilising deposits may prove disastrous, especially for RRBs as their chests would be depleted and in case of low recovery, which has become a common features with all RRBs, their liquidity may be impaired to an irreparable state.[7]

TABLE - 5.2

Growth of Deposits of RGB (Rupees in lakhs)

Year	*No. of Branches of RGB*	*No. of Accounts of RGB*	*Deposit Amounts (Incre-mental)*	*Cumulative deposits of RGB*	*Average Cumulative deposit per RGB Branch*
1	2	3	4	5	6
1981	7	1290	39.55	39.55	5.65
1982	25	11381	52.81 (33.52)	92.36 (133.5)	5.69
1983	36	22019	51.94 (-1.64)	144.30 (56.23)	4.00
1984	52	34708	65.10 (25.33)	209.40 (45.11)	4.02
1985	68	47737	100.49 (54.36)	309.08 (47.98)	4.55
1986	68	60142	140.19 (39.5)	450.08 (45.23)	6.61
1987	69	73990	224.49 (60.13)	674.57 (49.87)	9.77
1988-89	75	89309	187.51 (-16.47)	862.08 (27.79)	11.49

Contd.

TABLE 5.2 (Contd.)

1	2	3	4	5	6
1989-90	75	102505	354.35 (88.97)	1216.43 (41.1)	16.21
1990-91	75	113992	291.69 (-17.68)	1508.12 (23.97)	20.10
1991-92	75	125873	415.09 (42.30)	1923.21 (23.52)	25.64

Source : Annual Reports of RGB from 1981 to 1991-92.
Note : 1981 to 1987 are the calendar years and from 1988-89 onwards are the financial years. (Figures in the brackets indicate the percentage of incremental deposit in column '4' and percentage of cumulative deposit in column '5' of the table).

From the table 5.2 it is found that the RGB has increased its role in deposit mobilisation from year to year and has shown its involvement in expanding banking facilitres to the rural areas of the district. However in the year 1983, 1988-89 and 1990-91, the incremental deposit growth has a negative trend, which can be observed from the table 5.2 and the diagram 5.1. In the diagram 5.1, a comparative view of the incremental deposit growth and the cumulative deposit growth in percentage has been shown. It is seen that, while the incremental deposit growth has negative slopes in the years mentioned earlier, the cumulative growth is always positive with flactuations. The average cumulative deposit growth is always positive with flactuations. The average cumulative deposit per RGB branch has fallen from Rs. 5.65 lakhs to 3.69 lakhs in the year 1982 and thereafter upto 1985 and a slow growth has been witnessed as presented in the diagram 5.2. After 1985, the per branch growth of cumulative deposit is better and it has become Rs. 25.64 lakhs by March 1992.

In the year 1982 the bank has fixed a target for deposit mobilisation of Rs. 86.6 lakhs and it has exceeded that by Rs. 92.36 lakhs. As such the deposit mobilisation was satisfactory in the said year.[8] In the year 1983, the net increase of deposit was less than the deposit amounts of the previous year. The incremental deposit growth was (-1.64%) and the cumulative deposit growth for the said year was 56.23%. In comparison the growth of deposit with the previous year, the growth in the year 1983 has remained at a lower level both for cumulative and incremental deposits. Thus the performance of the bank in the said year is found unsatisfactory.

PERCENTAGE OF INCREMENTAL & CUMULATIVE DEPOSIT OF R.G.B.

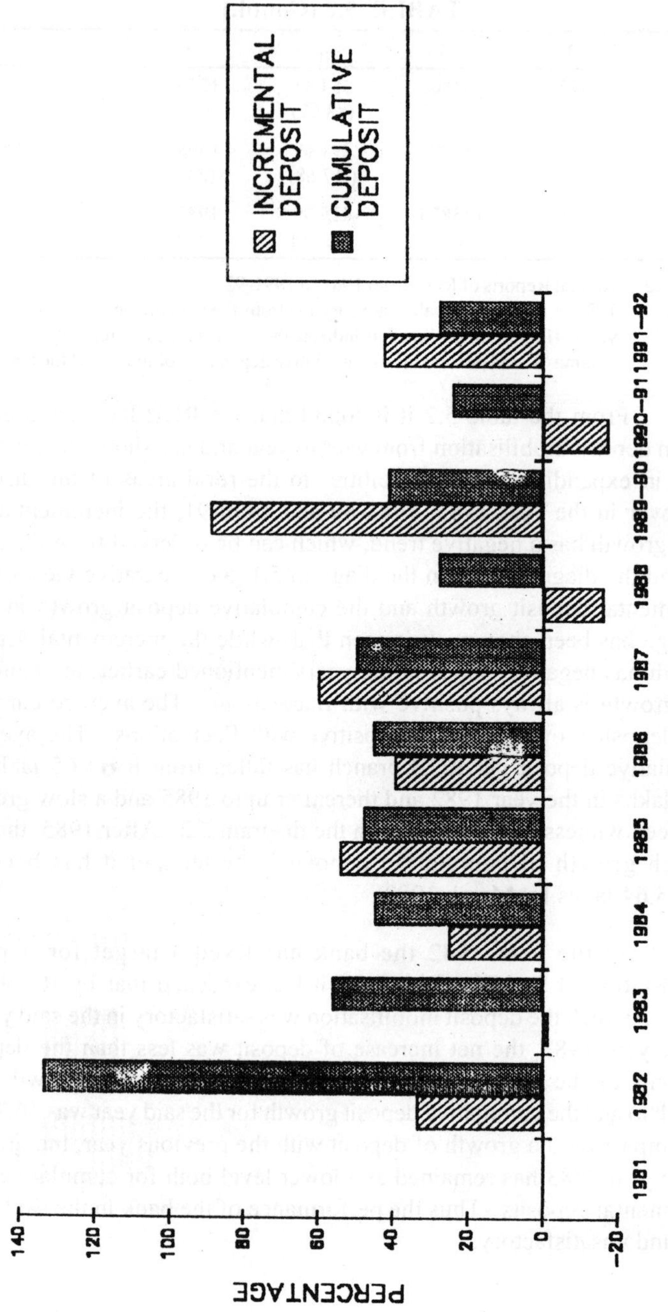

DIAGRAM No. 5.1 (SOURCE TAB. 5.2)

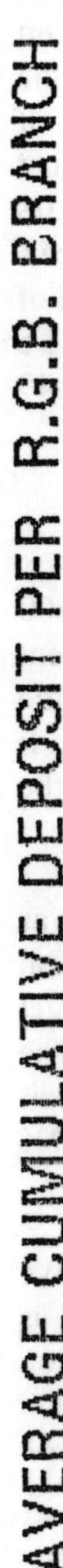

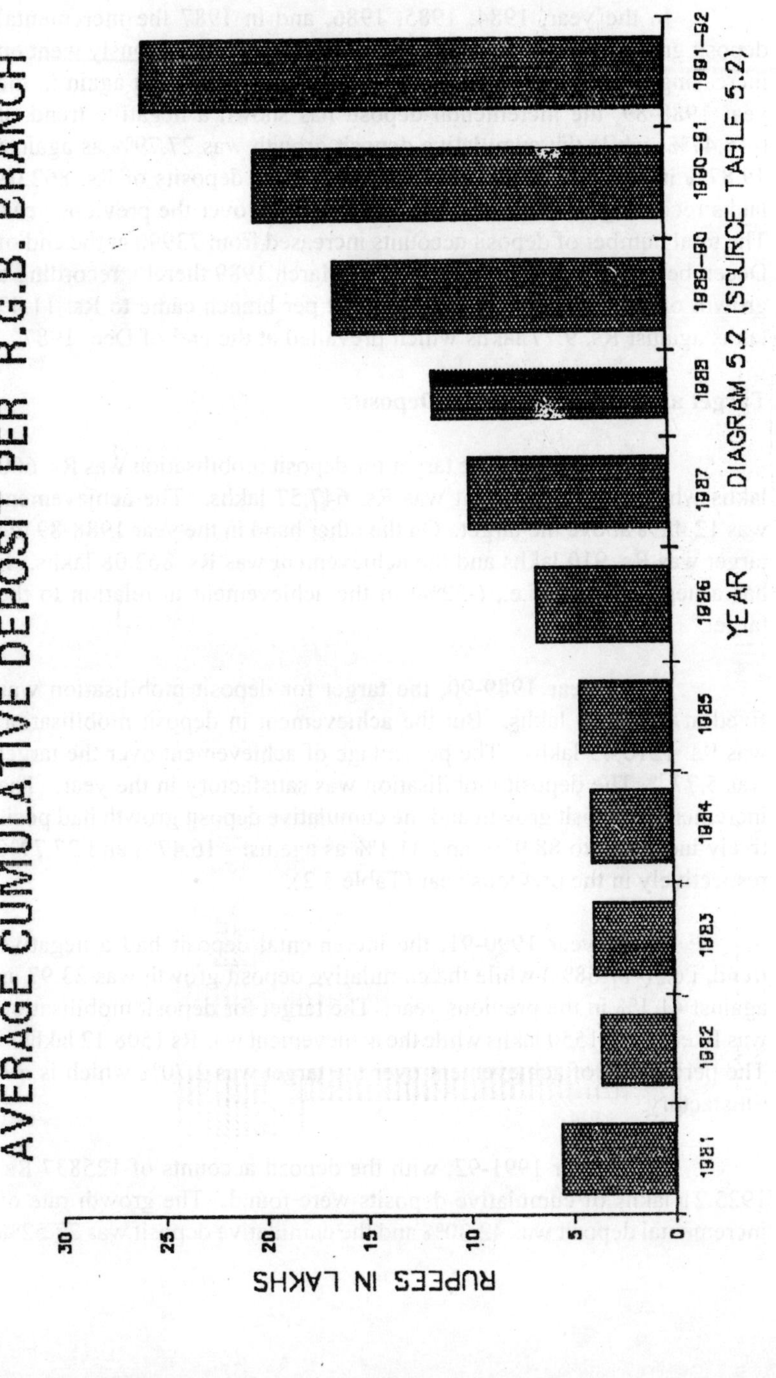
AVERAGE CUMULATIVE DEPOSIT PER R.G.B. BRANCH
RUPEES IN LAKHS
0
5
10
15
20
25
30
1981
1982
1983
1984
1985
1986
1987
1988
1989-90
1990-91
1991-92
YEAR
DIAGRAM 5.2 (SOURCE TABLE 5.2)

In the year, 1984, 1985, 1986, and in 1987 the incremental deposit growth and the cumulative deposit growth continuously went on increasing positively with fluctuations and variations. But again in the year 1988-89, the incremental deposit has shown a negative trend of (-16.47%) while the cumulative deposit growth was 27.79% as against 49.87% in the year 1987. The bank mobilised deposits of Rs. 862.08 lakhs recording as increase of Rs. 187.51 lakhs over the previous year. The total number of deposit accounts increased from 73990 at the end of December 1987 to 89309 at the end of March 1989 thereby recording a growth of 20.70%. The average deposit per branch came to Rs. 11.49 lakhs against Rs. 9.77 lakhs which prevailed at the end of Dec. 1987.

Target and Achievements of Deposits

In the year 1987 the target for deposit mobilisation was Rs. 600 lakhs while the achievement was Rs. 647.57 lakhs. The achievement was 12.42% above the target. On the other hand in the year 1988-89 the target was Rs. 910 lakhs and the achievement was Rs. 862.08 lakhs. It has a negative trend i.e., (-52%) in the achievement in relation to the target.[9]

In the year 1989-90, the target for deposit mobilisation was fixed at Rs. 1150 lakhs. But the achievement in deposit mobilisation was Rs. 1216.43 lakhs. The percentage of achievement over the target was 5.77.[10] The deposit mobilisation was satisfactory in the year. The incremental deposit growth and the cumulative deposit growth had positively increased to 88.97% and 41.1% as against - 16.47% and 27.79% respectively in the previous year (Table 5.2).

In the year 1990-91, the incremental deposit had a negative trend, i.e., (-17.68%) while the cumulative deposit growth was 23.97 as against 41.1% in the previous year. The target for deposit mobilisation was fixed at Rs. 1550 lakhs while the achievement was Rs 1508.12 lakhs.[11] The percentage of achievement over the target was 2.70% which is not satisfactory.

In the year 1991-92, with the deposit accounts of 125837 Rs. 1923.21 lakhs of cumulative deposits were found. The growth rate of incremental deposit was 42.30% and the cumulative deposit was 27.52%

over the previous year. The average deposit per RGB branch in the year was Rs. 25.64 lakhs.

The break up of deposits for the year ended 31st March 1992 (Table 5.3) is as follows :

TABLE - 5.3

Types of Deposits of RGB (By 31st March 1992)

Types of Deposit	*No of Accounts*	*Amounts (Rs. in lakhs)*
Current	954	35.25
Saving	101473	552.82
Term	23410	1335.14
Total	125837	1923.21

Source : Annual Report, RGB, 1991-92

With the expansion of branches, increasing in the deposit accounts, covering more and more villages in its service area and involving more and more members of the staff of the bank in its activities, the RGB played an effective role, which is indicated in table 5.4.

TABLE - 5.4

Per branch/per staff average deposit of RGB

(Rupees in thousand)

Year	*No of Villages covered*	*No of Branches operating*	*No of Staff*	*Deposit per Branch*	*Deposit per Staff*
1981	30	7	65	565	61
1985	702	68	17	456	177
1989-90	1817	75	232	1622	524
1990-91	1817	75	264	2011	571
1991-92	1833	75	342	2564	563

Source : RGB, Head Office, Berhampur (Ganjam).

In the year 1981, the RGB covered only 30 villages, by 1985 it increased to 702 and by 1989-90 it was 1817 villages. It had increased its coverage to 1833 villages in the year 1991-92. The branches opened in the first year was only 7 with 65 staff. It had increased to 68 in 1985 with 175 staff and further increased to 5 branches in the financial year 1988-89 (not found in table 5.4). It has remained stagnant with 75 thereafter. The details of the opening of the branches are cited in Annexure-1 for reference.

It is seen from table 5.4, that the deposit per branch as well as deposit per staff increased year after year. However in 1985, the deposit per branch was less than the deposit per branch in the first year of operation of RGB.

The RGB did not open any branch after 29.03.1989. However it increased the coverage of villages as cited in the table 5.4. It has not opened any new branch after the particular date due to the higher cost of rural lending, the continuous losses and other constraints which are taken up in the next chapter.

For making a comparison between the RGB and other institutions participating in the DCP, it is essential to know about the contribution of RGB in deposit mobilisation in the district. Thus in this study the District Credit Plans have been taken as the reference points. It was found that the data collected from RGB sources on deposits lightly vary from the data of DCP. When it was enquired at the lead Bank and RGB, no convincing answer was furnished by any one. However for the comparison the DCPs of Lead Bank are considered in table 5.5. The references were taken from the year 1984 only to minimise the differences on data between RGB sources and DCP.

The RGB has always remained at less than 5.78% of its contribution (share) upto March 1991 in the deposit mobilisation of the district. In the year 1984 its share in the total deposit was only 2.15% and its slowly increased upto March 1991. In deposit mobilisation the Co-operative Banks were in a superior position in the initial periods but by 1990-91 the difference was very less and even then they maintained their superiority by degree of differences as they cover both the target and non-target group in their operations. The seventeen commercial banks together with their branches were sharing more than 88% of the district as found in the table 5.5. However the comparison will be more reasonable, if it is made with individual banks, which can be seen from the

Annexure-6 at Col. 3. The deposit growth of all the financial institutions had fallen from 1986 to 1989-90 with a flactuation in the Co-operative sector. The deposit growth in relation to the deposits of the previous year in respect of Co-operatives are not satisfactory for the years 1985, 1988 and 1989-90 securing 3.03%, 2.34% and 0.66% respectively.

TABLE - 5.5

Deposit growth of all banks of Ganjam district

(Rupees in lakhs)

Year	RGB Banks	Commercial Banks	Cooperative (District)	All Banks
1984	210.00 (2.15)	8516.02 (87.37)	1028.34 (10.54)	9754.36 (100)
1985	325.83 (2.8)	10250.04	1059.54	11635.41
1986	478.60 (3.38)	12476.92	1192.07	14147.59
1987	688.85 (4.1)	14837.07	1264.12	16790.04
1988	861.01 (4.45)	17190.40	1293.74	19345.15
1989	1093.32 (4.99)	19415.20	1385.04	21893.56
1989-90	1259.81 (5.35)	20782.70	1394.19	23526.70
1990-91	1552.82 (5.78)	32732.58 (88.37)	1568.19 (5.83)	26853.59 (100)

Source : ACP, 1984, PP. 56, 58.
ACP, 1989-90, pp. 94, 95, 96.
ACP, 1990-91, pp. 60.
ACP, 1991-92, pp. 54, 55.

Note : The figures in the brackets indicate their respective percentage of contribution to the district (DCP).

The per account deposit for the financial year 1989-90, 1990-91 and 1991-92 for RGB is respectively Rs. 1186.00, Rs. 1223.00

and Rs. 1528.00. This shows an increasing trend of average deposit per account. This is mainly due to the Service Area Approach, which lays stress on banking activities in a particular area. However, the RGB should spread more and more branches to the non-banked areas of the district and should not remain stagnant at 75 number of branches. Out of the 75 branches of RGB, 49 banks have reached the targets of deposit by 31.3.90 and 26 branches have not reached the targets. Thus nearly 35% of the branches of RGB do not fulfil the targets of deposit.[12]

The performance of RGB can be studied by making a comparison of deposit mobilisation of RRBs of Orissa. Table 5.6 provides the information on deposit of RGB and other RRBs of Orissa as on March 1990.

According to table 5.6, the RGB has mobilised deposits of RS. 1093.32 lakhs and among the RRBs of Orissa during March 1990, its rank is 6th in deposit mobilisation. Out of the total deposits of Rs. 15031.47 lakhs, the deposit of RGB for the said period constitutes 7.27%. The deposit accounts of RGB to the total deposit accounts of the state constitute 6.7%.

The Cuttack Gramya Bank has contributed 24.61% of the total deposits of RRBs of Orissa, which is the highest. The Koraput Panchabati Gramya Bank is in the second position contributing 14.73% followed by Bolangir Anchala Gramya Bank at 13.15%, Puri Gramya Bank at 12.15%, Baitarani Gramya Bank at 8.52%. After Rushikulya Gramya Bank, the Balasore Gramya Bank ranked in the 7th position contributing 7.21%, Dhenkanala Gramya Bank at 8th position contributing 6.96% and the last being the Kalahandi Gramya Bank accounting for only 5.36% of the total deposit in the state.

In deposit mobilisation, RGB being a bank of rural people has to increase its role in Ganjam district by encouraging small savings by the small deposits in its small area of operation. The outstanding deposits of RGB are increasing. Then number of deposit accounts and the number of adopted villages are increasing, through the cluster approach of Service Area principle. The RGB by March 1990 reached the target through 49 branches out of its 75 branches. As such, one can say that the role of the bank is satisfactory one. But when the role of RGB is examined on the basis of its contribution or percentage of sharing to the total deposit mobilisation in the district and among all the RRBs of the State, it is most unsatisfactory. It gives a very discouraging picture about the effectiveness of the Gramya Bank in Ganjam district. In order to improve the viability of RGB, it is necessary to step up the efforts to mobilise more deposits in the district, as the deposits constitute an important source of lending and investment for RGB.

TABLE - 5.6

Comparative Deposit Statement of RRBs of Orissa as on 31.3.1990

(Rupees in lakhs)

Sl.	*Name of RRBs of Orissa*	*No. of Accounts*	*Deposit Amounts*	*Rank of RRBs*
1.	Puri Gramya Bank	167,796	1826.62	4th
2.	Bolangir Anchala Gramya Bank	301,139	1977.08	3rd
3.	Cuttack Gramya Bank	336,298	3700.40	1st
4.	Koraput Panchabati Gramya Bank	159,928	2214.69	2nd
5.	Kalahandi Anchal Gramya Bank	78,260	806.68	9th
6.	Baitarani Gramya Bank	124,311	1281.17	5th
7.	Balasore Gramya Bank	120,031	1083.88	7th
8.	Rushikulya Gramya Bank (RGB)	97,881	1093.32	6th
9.	Dhenkanal Gramya Bank	71,504	1047.63	8th
	Total Orissa	1459,148	15031.47	

Note : It is found that there is some variation in presentation of data in RGB by different sources. In DCP the deposit mobilisation by RGB during March 1990 as in table 5.5 in Rs. 1259.81 lakhs. But in table 5.6 which is a source from NABARD statistics it is Rs. 1093.32 lakhs and the Annual Plan provides the figure as 1216.43 for the said period. However for the comparison the data provided by national level organisations are considered there.

Source : Statement No. 4 RRB Statistics NABARD (1989-90) p-6.

At the national level, the 196 RRBs with their 14,531 branches, covering 385 districts have mobilised Rs. 5,141 crores of deposits by the end of September 1991, recording 20.5 percent of growth from the previous years deposit of Rs 4,267 crores.[13]

Refinances of RGB

Refinance is an important source of funds available to RGB for the purpose of lending. The RGB gets refinance (a) from NABARD (b) from Sponsored Bank. The details of refinances availed by RGB from NABARD and Sponsored Bank are discussed below :

(a) Refinance from NABARD

The Committee to Review Arrangements for Institutional Credit for Agriculture and Rural Development (CRAFICARD) appointed by RBI felt the need of combining the functions of Agricultural Refinance and Development Corporation (ARDC) and those departments of RBI concerned with rural credit which resulted in formation of NABARD in July 1982.[14]

NABARD is an apex institution for financing agricultural and rural sectors which provides by way of refinance loans and advances repayable on demand or on the expiry of fixed period not exceeding 18 months, to Commercial Banks, Regional Rural Banks, State Co-operative Banks and other financial institutions, which are approved by the Reserve Bank of India (RBI).[15]

Refinance provided by NABARD to state Co-operative Banks and Regional Rural Banks under section 21 of the NABARD Act is for periods not exceeding 18 months i.e., of a short term nature. Loans and advances granted by way of refinance to state Co-operative banks and Regional Rural Banks under section 22 of the Act are for periods between 18 months and 7 years. Similarly financial assistance granted for rescheduling loans and advances under section 23 is also for periods ranging between 18 months and 7 years. Long-term investment credit provided under section 25 could be granted for periods upto 25 years. Financial assistance granted to State Government under section 27 is for a period not exceeding 20 years.[16]

Commercial Banks and Regional Rural Banks and state Co-operative Banks get refinance from NABARD ranging between 80% and 90% i.e. for minor irrigation and land development schemes 90% for IRDP schemes 90% and for diversified purposes 80%.[17]

The NABARD as an apex agency for providing integrated credit support for overall development of rural Orissa and Ganjam has established a zonal office at Bhubaneswar and a district office at Berhampur.

The RGB being the rural bank for Ganjam district gets refinance facilities from NABARD at an interest rate which is 3% less than the Bank rate.

The table 5.7 provides the information on the yearwise refinance made by NABARD and the repayments made by RGB. It also provides the date on outstanding dues of NABARD refinance. In most of the cases the drawls made are less than the limits sanctioned for refinance. It shows that the bank was incapable of utilising the refinance facilities to the maximum level for the benefits of the rural people. After 1986-87, the refinance was made on the basis of medium term and short term refinance schemes. The outstanding figures of refinance presented in the table are for the period May to June, but not for April to March.

TABLE - 5.7

NABARD Refinance Availed by RGB and Outstandings

(Rupees in Lakhs)

Year	*Limit Sanctioned*	*Drawls made*	*Repayments made*	*Outstanding at the end June*
1	2	3	4	5
1981-82	30.00	17.20	–	17.20
1982-83	75.00	41.95	–	59.15
1983.84	100.00	40.85	–	100.00
1984-85	100.00	36.55	–	136.55
1985-86	200.00	62.61	–	199.16

(Contd.)

TABLE 5.7 (Contd.)

1	2	3	4	5
1986-87				
ST	125.00	10.32	–	85.00
MT	100.00	34.46	24.90	134.04
1987-88				
ST	175.00	20.78	–	105.78
MT	155.00	155.00	24.90	264.15
1988-89				
ST	175.00	101.78	136.35	71.21
MT	100.00	100.00	57.47	306.68
1989-90				
ST	185.00	158.92	101.78	128.35
MT	100.00	100.00	94.72	311.96
1990-91				
ST	200.00	150.54	141.96	136.93
MT	125.00	125.00	103.07	333.89
Total of 10 Years	2005.00	1155.96	685.15	470.82

Source : Statistics section, RGB Head Office, (During May 1991)

Note : MT = Medium Term
ST = Short Term

During the period 1990-91, the limits sanctioned for short term and medium term refinance facilities are Rs.200 lakhs and Rs. 125 lakhs respectively. The drawls made are Rs. 150.54 lakhs in short term and Rs. 125 lakhs in medium term, which are less than the limits fixed - The RGB made payments of Rs. 141.96 lakhs towards the short-term and Rs. 103.07 lakhs towards the medium term refinance of NABARD. The outstanding dues of RGB to NABARD in short-term by June 1991 is Rs. 136.93 lakhs and in medium term is Rs. 333.89 lakhs.

The details of refinance made by NABARD as on 31.3.1992 are presented below in table 5.8

TABLE - 5.8

NABARD Refinance to RGB During the Year 1991-92

(Rupees in lakhs)

Types Scheme	*Limit Sanctioned*	*Refinance Availed*	*Repayments Made*	*Outstanding as on 31.3.92*
ST (SAO)	200.00	180.32	156.94	180.32
ST (OSAO)	15.00	–	–	–
Total short terms	215.00	180.32	156.94	18032
MT (NS)	100.00	100.00	122.79	355.38
MT (Sch)	–	147.99	103.25	324.14
Total	100.00	247.99	226.04	679.52'

Source : 11th Annual Report, RGB (1991-92).

The limits sanctioned in the short term was Rs. 215 lakhs, but refinance availed for Seasonal Agricultural Operations only for Rs. 180.32 lakhs and repayment made for Rs. 156.94. The outstanding refinance dues of RGB by 31.3.92 was Rs. 180.32 lakhs. Similarly in Medium term refinance the limit sanctioned for non-schematic loans was Rs. 100 lakhs and the whole amounts were drawn for the purpose of the beneficiaries. The repayments made to NABARD were Rs. 122.79 lakhs and the outstanding dues were Rs. 335.38 lakhs during the period under report. On the other hand, in schematic lending (Medium term) there were no limits fixed. However Rs. 147.99 lakhs were withdrawn and repayments made for Rs. 103.25 lakhs. The outstanding dues in the schematics was Rs. 324.14 lakhs. The total outstanding, medium term dues to NABARD constitute Rs. 679.52 lakhs by 31.3.1992.

The refinance from NABARD to different RRBs of Orissa by March 1990 are presented in table 5.9 for a comparison. The refinances are generally made on the basis of performances of RRBs and of regular repayments.

TABLE - 5.9

NABARD Refinance to RBBs of Orissa (As. on 31.3.1990)

Sl. No.	*Name of the RRBs*	*Rs. in Lakhs*
1.	Puri Gramya Bank	1633.48
2.	Balangir Gramya Bank	2729.28
3.	Cuttack Gramya Bank	1370.40
4.	Koraput Panchabati Gramya Bank	1755.86
5.	Kalahandi Gramya Bank	1196.48
6.	Baitarni Gramya Bank	708.56
7.	Rushikulya Gramya Bank	695.18
8.	Dhenkanal Gramya Bank	463.85
9.	Balesore Gramya Bank	464.27
	Total	11017.36

Source : RRB Statistics, NABARD 1989-90 P-134

The Rushikulya Gramya Bank got 6.3% of the total RRB NABARD refinance of Orissa during 31.3.1990. At the national level the following (table 5.10) is the refinance from NABARD to RRBs at the end of March 1992.

TABLE - 5.10

National Level NABARD Refinances to RRBs

(Rupees in crores)

Type of refinance	*Limit santioned*	*Amount outstanding*
Short Term	Rs. 484.54	Rs. 451.95
Medium Term		
(a) Non schematic	Rs. 71.69	Rs. 246.25
(b) Conversion loans	Rs. 1.53	Rs. 11.31
Long Term	Rs. 2,276.17	Rs. 2,012.37
Total :	Rs. 2,833.93	Rs. 2,721.88

Source : Table 11.15, RBI, Bulletin, January - 93., P-42

By the end of Sept. 1991, the refinance facilities by NABARD to RRBs of the Nation was Rs. 142188.90 lakhs and out of the said amounts of refinance the share of RRBs of Orissa was Rs 11734.40 lakhs, which constitutes 8.25% of the total.[18]

The NABARD has a R & D fund, which is providing assistance to the RRBs from its Technical Monitoring and Evaluation (TNE) cells for preparation and evaluation of schemes under project lending. Out of 196 RRBs, 96 have taken advantage of the scheme.[19]

(b) Refinance from the Sponsor Bank

The RRB Act has cast a responsibility on sponsor banks to aid and assist RRBs and to provide managerial and financial assistance. In accordance with the statutory responsibility, sponsor banks provide financial accommodation usually upto 35% of RRB's loans.[20]

TABLE - 5.11
Refinances to RGB by the Sponsor Bank

(Rupees in Lakhs)

Year	*Limit Sanctioned*	*Drawls made*	*Repayments made*	*Outstanding at the end June*
1	2 3	4	5	6
1981-82	–	12.63	–	12.63
1982-83	83.25	21.93	–	34.56
1983-84	60.00	25.44	–	60.00
1984-85	–			60.00
1985-86	110.00	50.00	–	110.00
1986-87	210.00	54.78	–	164.78
ST	57.00	–		56.17
MT	115.00	–	21.72	86.89
1987-88	–			
ST	–		56.17	
MT	50.00	50.00	–	136.89
1988-89	75.00	51.34	56.17	51.34
ST	80.00	62.80	69.37	54.77
MT	55.00	55.00	71.17	139.00
1990-91				
ST	200.00	150.54	41.96	136.93
MT	125.00	125.00	103.07	333.89
Total of 10 Years	935.250	423.92	230.15	193.77

(Contd)

TABLE 5.11 (Contd.)

1	2	3	4	5	6
1991-92					
ST (SAO)		80.00	73.68	64.35	72.13
ST (OSAO)		6.00	–	–	–
DRI		–	–	13.49	9.16
MT (NS)		35.00	38.80	57.68	155.76

Source : Statistics section, RGB Head Office, Berhampur and 11th Annual Report of RGB, 1991-92.

The sponsor bank i.e., the Andhra Bank has sanctioned the limit of Rs. 935.25 lakhs from the period 1981-82 (June) to 1990-91 (June) and the RGB has availed the refinance of Rs. 423.92 lakhs which constitutes 45.22% of the limits. As such it could not avail 54.78% of refinance facilities during the period. It has made repayment to the Sponsor Bank of Rs. 230.15 lakhs towards the drawl of Rs. 423.92 lakhs. The repayments constitute 54.29% of the amounts drawn upto June 1991.

During the period 1991-92 (March) an amount of Rs. 121 lakhs of limit was sanctioned by the Andhra Bank (Sponsor Bank) to RGB. RGB has availed the refinance facilities for Rs. 112.48 lakhs, which is 92.95% of the limit. It has made repayment during the said year for Rs. 135.52 lakhs and the outstanding dues to Andhra Bank as on 31.3.92 was Rs. 237.05 lakhs.

The table 5.12 provides a comparative view of the RRBs of Orissa in availing the refinance facilities from their respective Sponsor Bank.

It is to be seen form table 5.12 that out of Rs. 3724.45 of refinances of different Sponsor Banks to RRBs in Orissa, the Andhra Bank's refinance to RGB constitutes 6% only. The amount of refinance availed of by 196 RRBs of the country from their Sponsor banks stood at Rs. 305 crore at the end of September 1991 as against Rs. 328 crores at the end of September 1990. The RRBs had also availed of refinance to the tune of Rs. 23 crore from IDBI and Rs. 12.62 crore from other institutions.[21] But by March 1990 (table 5.10) in Orissa Cuttack Gramya Bank is only RRB to get refinance facilities of Rs. 9.99 lakhs from such other sources.[22] The RGB has no such other refinancing sources in the said year.

TABLE - 5.12

Refinances from Sponsor Banks (All RRBs of Orissa) (As on March 1990)

(Amount in lakhs)

Sl. No.	*Name of the Banks*	*Amounts of Refinance*
1.	Puri Gramya Bank	445.38
2.	Bolangir Gramya Bank	585.78
3.	Cuttack Gramya Bank	1219.45
4.	Koraput Panchabati Gramya Bank	493.30
5.	Kalahandi Anchal Gramya Bank	279.76
6.	Baitarani Gramya Bank	241.34
7.	Balasore Gramya Bank	95.09
8.	Rushikulya Gramya Bank	224.97
9.	Dhenkanal Gramya Bank	139.38
	Total	3724.45

Source : RRB Statistic, (1989-90), NABARD, P. 134.

Recovery of Loans

Credit can generate accelerated economic growth only when the amounts taken are repaid in time. "The Problem of accumulated overdues and arrears of interest amount need to be solved immediately and once for all. The accumulated overdues have posed a good many problems and if not solved it would continue to pose problems in the issuance of future loans".[23] The Regional Rural Banks, being an organisation for development, provide cheap credit to the deserving target groups with the objective that the credit so provided will result in incremental income of the loanees, who shall repay the loan in easy instalments in accordance with the phased repayment schedule, which is prescribed.

The financial resources of RGB are limited. It cannot continuously go on lending without getting them back for recycling. Recovery of loan is a major economic strength for RGB or to any rural branch of a bank for its survival by which it can be in continuous service of pumping the credit to the empty hands of needy small investors and entreprenuers of the rural sector. Thus, there can be no difference of opinion about the need for timely recycling of funds. "Inadequate recovery of loans not only inhibits the ability of the system to recycle the funds but also denies the benefits of borrowing to other needy people. Better recovery of loans helps in building confidence of general public."[24]

Heavy and mounting overdues pose a serious threat to the process of institutionalising rural credit. This problem is common to all the institutions of credit like Co-operatives, Commercial Banks as also Regional Rural Banks.[25]

The Regional Rural Bank or the Rushikulya Gramya Bank in Ganjam District of Orissa is by no means a charitable institution and it cannot exist if it goes on lending without the recoveries. Profit or no profit, a credit institution, however pious its objectives, cannot afford to incur losses. Money must flow in a circular way. The loanable funds must go from RRBs to the weaker sections for generating investment and income. It should return through instalments with periodic intervals for further loan loans. This cycle and recycle must continue for the viability of RRBs or any other lending institution.

Recovery of loans play a very important role in an economic of building confidence of the general public in the soundness of the banking system. It also reduces the cost of credit operations appreciably by avoiding litigation. It also improves the efficiency of the operational staff and helps them to devote more time for development work rather than keeping themselves busy in recovering loans.

The Demand, Collection, Balance (DCB) and Overdues of Loans of Rushikulya Gramya Bank (RGB)

The statistical section of RGB provided the information that quite a large number and percentage of the total borrowers belonging to weaker section have not repaid the loans. The repayment position was found low in case of landless and agricultural labourers, and rural artisans including the small entreprenuers.

The table 5.13 presents the DCB and overdues of RGB from 1983 to 1989 March.

TABLE 5.13

DCB Position and Overdues of RGB (From 1983 to 1988-89)

(Rupees in lakhs)

Years (Jan - Dec)	*Demand*	*Collection*	*Balance*	*% of Overdues*	*% of Recoveries*
1983	27.34	18.29	9.05	33%	67%
1984	41.34	21.03	20.31	49%	51%
1985	122.42	64.62	57.80	47%	53%
1986	147.06	77.83	69.23	47%	53%
1987	278.12	161.22	116.90	42%	58%
1988	536.40	319.57	216.83	40%	60.%
1988-89 (Apr - March)	707.01	401.76	285.25	40%	60%

Source : Statistics sections, RGB Head Office, Berhampur Ganjam.

It has been observed from the table 5.13 that in the year 1983 the percentage of overdues was 33% and afterwards it has remained above 40%. During the year 1984 it was at a maximum being 49% and in 1985, 1986 it was at 47% and thereafter it has fallen to 42% in the year 1987 and in the Year 1988, 1989 (March) to 40%.

The table 5.13 indicates the sectorwise overdues of RGB for June 1990, 1991, 92. The overdues by June 90 is found after the adjustment made as per the Agricultural and Rural Debt Relief Scheme (ARDRS) during 1990. The scheme was introduced from May 15, 1990. According to this scheme the Commercial Banks (Public Sector and

Regional Rural Banks are to exempt the loans of rural people to the extent of Rs. 10,000/- as debt relief to the borrowers who availed the loans on or after 1st April, 1986, and instalments of loan falling due after October 2nd 1986, which are overdue to a bank on October 2nd, 1989. The relief will be available to a non-wilful defaulter only.[26]

TABLE - 5.14

DCB Position and Overdues on RGB (From June 1990 to June 1992)

(Rupees in lakhs)

	June 1990	*June 1991*	*June 1992*
Agri. Crop Loan			
Demand	237.85	301.24	349.38
Collection	111.07	122.08	183.71
Balance	126.78	179.16	165.67
% of overdues	53.3	59.4	47.4
Agri. Term Loan			
Demand	153.69	167.38	261.74
Collection	78.91	32.07	50.49
Balance	74.78	165.31	211.25
% of overdues	48.6	83.7	80.00
SSI, Tertiary and Consumption Loans			
Demand	471.08	603.07	629.99
Collection	244.67	236.05	258.13
Balance	226.41	367.02	371.86
% of overdues	48.00	60.8	59.00
Total			
Demand	862.62	1101.69	1241.11
Collection	434.65	390.20	492.33
Balance	727.97	711.49	748.78
% of overdues	49.6	64.5	60.33

Source : Statistics Section, RGB Head Office Berhampur, Ganjam.

It is found from the table 5.14 that the overdues of RGB in the agricultural sector (After the debt reliefs) was 53% for crop loan and 48.6% in term loans by June 1990, and by June 1991 it was 57.4% for crop loan and 83.7% for term loan. In the same way by June 1992 the percentage of overdues in crop loan was 47.4% and for the term loan was 80%.

In the year June 1991 both the crop loan and term loan overdues were higher than they had been for the other two years. In a comparison between the overdues of crop loan and term loan, for 1991, and 1992 (June) the overdues of term loans are much higher than the overdues of crop loans. On the otherhand, in June 90, the overdues of crop loan was slightly higher than the overdues of term loans.

The overdues of S.S.I. sector, tertiary sector and the consumption loans are expressed together in table 5.14. The percentage of overdues in these sectors together are 48%, 60.8% and 59% by the end of June 1990, 1991, and 1992 respectively. In the same way, the total overdues for RGB in June 1990, 1991 and 1992 are respectively 49.6%, 64.5% and 60.33%.

TABLE - 5.15

Comparative Data on Overdues of All the Banks As on June 1990 (Ganjam District)

(Amounts in Lakhs)

Sl. No.	*Name of the Bank*	*Demand (Amounts)*	*Collection (Amounts)*	*Balance (Amounts)*	*% of Overdues*
1	2	3	4	5	6
1.	Allahabad Bank	58.18	10.47	47.71	82
2.	Andhra Bank	349.02	145.52	203.50	58
3.	Bank of Baroda	54.93	10.35	44.58	81
4.	Bank of India	46.25	7.72	39.03	83
5.	Canara Bank	305.67	169.53	136.14	45
6.	Central Bank of India	54.49	7.62	46.87	86
7.	Indian Overseas Bank	278.85	115.99	162.86	58
8.	Indian Bank	169.32	38.17	131.15	77
9.	Punjab National Bank	13.57	3.68	9.89	73
10.	State Bank of Hyderabad	2.23	–	2.23	100
11.	State Bank of India	1903.11	928.61	974.50	51
12.	Syndicate Bank	237.97	32.31	205.66	86
13.	Union Bank of India	25.07	3.32	21.75	87
14.	United Bank of India	102.01	33.17	68.34	67
15.	United Commercial Bank	360.08	27.31	332.77	92
16.	Vijaya Bank	64.09	20.52	43.57	68

Contd

TABLE 5.15 (Contd.)

1	2	3	4	5	6
17.	Vysya Bank	3.59	1.83	1.76	49
	Commercial Banks	4028.93	1556.12	2472.81	61
	RGB	862.62	434.65	427.97	49.6%
	All Banks (Dist.)	4891.55	1990.77	2900.78	59.3%

Source : Regional Office, Andhra Bank, Berhampur, Ganjam.

The comparative statement of overdues presented in table 5.15 shows the position of overdues in Ganjam district (Banking sector) by June 1990. The Canara Bank in Ganjam district has the lowest overdues i.e., 45%. The district average picture in the overdues is 59.3%, while excluding RGB the commercial banks in total have 61%. The RGB has 59.3% of overdues during the said period.

Thus it is clear that the overdues is not only a problem for RGB but it is a general problem of the banks as a whole in the district.

The percentage of overdues to outstanding advances during March 1990 in case of all the 9 RRBs of Orissa is presented in table 5.16.

TABLE - 5.16

Percentage of Overdues of All RRBs of Orissa (As on March 1990)

Sl. No.	*Name of the Bank*	*Percentage*
1.	Puri Gramya Bank	28.2%
2.	Bolangir Anchal Gramya Bank	15.5%
3.	Cuttack Gramya Bank	37.8%
4.	Koraput Panchabati Gramya Bank	14.6%
5.	Kalahandi Anchala Gramya Bank	10.4%
6.	Baitarani Gramya Bank	23.5%
7.	Balesore Gramya Bank	28.7%
8.	Rushikulya Gramya Bank	19.7%
9.	Dhenkanal Gramya Bank	16.8%
	Total	23.2%

Source : RRB statistics (NABARD) 1989-90 Statement No. 4, P.-6.

Table 5.16 presented the trend of overdues in relation to the outstanding advances of all RRBs of the State. The Cuttack Gramya Bank occupies the top place in overdues being 37.8%. The RGB has 19.7% of overdues out of the outstanding advances during the reporting period. The overdue percentage for Orissa in RRB sector is 23.2% by March 1990. The percentage of overdues to outstanding advances of RRBs increased marginally from 32.1% as at the end of September 1990 to 32.93 per cent in September 1991 at the national level.[27]

Profits as A Source of Capital

"Profit is the ultimate output of a company and it will have no future if it fails to make sufficient profit".[28] The RGB being a commercial bank should optimise its income on lending operations. The RGB and the Rural Banks get concessional refinances and supply loans at concessional rate of interest. Only recently the rate of interest was made uniform keeping relation of interest to the quantity of loans. (As discussed in chapter-4). But for rural development a concessional rate of interest is not the main requirement. There is the requirement of timely supply of credit to the right persons for the right purpose. The concessional rate of interest of lending is not necessary for rural development, what is required is timely and adequate amount of credit. "A credit institution is considered financially viable if it attains a level of business giving an income level which would enable it to meet not only all the expenses, but also help it to build of a minimum reserve over a period of time."[29] A credit institution should be structurally sound and should have the ability to generate on its own profits to take care of :

(a) expenses for developing its business.

(b) supervision of end-use of credit.

(c) training and effective supervison of staff ; and

(d) other incidental liabilities including provisions for bad and doubtful debts

It is, therefore, necessary to realistically determine how these institutions turn into self supporting and financially sound institutions.

As the rural development process gathers momentum, the rural community will also expect other banking services - other than credit. In the long-run, the interests of the weaker sections can be served effectively only by institutions which are financially and structurally strong and can respond to the changing needs of the community".[30]

Thus the earnings of RGB have to be positive if it is to survive as an agent of rural lending in Ganjam district. The factors that generally influence the credit earning of any financial institution are as follows :

(a) Nature of Business.

(b) Risk involved

(c) Risk of inflation

(d) Comparative rate of return on gilt - edged securities.

(e) Flactuations of external economic conditions.

As the RGB is a state sponsored Credit organisation, the factors like business risk do not come under consideration. It is expected to act as a catalyst to usher in an era of rural prosperity.[31] Even the comparative rate of returns on gilt-edged securities do not exercise any far-reaching impact on the activities of RRBs. The Government has extended shielding patronage to them and therefore, the general monetary theories are not of much applicability in their case.[32]

Inspite of a number of concessions and privileges, RRBs in Orissa and specially RGB in Ganjam district fared very badly in terms of profit earnings.

In the analysis of the facts of the table 5.17, it is to be found that among 9 RRBs of Orissa only one RRB i.e., Koraput Panchabati Gramya Bank, sponsored by State Bank of India, established with effect from 13.11.1976 has fared well and made profits continuously from March 1983 to March 1990.

TABLE - 5.17

Profits and Losses of RRBs of Orissa
(From Dec. 1983 to Dec. 1986)

(Rs. in lakhs)

Name of RRBs	*1983*		*1984*		*1985*		*1986*	
	P	*L*	*P*	*L*	*P*	*L*	*P*	*L*
Puri G.B.	4.28	–	–	-12.27	–	-25.93	–	-58.54
Bolangir Ach. G.B.	–	-18.42	–	-50.55	–	-80.64	–	-40.39
Cuttack G.B.	6.63	–	4.10	–	–	-17.42	–	-19.28
Koraput Panch. G.B.	14.60	–	17.34	–	15.30	–	1.35	–
Kalahandi Anch. G.B.	–	-16.5	–	-13.22	–	-9.96	–	-16.66
Boitarani G.B.	–	-2.79	–	-10.77	–	-12.15	–	-33.50
Balesore G.B.	–	-18.70	–	28.90	–	-35.27	–	-48.93
RGB (Ganjam)	–	-5.59	–	-10.98	–	-18.93	–	-28.14
Dhenkanal G.B.	–	-7.25	–	-14.94	–	-19.49	–	-26.18
Orissa	25.51	-68.80	21.44	-141.63	15.30	-219.82	1.35	-271.62

Name of RRBs	*1987*		*1988-89*		*1989-90*			*Accumulated Losses as on March 1990.*
	P	*L*	*P*	*L*	*P*	*L*		
Puri G.B.	–	-65.37	–	-91.58	–	-115.18		-424.85
Bolangir Ach. G.B.	4.95	–	–	-337.37	–	-276.96	–	-807.22
Cuttack G.B.	–	-29.28	–	-172.41	–	-89.60	–	-309.01
Koraput Panch. G.B.	2.50	–	4.41	–	18.27	–	–	–
Kalahandi Anch. G.B.	–	-20.79	–	-10.39	–	-28.00	–	-124.72
Boitarani G.B.	–	-51.69	–	-127.28	–	-144.27	–	-403.10
Balesore G.B.	–	-61.92	–	-91.40	–	-73.33	–	-384.67
RGB (Ganjam)	–	-35.31	–	-37.16	–	-62.03	–	-202.99
Dhenkanal G.B.	–	-19.22	–	-18.58	–	-14.08	–	-108.03
Orissa	7.45	-283.58	4.41	-886.17	18.27	-802.43		2784.59

Source : RRB Statistics (1989-90), P. 164.

Note : P = Profit, L = Loss.

The Puri Gramya Bank and Cuttack Gramya Bank did make profit in the year 1983 including the Koraput Panchabati Gramya Bank. But afterwords the profit making capacity of Puri Gramya Bank has disappeared seen. It has incurred losses continuously. The accumulated losses of Puri Gramya Bank by March 1990 is Rs. 424.85 lakhs.

The Cuttack Gramya Bank could continue making profit upto March 1984. But thereafter it faced continuous losses and the accumulated loss of the said bank by March 1990 is Rs. 309.01 lakhs.

In between the years under discussion the Balangir Anchal Gramya Bank could make profit during the year 1987 of Rs. 4.95 lakhs only.

As such excluding the Koraput Panchabati Gramya Bank, all other banks have accumulated losses by March 1990. The profit of Koraput panchabati Gramya Bank also became negligible between 1986 to 1988-89, flactuating between 1.35 lakhs to 4.41 lakhs.

The Rushikulya Gramya bank is continuously facing losses and the accumulated loss of RGB by March 1990 was Rs. 202.99 lakhs. The accumulated losses for the year 1990-91 (March) and 1991-92 (March) were Rs. 260.21 lakhs and Rs. 417.18 lakhs causing yearwise losses of Rs. 57.22 lakhs and Rs. 156.97 lakhs respectively.[33]

By analysing the performance of RRBs of Orissa from the facts of the table 5.17, one can clearly say that RRBs in Orissa as a business organisation have no viability and one fine day they will be happy to close-down their operations. Excepting the RRB of Koraput district, all other RRBs are incurring heavy losses. By the end of March 1990, the accumulated losses of RRBs of Orissa was Rs. 2784.59 lakhs. "It is believed that new branches of old RRBs act as a drag on their profits. Consequently, the profits of old RRBs with large number of new branches get eroded."[34]. It is found from the study of facts that the more the number of branches and older the RRB the higher are the losses and in the same way the losses of RGB are also rising regularly.

TABLE - 5.18

Income and Expenditure (RGB/All RRBs of Orissa) (As on end of March 1990)

(Rupees in lakhs)

Incomes	*RGB*	*All RRBs of Orissa*	*Expenditure*	*RRB*	*All RRBs of Orissa*
Interest	180.09	2472.08	Interest paid	138.05	1818.30
Commissions	1.37	27.94	Salaries	81.73	988.83
Ineidental	Nil	0.31	DIR fees	Nil	0.04
Subsidy from sponsor bank	4.40	28.69	Rent	21.51	283.98
Other receipts	0.53	30.66	Postage	1.00	12.43
			Audit fees	0.25	3.65
			Depreciation	2.50	25.91
			Stationary	2.58	28.05
			Other Expenditure	0.80	181.65
Total Incomes	186.39	2559.68	Total Expenditure	248.42	3343.84

RGB Losses by March 1990 = (Rs. 186.39 lakhs - Rs. 248.42 lakhs) = Rs. -62.03 lakhs

Losses of RRBs of Orissa by March 1990 = (Rs. 2559.68 lakhs - Rs. 3343.84 lakhs) = Rs. -784.16 lakhs

Source : RRB statistics, NABARD, Bombay, 1989-90, PP. 150,151.

The income and expenditure sides of RGB for the year March 1989-90 has been presented on the previous page. The facts and figures of the Balance Sheet (Table 5.18) reveal that the salaries of the staff of RGB constitute percentage of salaries and allowances to total expenditure for the year 1990-91 (March) and 1991-92 (March) constitute 32.66% and 34.27% respectively.[35] "The recent wages settlement has already pushed up the staff costs".[36] The interest payments of RGB towards the depositers constitute 55.57% of the total expenditure of RGB in the year 1989-90. " It is thus understood that the interest charges constituted more than half the total cost. Therefore, every effort should be made by the bank to reorganise the deposits, borrowings - mix in such a way that the interest cost is brought down to the maximum possible extent.[37] Similarly the rent paid for the Bank constitute 8.65% of the total expenditure during the said period. The other expenditures constitute 2.88% of the total expenditure during 1989-90 (Table 5.18). The percentage of interest paid on deposits and borrowings to total expenditure for the year 1990-91 (March) and 1991-92 (March) constitute 55.54% and 47.74% respectively.[38]

The above analysis shows that the cost of RGB is increasing with increase in losses and thus the RGB's capital is giving negative returns.

With a smaller contribution of deposits to the district and not achieving the deposit target in certain years and if achieved not to a greater extent, the main source of capital is limited in the hands of the RGB. It is mostly dependent upon refinances from NABARD and Sponsored Bank for its business. The RGB has not made profit in any of the years. There are heavy overdues and collections in most of the cases are doubtful. Due to the continuous losses, the share capital and reserve funds as sources of capital for RGB have lost their importance. The continuous increase in the overdues and increased cost of banking to RGB is a main constraint and negatively affects the capital structure of RGB. Thus the main source of RGB and RRBs are the refinances from sponsor bank to some extent and the refinances of NABARD to a greater extent. "The justification of the emergence and continuation of rural banks lie in providing cheaper credit than others to their clientele. At present they are unable to do so because of higher cost of their funds. The cost is high because (a) their paid up capital, a cost free component is meagre, (b) their current deposits, an interest free component, are relatively small (c) refinance facilities provided by the sponsor banks are dearer and (d) the borrowing from the sponsor banks under refinance facility are considered as their deposits for provisions of minimum statutory reserves. Sometimes the banks feel that inspite of much propaganda the promised and necessary assistance is not forthcoming at right time and in right manner even in reasonable cases. This is a peculier paradox and needs to be looked into and resolved.[39] It is important to prevent misdirection and leakages of credit so that the recovery of loans becomes an easy task.[40]

RGB as a bank has to obtain deposits from prosperous clients, institutions and corporations a situated in the nearby areas and it has to welcome funds from Government and Semi-Government, block level organisations. But in practice, it is found that the funds of the Government lie with the State Bank of India and with other nationalised Banks and they do not flow into the deposit liabilities of RGB at the block level and in rural areas.

In the next chapter the constraints of RGB have been taken up with case studies. However the present chapter with the detailed discussions on the factors which influence the capital sources of RGB provides the conclusion that, RGB as a RRB for its capital basically depends upon the refinances and continuous overdues which endangers its viability.

Conclusion

RGB being a small bank for small men belonging to a well defined but small area has very limited funds to cater to the needs of the people. It mostly depends upon the refinances and subsidies for lending under different schemes of State and Central Governments. The nature, style of functioning and organisational pattern of Rushikulya Gramya Bank are quite different from those of Commercial Banks functioning in the district.

The following constitute the main source of capital for the RGB.

(1) Share Capital

(2) Deposits.

(3) Refinance from NABARD

(4) Refinance from Sponsor Bank

(5) Recovery of loans

(6) Accumulated Profits.

The RGB has an authorised capital of rupees one crore and paid up share of Rs. 50 lakhs contributed by the Central Government, the sponsor bank and the State Government in the ratio of 50 : 35 : 15 per cent respectively. The RGB has been incurring losses right from its inception.

The deposit mobilisation of RGB has a significant role in both the district economy and to the Bank's financial self-sufficiency. It enables the bank for recycling the deposits in credit deployments. By 1991-92, RGB with its 75 branches in 1833 adopted villages, with 342 staff has mobilised deposit for Rs. 1923.21 lakhs in 125837 accounts as against 7 branches of RGB in 30 adopted villages, involving 65 staff mobilising Rs. 39.55 lakhs in 1290 accounts in the year of inception i.e. in 1981. The average deposit per branch of RGB was Rs. 5.65 lakhs in 1981 and the same had increased to Rs. 25.64 lakhs in the year 1991-92. The branches of RGB have remained unchanged at 75 numbers from 1989 onwards. With an increase in the number of branches (upto 1989), expansion in accounts covering more and more villagès in its operational field, the RGB increased its deposits. But its share in Banking sector in mobilisation of deposits of the district is not satisfactory. In the Banking sector of the district in mobilisation of the deposits, the share of RGB is less than 6% by March 1991. The deposit contribution of RGB slowly increased in the district from 2.15% in Dec. 1981 to 5.78% in March 1991. The percentage growth of the deposits of RGB remained always above the percentage growth of the district, 'which can be worked out from table 5.5. The RGB occupies the 6th position in deposit mobilisation among the 9 RRBs of the state during March 1990, according to date of NABARD. It contributes 7.27% of deposits of the total RRB deposits of the State. The Cuttack gramya Bank, contributing 24.61% of the deposits is highest among the RRBs of the State. In most of the years, RGB also failed to achieve the targets of deposit mobilisation. The foregoing analysis points out that even though the growth rate in percentage terms is good in respect of RGB in the district, in quantitative terms the achievement is not vary much satisfactory. The RGB has to do a lot to attract more depositors in the rural sector.

Like any other RRB, the RGB gets refinance facilities from NABARD and its sponsor Bank. NABARD refinance is the main source for its lending operations in Government sponsored programmes. As on 31.3.1990 for the financial year 1989-90 the RGB has got only 6.3% of the total refinances among the 9 RRBs of the state. The NABARD has refinanced to RGB from 1981-82 (June) to 1990-91 (June) Rs. 1155.96 lakhs out of the sanctioned limit of Rs. 2005.00 lakhs. The refinance availed constitute 57.65% of the total limits sanctioned during the ten years. It has made repayment of Rs. 685.15 lakhs and the outstanding due to NABARD is Rs. 470.82 lakhs during June1991. However by March 1991-92 the outstanding dues to NABARD was Rs. 679.52 lakhs. During the year 1991-92, out of the total limit of Rs. 315 lakhs the RGB has drawn Rs. 180.32 lakhs in ST and Rs. 147.99 lakhs in M.T. i.e., total of Rs. 428.31 lakhs, which has crossed the limit fixed. It shows an increasing role of RGB in lending to the Govt. sponsored programmes availing the refinance facilities during the year 1991-92. The RGB has to do a lot to attract more depositers in the rural sector.

The sponsor bank has provided Rs. 935.25 lakhs as refinance limits during the ten years tenure from 1981 to 1991 (June) and the bank has availed refinance for Rs. 423.92 lakhs, which is 45.22% of the limits sanctioned. During the period 1991-92 as on 3.3.1992 the sponsor bank has an outstanding claim on RGB in refinance for Rs. 237.05 lakhs. The refinances, as an important source of capital in the hands of RGB are helping it in making the loans to its beneficiaries.

Recovery of loans is a general problems for any bank that finances the rural sector. But increase of RGB it is very serious as it is to lend to the target group of people in the rural sector, who are economically poor, illiterate and undeveloped in many respects in comparison to the beneficiaries of commercial banks. The district level overdue percent (of all the banks) is 59.6% as on June 1990, while for RGB it is 50% and for all the 17 commercial Banks it is 61% (Table 5.15). Thus, with the non-repayment of 50% of loans, and with the bad effects of ARDRS of 1990 the recycling for loans of RGB is not satisfactory and the sources of capital in the hand of RGB becomes scarce.

The RGB with its ever-rising expenditure and with its low income has been incurring losses continuously. By March 1990, the accumulated losses were Rs. 202.99 lakhs which constitute 7.28% of the total losses of RRBs of Orissa. (Table 5.17) By the end of March 1992, the accumulated loss for RGB is Rs. 417.18 lakhs. With the increase in the salaries and other expenditures the RGB has to face increasing losses. Thus the capital base of RGB is very weak and it is doubtful if it can become viable in the near future at all.

References

1. RGB Head Office, (Rural Development Officer - Interview. May ' 1991).

2. Ibid.

3. Annual Report, 1990-91, RGB Head Office, Berhampur, Ganjam.

4. RRB Act, 1976, Chapter, 11-3.

5. "RRB (Amendment) Act, 1987", RBI Bulletin, (Supplement) Report on trend and progress of Banking in *India, 1988 - 1989 (July - June)*, Bombay, October, 1989, PP. 64, 65.

6. Varma, M.L., *Rural Banking in India*, Jaipur (Rajastan), Kuber Associates and Publishers, 1st Edition, 1988, P. 124.

7. Vyas, M.R., *Financial Performance of Regional Rural Banks*, Jaipur (Rajastan), Arihant Publishers, 1991, P. 81.

8. "Report of Board of Directors" : *Annual Report of RGB*, 1982.

9. Statistics section, Head Office, RGB, Berhampur, Ganjam (Enquiry).

10. Ibid.

11. Ibid.

12. Ibid.

13. Table 11-13, *RBI Bulletin, (Supplement)*, January, 1993, P. 40.

14. Sardesai, A.V., "Institutional arrangements for Rural Credit in India", (Mimiograph), College of Agricultural Banking (RBI), Pune.

15. Lall, G.S., (Edt.), "National Bank for Agricultural and Rural Development", *The Journal of Banking studies*, Vol. X, NO. 3, July - Sept., 1987, P. 180.

16. Iyer, V.D., "NABARD : Functions and working" (Mimiograph), College of Agricultural banking, RBI, Pune.

17. Ibid.

18. Table 11-13, *RBI Bulletin (Supplementary)*, January, 1993, P. 40.

19. Ibid, P. 43.

20. Khandewal, Anil Kumar, *Hand Book on Personal Management and Industrial Relations for Rural Banking*, Jaipur (Rajastan), Rawat Publication, 1987, P. 7.

21. RBI Bulletin (Supplementary), 1993, *Op.cit.*, P. 43.

22. RRB Statistics, (1989-90), NABARD, P. 134.

23. Patel, K.V., Shah, A.C., Mello, L.D., "Accumulated overdues", *Rural Economics*, Bombay, The Indian Institute of Bankers, (1st Edition, 1984, Reprint 1987), P. 447.

24. Kumari Gita (Economic Officer, Punjab National Bank, New Delhi), "Recovery Ethics in Rural Lending", *IBA Bulletin*, Vol. X, No. 12, December, 1988, P. 258.

25. Lall, G.S. (Edited), "Agricultural Finance and Commercial Banks - Problems of regular recoveries", *The Journal of Banking Studies*, Vol. XI, No. 2, April - June, 1988, P. 21.

26. Annonymous, "Agricultural and Rural Debt Relief Scheme - 1990", *RBI Bulletin (Supplement)*, Bombay, 1991, March, P. 67.

27. Annonymous, "Overdues", *RBI Bulletin (Supplement)*, Bombay, January, 1993, P. 41.

28. Pandey, I.M., *Financial Management*, New Delhi, Vikas Publishing House, P. 18.

29. Singh, R.K.R., Singh, R.P.N., Singh, B.B., "Financial viability of commercial and Regional Rural Banks in Bihar - A case study", *The Journal of Indian Institute of Bankers*, Vol. 58, No. 9, (April-June), 1987, P. 83.

30. Malhotra, R.N., "Bank Branch profitability, evaluation of commercial banks' performance, problems of RRBs and Developments in Capital Markets", *The Journal of Indian Institute of Bankers*, Vol. 58, No. 4 (October - December), 1987, P. 173.

31. Vyas, M.R., *Op.cit*, P. 96.

32. Ibid.

33. Patjoshi, P.C., Statistical Officer, RGB Head Office, Berhampur, Ganjam. (During January, 1990).

34. Jethwaney, Sonika, "Regional Rural Banks - A review", *IBA Bulletin (Rural Development Issue)*. Vol. X, No. 12, December, 1989, P. 249.

35. Statistics section, RGB Head Office, Berhampur, (Enquiry)

36. Satyamurty, B., "Bank costs and profitability concepts, evaluation techniques and

strategies for improvement", *The Journal of Indian Institute of Bankers*, Vol. 61, No. 3, July - September 1990, P. 119.

37. Abdul, Noorbasha and M. Jyoti, "Viability of RRBs - A case study", *Yojana*, Vol. 33, No. 9, March (16 to 31), 1989, P. 19.

38. Statistics section, RGB Head Office, Berhampur (Enquiry).

39. Verm, M.L., *Op.cit.* P. 20.1

40. Malhotra, R.N., *Op.cit*, P. 171.

6

The Role of RGB in Income Generation and the Operational Constraints

The Rushikulya Gramya Bank, like its counterparts elsewhere in the country, is specially designed to serve the developmental credit needs of the weaker sections which are not fulfilled by other institutional sources of credit in the field like the commercial banks and the credit cooperatives. The RRBs have come to be accepted as useful instruments for promotion of growth with social justice in rural India. By providing productive credit to the economically weak they furnish their clientele with a new means to improve their lot as also contribute to improvement of the locality as a whole.[1]

It was generally felt that in the initial stages, while performing the assigned social function, the RRBs might sustain losses. But once in the swing they would earn their way and become automatically self-sustaining to ensure their own survival. Thus issues of social service and viability of the institution become necessarily related. It, therefore, is natural to consider in the present chapter the issues of viability and other operational constraints along with income generation potential of the credit support extended by the RGB.

It is not possible to examine the effectiveness of all the RRBs of the country or of the state in connection with income generation, employment creation and production of larger output as a result of credit extention to the weaker sections. It may not even be possible to examine even all the branches of RGB and all beneficiaries with all types of information. What is feasible is a sample study of some branch or branches for analysing the impact of credit on employment, income and output of a particular locality in which the branch works. Accordingly, an indepth analysis has been carried out in this chapter taking two sample branches of RGB from two sample blocks of Ganjam district of Orissa. As such, an attempt is made to study the impact of RGB credit on the rural .poor of Purusottampur block and Hinjilicut block, taking the branches of RGB Jarado, Sikiri and Samarjhola from the respective blocks.

Through case studies of the two branches of RGB in Hinjilicut block and one from Purushotampur block we have to ascertain the extent to which the rural poor of the respective areas are able to improve their economic condition as a result of deployment of credit. The impact of RGB lending for income generation, employment creation and asset formation on the target-people is examined.

In this chapter an attempt has been made to identify the various constraints which the RGB faces in the discharge of its functions. For identification of the constraints some individual case studies have been made in two RGB branches of Hinjilicut block and one branch in purusottampur block. To identify and examine the constraints the beneficiaries of Sikiri, Samarjhola branches of Hinjilicut block and Jarado branch of Purusottampur block were personally interviewed by the scholar on the basis on a semi-structured schedule. As a whole this chapter highlights three major aspects i.e., (1) Impact of loans (2) Viability of the bank (3) and Constraints.

The Case study of Jarado branch was made during January 1989 and the year 1985 (January - December) was chosen as the base year to find out the impact of loans given in the said year over the post loan period. The case study of Sikiri branch was conducted during April 1992 and the base period for the beneficiaries was taken as 1989 (January - December). The field level studies were made in two branches of RGB. These case studies represent the trend of economic growth, overdues and the manner of utilisation of RGB loans in two different branches of two different areas and in two different periods. In jarado branch 90% of the beneficiaries of 1985 were interviewed while in Sikiri branch of RGB 70% of the beneficiaries of the year 1989 were interviewed. The conclusions, the impact of RGB credit on the beneficiaries of the two blocks have been drawn after a careful comparison. In Samarjhola branch some cases have been studied to find out operational constraints, if any.

Jarado branch of RGB was opened on 2.9.1982 at Jarado village of Purusottampur block of Chatrapur sub-division in Ganjam district. It is one of the five branches of RGB in the block. In the said block a branch of Andhra Bank and two branches of State Bank of India are also operating. The total number of bank branches in this area is eight. There is also one branch of the District Central Co-operative Bank. Twenty three recognised and four unrecognised primary Agricultural Societies exist in the block. Thus the block has a good scope of institutional flow of credit to the needy sections.

In case studies of Jarado branch, the analysis has been carried out on beneficiaries in two categories (1) Dairy and Goatry (2) Bullock, bullock-cart, Dugwell. The case studies of Jarado branch are basically on term loans of Agriculture and allied activities. On the other hand, the case studies of Sikiri branch have been carried out village-wise. However in both the case studies, the aim is to findout the incremental income, employment and output accorded to the beneficiaries in the post-loan period.

The identification of beneficiaries was done by taking their names from the respective Branch Managers. The date of loans, amounts sanctioned, the recovery, and the outstanding dues were collected from the bank offices, while the utilisation of loans and improvement of income, loans taken from other sources etc., are based on a field level study conducted with the help of a questionnaire (Annexure - 7).

The field level study is based on the statistical surveys in the areas of the branch of the Bank. The beneficiaries of the branches of RGB are from the target group, weaker sections of the locality. 80% of them are uneducated, illiterate and they are lacking in knowledge of banking. They do not furnish any concrete information about their own income as they do not feel it necessary to keep any account or any record of the same. As such, the incomes of the pre-loan period and post-loan period are not to be taken as exact incomes but only as approximate incomes of the beneficiaries. The incomes of the beneficiaries may not be treated as accurate incomes because, most of them do not provide proper information either deliberately or out of ignorance. This is the main constraint to assess the credit needs and the impact of credit.

Income, employment and production are inter-related with each other. They move in the same direction. Increased output contributes to the growth of income and increased savings and investment. Higher level of investment results in more production and more employment opportunities, generating thereby additional income. Thus, credit should be used in a purposeful manner so that the overall development of the rural economy can take place in the command area of a bank branch.

The objectives of the present case studies are :

(i) to assess the improvement of income, employment and production in the post sanction period over the pre-sanction period.

(ii) to find out the role of the branches of RGB in rural development of the areas concerned.

(iii) to interview some of the beneficiaries who availed themselves of the loan facilities with a view to as certain difficulties faces by them in getting services.

(iv) to present the observations with suggestions.

Before starting the analysis of impact of RGB credit on beneficiaries of Jarado branch, it is essential to have some knowledge of the demographic features of the Purusottampur block in which it is located.

The Purusottampur block is one of the eight blocks in the Chatrapur administrative sub-division. It has 108 inhabited villages and 23 Grampanchayats.[2] The block has a total population of 1,15,776 and the scheduled caste/scheduled tribe population constitute 15.19% and 0.64% respectively of the total.[3] The rural population constitute 90.72% of the total population. The cultivators constitute 50.26%, the agricultural labourers 36.97%, people engaged in the cottage industries and household industries 2.14% of the total population. People engaged in other industries constituted 0.41%, those engaged in trade and commerce constitute 2.62% and the unaccounted balance constitutes 7.57% of the total working-force of the block as per 1981 census. The net cultivated area is 80.78% of the total reporting area of the block.[4] The density of population of the block is 410 per sq. km.[5]

Table 6.1 provides the information on the beneficiaries of Jarado branch for the year 1985 (January - December). 14 beneficiaries on Goatary and Dairy were interviewed in different villages of Jarado branch during January 1989. In case of Goatry the net increase in income is a positive one. While in dairy it is negative.

Table 6.1 on next page is a consolidation of the data collected from the concerned branch and the information elicited from individual beneficiaries through the questionnaire method.

In the interviews of the beneficiaries given in Table - 6.1, the beneficiary having serial No. 4 said that before the RGB finance he was taking hand loans from rich persons and friends of the village at a higher rate of interest. He answered that the RGB loan is better as the instalments for repayment are many and interest is low. The instalments of the repayment is a small fraction of the income (which is derived from the loan capital).

Most of the beneficiaries are wilful defaulters. They anticipate the Dept Relief schemes of Government of State and Centre to come to their rescue. Some of the defaulters encourage others not to repay the loan.

Incomes before the sanction of loan refers to the incomes of some activities for which the present loan has been sanctioned. Serial No. 1, 4 and 8 were doing earlier resources and own arrangements. However after the availability of credit from RGB, they have also improved their income. The other beneficiaries are mostly the daily labourers who could not give out the exact increase in their income as the income was inadequate for maintenance and it fluctuated from time to time.

Serial No. 11, Jaya Nahak of Mohacha village, was not available for interview even after three visits to him. As such his case need not be taken into consideration.

TABLE - 6.1

Loan to Dairy, Goatry Activities by Jarado Branch 1985 (Jan - Dec)

(Amount in Rupees)

S. No.	*Name of the Beneficiary (Village, Date, Purpose, Scheme)*	*Amounts Sanctioned*	*Subsidy Amount*	*Recovary by Dec '88*	*Outstanding Dues by Dec '88*	*Income before Loan (PM)*	*Income after Loan (PM)*
1	2	3	4	5	6	7	8
1.	Kasi Jena, Jarado, 21-11-85 Goatry, AGTL (A)	2200	833	260	1668	200	500
2.	Krishna Nahak, Tiadiapalli, 30-08-85, Goatry, AGTL (A)	2200	733	190	1791	–	250
3.	Satrughna Nahak, Tiadiapalli, 25-09-85, Goatry, AGTL (A)	2200	733	500	1434	–	350
4.	Surendra Nahak, Tiadiapalli, 25-09-85, Goatry, AGTL (A)	2200	733	1020	871	300	600
5.	Bansi Nahak, Tiadiapalli, 25-09-85, Goatry, AGTL (A)	2200	733	400	1504	–	300
6.	Nila Nahak, Tiadiapalli, 18-10-85, Goatry, AGTL (A)	2200	733	1550	244	–	300

(Contd.)

TABLE - 6.1 (Contd.)

1	2	3	4	5	6	7	8
7.	Indra Nahak, Tiadiapalli, 25-09-85, Goatry, AGTL (A)	2200	733	100	1903	–	300
8.	Rama Nahak, Tiadiapalli, 18-10-85, Goatry, AGTL (A)	2200	733	925	871	250	450
9.	Krushna Nahak, Tiadiapalli, Ambila Palli, 24-06-85	2200	666	Nil	1886	–	400
10.	Dhana Nahak, Tankachai, 03-06-85, Goatry	1800	1350	203	300	–	400
11.	Jaya Nahak, Mohachai, Goatry, 03-06-85	2200	1650+260	Nil	377	–	–
12.	Ananda Nahak, Jarado, Dairy-Cow, AGTL, 03-09-85	2500	833	Nil	2308	–	–
13.	Bancha Panda, Mohachai, She-Bafalow, AGTL (A)	2500	833	Nil	2308	–	–
14.	Prahallad Dakua, Mohachai, She-Baffalow, 29-12-85	2500	833	Nil	2247	–	–

Field Level Study (Jan - 1989)

Remarks of beneficiaries according to the serial number

1. He was earning Rs. 200/- in preloan period in goatry. After the loan the income increased to Rs. 500/-. He is a willful defaulter.

2. He got net increase of Rs. 250/- PM after the loan. Before he was a labourer. He is a willful defaulter.

3. He got net increase of Rs. 250/- PM after the loan. Before he was a labourer. He is a willful defaulter.

4. Repayment is better. Earlier he was getting Rs. 300/- from the said activities. He was taking loan from rich persons earlier. He is a willful defaulter.

5. He was a labourer in preloan period. He is a willful defaulter.

6. He was a labourer in preloan period. He is a willful defaulter.

7. He was a labourer in preloan period. He is a willful defaulter.

8. He was getting Rs. 200/- before the loan from the said activities. He is a willful defaulter.

9. He was a labourer before the loan. He is expecting a debt relief scheme in future.

10. He was a labourer before the loan. He is expecting a debt relief scheme in future

11. He was not available for interview, even after three visits paid to him.

12. No asset is available. Doing mini labour contractor. He is a willful defaulter. Loan became unproductive.

13. He has disposed the she-buffalow for Rs. 1400/-. He went outside of the state for small business. He is willful defaulter. Recovery is doubtful. His wife got DRI loan of Rs. 3000/-.

14. Working in a Jute Mill of Calcutta. Assets are disposed. Recovery doubtful. He is a willful defaulter.

The loans given for the purpose of Dairy, and purchase of she bufallows were most unproductive. Ananda Nahak of Jarado village (Serial No. : 12) has disposed of the assets and he is doing the work of a mini labour contractor. He is a wilful defaulter and paid only Rs. 70/- towards the repayment of loan. He has not used the loan amounts for the specific productive activities. Similarly Bancha Panda (Serial No. 13) has also disposed of the she bufallow for only Rs. 1400/- and went outside the State to do small business. His wife has availed herself of another loan under the DRI scheme at a nominal rate of interest from RGB. The loans are doubtful of recovery and they are not used for the purpose for which these loans were given. The last beneficiary serial No. 14, Prahallad Dakua of Mohachai village has disposed of the asset and went to Calcutta to work as a labourer in a Jute Mill.

It is observed that the beneficiaries of Goatry have utilised the loan for generating the income and employment. The loans given for Dairy purpose are most unproductive in all the three sample cases.

Out of the 14 cases one case at Sl. No. 11, was not available for the interview. So far an average analysis of net income after the loan (Post-loan period) comes to Rs. 238.46 per month. (Total post loan period income minus the total pre loan period income = The total net increamental income. Total net increment in income will be divided by 13 beneficiaries = Rs. 238.46) Out of 13 interviewed 9 have reported that the loan amounts were not adequate to them.

Table 6.2 provides the consolidated date of the beneficiaries of Dugwell, Bullock and Bullock Carts. While examining the 13 cases of Bullock, Ballockcart and Dugwell loans it is found from serial No. : 2 and 3 that they have disposed of their assets. But their repayment of loan is satisfactory. They have repaid their loan out of the income from their dialy labour. As such the loan has not generated income or employment for them. Similarly serial No. 9 has also not completed the unit and the loan amounts were not utilised for the purpose. This is again another example of non-utilisation of loans for generating income.

Out of 13 cases, three did not create any employment. Thus the loan has the employment generating of 77% in that year as per table 6.2. In table 6.1 also the total number of persons who had utilised the loan for creating income were ten and persons interviewed were (14-1) = 13 in number. Thus the percentage of loan utilisation or the employment creation is also 77%.

Hence, during 1985, through the different loans, the Jarado branch created 77% of employment and generated average income of Rs. 238.46 as seen in table 6.1 and, in the table 6.2. Thus in total for the year the average income comes to Rs. 246.15 per month (238.46 + 253.84 = 492.30 / 2 = Rs. 246.15 per month) (The average is out of the 13+13 = 26 beneficiaries).

TABLE - 6.2

Jarado Branch RGB Finances for Dugwell, Pumpset and Bullock, Bullock Cart

(Amount in Rupees)

S. No.	*Name of the Beneficiary (Village, Date, Purpose)*	*Amounts of the loan*	*Subsidy Amount*	*Recovary by Dec '88*	*Outstanding Dues by Dec '88*	*Income before Loan (PM)*	*Income after Loan (PM)*
1	2	3	4	5	6	7	8
1.	Deenabandhu Nayak, Jarado, 23-02-85 Bullock	2000	666	540	1238	300	500
2.	Bhima Nayak, Bullock Jarado, 23-02-85	2000	666	970	711	–	–
3.	Surendra Nayak, Jarado, Bullock, 07-06-85	2000	666	1050	507	–	–
4.	Arakhita Nayak, Jarado Bullock, 07-06-85	2000	666	200	1664	200	500
5.	Dhanu Nayak, Tiadipalli, Bullock, 11-06-85	2000	666	–	1898	250	500
6.	Subash Ch. Jena, Jarado, Bullock Cart (DRI) 27-12-85	4390	2195	1060	1335	350	800

(Contd.)

TABLE - 6.2 (Contd.)

1	2	3	4	5	6	7	8
7.	Bansidhar Swain, Tankachai, Bullock Cart, 15-07-85	5000	3750	550	832	400	800
8.	Prakash Ch. Nahak, Tiadipalli, Bullock, 11-06-85	2000	666	800	825	200	500
9.	Subash Ch. Swain, Jarado, Dugwell, 17-06-85	4000	–	200	3440	–	–
10.	Bauribandhu Jena, Jarado, Dugwell, 10-08-85	3500	1167	1000	1917	–	350
11.	Bhimsen Padhi, Jarado, Dugwell, 10-08-85	4390	2195	1060	1335	–	400
12.	Kasinath Choudhary, Jhadabandha, Pumpset, 18-04-85	9000	2250	–	9891	–	300
13.	Bijoya Kumar Swain, Jhadabandha Energisation of Dugwell 18-04-85	9000	2250	50	9832	–	350

Remarks of beneficiaries according to the serial number

1. He cultivated 3 Acres of land as a Tanent. He has the asset.

2. No assets. He has 80 cents of land. Doing labour his 3 sons doing labour at Colliary.

3. Assets are not available made payments out of the income of his labour.

4. Assets are with him willful defaulter.

5. Assets are with him willful defaulter.

6. Assets are with him willful defaulter.

7. Assets are with him willful defaulter.

8. Assets are with him willful defaulter.

9. Not completed the unit willful defaulter.

10. He could save 350 willful defaulter.

11. Saved Rs. 400/- willful defaulter.

12. Saved Rs. 300/- per month which earlier was paying for irrigation.

13. Saved Rs. 350/- from irrigation willful defaulter.

The Jarado branch during 1985 has created employment to the extent of 77% of its beneficiaries and provided an average income of Rs. 246.15 per month to the beneficiaries. Thus in employment creation the bank has not crossed 100% and the reason behind it is the beneficiaries are not properly utilising the loan as most of them have disposed of the assets, which appears as a constraint in the functioning of the bank. More than 90% of the beneficiaries are wilful defaulters.

Before taking up the case study on Sikiri branch, it is also essential to know something about the Hinjilicut Block. The, Hinjilicut block forms part of the Chatrapur administrative Sub-division. Though the block head quarters have been located at Hinjilicut town, the block's jurisdiction does not cover Hinjilicut town area, since it has been declared an NAC. The block has 51 inhabited villages divided into 18 Grama Panchayats. The block has a total population of 1,07,418 and the rural population constitutes 86.42%.[6] The block is densly populated. The density of population of the block is 559 per sqr. km.[7] The scheduled caste population constitutes 7% of the total population of the block[8]. The total working force of the block constitute only 31.66% of the total population[9]. The cultivators constitute 40.57%, the agricultural labourers constitute 37.93%, the cottage industry and house hold industry constitute 10.42%, other industrial engagements constitute 0.33%, the trade and commerce constitute 1.75% and others constitute 8.97% of the total working force of the block.[10] The net cultivated area of the block is 84.66% of the total reporting area and 80% of both Khariff and Rabi areas are irrigated in the block. There are two State Bank of India branches, three other public sector bank branches and three RGB branches in the block. In the co-operative sector one branch of the District central Co-operative bank and 23 PACs are also functioning in the block. " The Sikiri branch of RGB is one functioning from 19.10.84. The other two branches of RGB are located at Ralaba and Samarajhala respectively.

Some cases of Samarajhala branch also been studied in this chapter under the sub-head of the constraints of RGB in the district.

As stated earlier, the case studies for income and employment generation of the Sikiri branch have been carried out village wise. The Village under the purview of Sikiri RGB branch are Giria, Sikiri and Kharida of Hinjilicut Block. The case study was conducted during December 1992 and the base period (for considering the pre-loan period) was taken as the year 1989 (January to December).

In the year 1989, the RGB branch of Sikiri has provided loans to 33 beneficiaries.[11] Out of the 33 cases 24 cases have been interviewed by the scholar through the same questionnaire method as followed for Jarado branch of RGB during January 1989. The beneficiaries taken for study constitute 72.72% of the total beneficiaries of the year 1989. The loans were given for service sector under small loan category both directly by the branch and under the sponsored programmes. The direct loans are not backed by subsidies while the loans through sponsored programmes are associated with subsidies. The different purposes and programmes followed by the branch are ERRPCA Agriculture croploan, IRDP small loan and loans for Betelvine.

In the case study of Sikiri, five case beneficiaries are taken into the study. Table 6.3 provides the information on them.

TABLE - 6.3

Loans Provided (Sample Cases) to the Beneficiaries Year 1989 (Jan - Dec) of Sikiri Village by RGB - Sikiri

(Amount in Rupees)

S. No.	*Name of the Beneficiary, Date (Purpose, of Loan, Scheme of loan)*	*Amounts of the loan*	*Subsidy Amount*	*Recovary by Dec '92*	*Outstanding Dues by Dec '92*	*Income before Loan (PM)*	*Income after Loan (PM)*
1	2	3	4	5	6	7	8
1.	Biswanath Padhi, Small Loan - (Direct) Grocery Shop 20-03-89	3000	–	3323	Closed A/C	300	600
2.	Brundavan Ch. Palo, Rabi Crop. (Direce) 07-12-89	2500	–	–	–	–	–
3.	Uchab Routa, Rabi Crop - Crop Loan, (Direct) 19-12-89	2000	–	2115	Closed A/C	–	–
4.	Heena Sethi, Batelevine (SC) (Direct) 20-03-89	3500	–	1400	He has not Closed A/C	300	1200
5.	Choudhary Swain, Betelewine (Direct) 15-12-89	3000	–	2362	–	300	1200

Field Level Study (Jan - 89)

Remarks of the beneficiaries according to the serial number

1. **He was taking loans paying higher interest to the private individuals.**

2. **He got affected by the flood of 1990 the crop loan was converted to the term loan. He has not paid any instalment. He is expecting a debt relief by govt.**

3. **He reported that out of the investment of 2000/- he got net benefit of 2400 rupees in the Crop.**

4. **Willful defaulter.**

5. **He is paying the instalments and will close the Account.**

All the loans provided to the beneficiaries of Sikiri village in the sample analysis are given directly by the branch without any sponsored programmes. As such, no beneficiaries got any subsidy. Biswanath Padhi took loan directly for the purpose of a Grocery shop. Before the bank loan he was depending on the rich person of the village for loans and was paying a higher rate of interest and repaid the loans in less number of instalments. But after the loan from RGB he could earn more. He has doubled his income per month which varied from Rs. 300/- to Rs. 600/-. He has also closed the account by paying the instalments properly.

The second person (beneficiary) Brandavan Padhi has taken loan for rabi crop. His crops were washed away by the flood of 1990 and he could not generate any income. His crop loan has been converted into a term loan. Till the end of December 1992, he has not paid a single instalment. His dues with the bank are continuing and the recovery is doubtful. He is expecting some debt relief to be extended to him as he gave us to understand.

The third beneficiary was Uchaba Routa. He also took loan for rabicrop. He said that with the loan amounts he purchased fertiliser, HYV seeds and irrigated the cultivated land. His net benefit out of the investment is Rs. 2,400/- in that Crop. As such in this case he has 120% increase in the income.

Hina Sethi and Choudhury Swain have taken direct loans for Betelvine production. Heena Sethi is a scheduled Caste beneficiary. He has only repaid Rs. 1400/- to the bank, eventhough he got the loan on 20.3.1989. On the otherhand Choudhury Swain has got the loan on 15.12.1989, and has repaid Rs. 2362/- towards his instalment. Both of them are defaulters and they are wilful defaulters. But they have admitted that each of them could raise their income four fold i.e., from 300 to Rs. 1200 per month due to the benefit of the loan. In the 4 cents of land that each one of them had they get output generally four times in a month and their net income varies between Rs. 1200/- and Rs. 1400/- per month. The presentation of income in table 6.3 is the likely income of the beneficiaries as given by them. There is no scientific and logical reason for accepting them as the true income. However out of five beneficiaries, four have utilised the loan for creating additional income. Thus in the sample analysis, there is 80% of employment and average income of Rs. 500/- p.m.

The net income from

1st case = Rs. 300/- pm

2nd case = nil

3rd case = Rs. 400/- pm

4th & 5th case = Rs. 900/- pm

i.e., a total of Rs. 2,500/-, when Rs. 2,500/- is divided among the five beneficiaries the average is Rs. 500/- pm.

TABLE - 6.4

RGB - Sikiri **Village - Giria** ***Amount in Rupees***

S. No.	*Name of the Beneficiary (Date of Loan, Scheme of Loan)*	*Purpose of loan*	*Amounts of Loan*	*Subsidy Amount*	*Recovary by Dec '92*	*Income before Loan (PM)*	*Income after.. Loan (PM)*
1	2	3	4	5	6	7	8
1.	Nandi Dalai, Small Loan Direct 23-03-89	Grocery	2500	–	245	200	450
2.	Daka Dalai, Small Loan (IRDP) 23-10-89	Cycle Mart	4800	1600	125	–	400
3.	Uchab Dalai, (IRDP) Small Loan 23-10-89	Trolly Rickshaw	2000	666	246	–	500
4.	Naba Parida, (IRDP) Small Loan 26-12-89	Rice Selling	4000	1333	4345	–	500
5.	Smt. Kuntala Devi, Ag. Term Loan 25-01-89	Betele vine	3000	–	700	300	1200
6.	Udaya Sethi, (Sc) Ag. Term Loan 07-02-89 (Direct)	-Do-	3500	–	3000	300	1400
7.	Haribandhu Dalai, Ag. Term Loan 11-07-89 (Direct)	-Do-	3500	–	500	300	1400

(Contd.)

TABLE - 6.4 (Contd.)

1	2	3	4	5	6	7	8
8.	Ananda Dalai, Ag. Term Loan 13-11-89 (Direct)	-Do-	2500	–	–	300	1000
9.	Jagannath Dalai, IRDP 22-12-89	-Do-	3550	333	850	300	1500
10.	Balaram Panda, IRDP, 22-12-89	-Do-	3550	333	900	300	1500
					Total	2000	9850
						= Nett income Rs. 7850/-	

Remarks of the beneficiaries according to the serial number

1. **Before this loan he was having a small shop.**
2. **He was unemployed willful defaulter.**
3. **He was a labourer. After Rickshaw he is happy. Wilful defaulter.**
4. **Repaid the loan, Before loan from RGB he was availing loans from individuals at higher rate.**
5. **She has been influenced by others not to repay the loan.**
6. **Utilised the loan and willful defaulters.**
7. **Utilised the loan and willful defaulters.**
8. **Utilised the loan and willful defaulters, Articipating debt reliefs.**
9. **Utilised the loan and willful defaulters.**
10. **Utilised the loan and willful defaulters.**

In analysing the table 6.4, it is found that before the sanction of loan, out of ten beneficiaries seven had some income in the same activity for the improvement of which they wanted a loan from RGB. None of the beneficiaries from among the ten sample beneficiaries and taken loan from any bank other than RGB. Only Udaya Sethi serial no. 6 of the Table 6.4 has taken a loan from other sources, serial no. 2, 3 and 4 worked as daily labourers and were earning Rs. 15 to 20 per day which was insufficient for their subsistence needs. It has been worked out from the date of the table that the net total income of all the ten beneficiaries is Rs. 7850 per month. The average income is Rs. 785/- after the loan. In this village the loan has created 100% of employment as all villagers have utilised the loan property and created an income. No one except serial no. 4 of the table has repaid the loan. Serial No. 6 is interested to make a loan again. As such he told us that he would repay the loan in the near future. He also told us that the loan amounts are not sufficient. But as the loan procedure is simple and instalments with interest are convenient he likes to take loan from RGB again and again. Before the RGB loan he was taking loans from private individuals and was paying higher rate of interest and there were no instalment repayments. He was sometimes left with no surplus of income. Thus RGB finance has improved his economic condition. The betelvine cultivators take loans to purchase bamboos for making fences and for irrigation purposes. The beneficiaries of betelvine in the Table 6.4, including Udaya Sethy are marginal farmers. Udaya Sethi is a scheduled caste beneficiary and he has not obtained any subsidy benefit as the loans are direct loans. Out of six betelvine loans four are direct loans and the remaining two are provided to Jagannath Dalai and Balaram Panda in IRDP on 22.12.1989. Ananda Dalai has not paid any instalment after taking the loan. He is capable of repaying the loan but he deliberately has not repaid anticipating write-off of the loan through some debt relief schemes in future.

Table 6.5 provides the information of income generation and employment creation from the loans of RGB branch of Sikiri, from the Kharida village of Hinjililcut Block.

Of the eight beneficiaries of Kharida village taken for consideration Duraydhan Behera (Serial No. 3) of table 6.5 has got a direct loan without any subsidy facility and he is continuing with overdues. All others of the table i.e., nine others, have availed the subsidies. ERRP is a state level programme under the IRDP. Six beneficiaries were given loans under the ERRP scheme. Under the scheme the poorest among the poor are selected for loans. Serial No. 2 got loan facilities under the IRDP scheme.

The last mentioned (8) beneficiary was provided loan for the purchase of a she bufallow. He could not provide good food to the bufallow. The follow up action and training regarding the maintenance of a she bufallow was not given to him by the Government departments of the block. The beneficiary faced severe damage to his property and house during the flood of 1990. He could not generate any employment and income and as such did not repay the loan. He said that when he had not enough to meet his own needs, he could not feed the bufallow which is an additional burden on him. He is providing the normal breast feedings to the she bufallow which is not increasing the milk yield capacity of the same. Thus out of ten loanees under the scheme only nine persons have utilised the loan creating 90% of employment as per the sample analysis.

TABLE - 6.5

Kharida Village, Sikiri Branch R.G.B.

Amount in Rupees

S. No.	*Name of the Beneficiary Date of Loan, Scheme of Loan*	*Purpose of loan*	*Amounts of Loan*	*Subsidy of Loan*	*Recovary by Dec '92*	*Income before Loan (PM)*	*Income after Loan (PM)*
1	2	3	4	5	6	7	8
1.	Smt. Duhiti Nayak, ERRP Non Agriculture 21-10-89	Rice Selling	1200	600	1266	–	700
2.	Mohan N. Nayak IRDP Small Loan 22-12-89	Vegitable Vender	1350	450	500	–	800
3.	Duryodhan Behera, Small Loan Direct 19-12-89	-Do-	1000	–	140	–	800
4.	Smt. Nanda Nayak ERRP Non Agriculture 21-10-89	-Do-	1200	600	1266	–	800
5.	Smt. Phala Nayak ERRP Non Agrl. 21-10-89	-Do-	1200	600	1266	–	1000
6.	Smt. Naikani Nayak ERRP Non Agriculture 21-10-89	Fish Vender	1200	600	1266	–	1000
7.	Smt. Malati Nayak ERRP Non Agriculture 21-10-89	-Do-	1200	600	1266	–	1000
8.	Haria Nayak ERRP (Agriculture) 27-03-89	She Buffallow	4624	2312	–	–	–

Remarks of the beneficiaries according to the serial number

1. Closed the account.

2. Willful defaulters.

3. Willful defaulters.

4. Closed the account.

5. Closed the account.

6. Closed the account.

7. Closed the account.

8. Flood affected. No maintenance of the She-buffalow. Non willful net inner.

All the beneficiaries said that before the loan they did not have any income from any other sources. They were either dependent upon daily labour or on hand loans for consumption purposes.

Out of the eight beneficiaries five constituting 62.5% are the women beneficiaries. They all are widows and they didnot have any income before hand. It is a pleasant thing to note that all the five widows have repaid the loan accounts and proved worthy in creating earnings and employment for themselves.

The net average per month income from the loans came to Rs. 590 with 90% employment arising out of loans at Kharida village. The recovery performance is better except for the case in serial No. 8.

It is observed from the case studies of both Jarado and Sikiri branches that the RGB credit has brought a major change in the traditional economic conditions of the rural beneficiaries of the blocks. But development and change in the economic condition do not depend only upon cheap credit but on many other factors like, training, involvement, insfrastructural facilities, proper education, the public media and a regular easy recovery of loans, which will increase the scope of availability of loans to others.

It is observed that the dairy and dugwell loans are hot utilised properly and they have given negative results. However, as a whole, the

RGB branches have provided easy capital to small businessmen, marginal farmers and self-employed persons in the blocks under study. The betelvine cultivators of Sikiri branch utilised the loans and generated income. The RGB being a weaker sector-oriented rural credit institution has played an effective role inspite of its limitations and constraints.

The RGB being a service-oriented financial institution, any initial loss for a short period may well be a price worth paying for achieving a longer social objective.[12] Similarly, for the viability of the bank of area where the Regional Rural Bank operates should hold promise of development and besides the Regional Rural Bank (RGB) should work on a low cost budget in respect of staffing pattern, salary structure and other establishment expenses.

The regional rural banks should use the locally obtained funds for effective and efficient disbursement of rural finance[13].

The RRBs in general and the RGB in Ganjam district in particular have been functioning under several constraints. The constraints which adversely affect the viability of RGB in Ganjam district have been studied carefully with some field level observations.

The function of RGB is confined to the specific target groups consisting of the small / marginal farmers agricultural labourers, and rural artisans. They are poor, illiterate and ignorant. "The major constraints are the lack of financial knowledge and limited options available to rural households and business thus limiting the ability of these groups to make sound financial decisions"[14]. In this connection in February 1993, the scholar met and interviewed three beneficiaries of Giria village of Hinjilicut Block. The beneficiaries are uneducated and illiterate. They are also very poor and their economic conditions has not improved even after the financial assistance given to them by the Sikiri branch of RGB.

The beneficiaries are :

(1) Congress Muni s/o. Kandha Muni

(2) Shyama Muni s/o Bankia Muni

(3) Uchaba Dalai s/o Khali Dalai.

The above mentioned three persons got loan benefits under the IRDP scheme. The first two persons got an amount of Rs. 2500/- each and the third man got a loan of Rs 3300/-. This was not paid in cash but was provided in the form of assets (cows). Congress Muni could not provide proper food to the cow and treated the cow on the same line as a country cow. After some days the cow became very weak and therefore he disposed of the cow for Rs. 150/- only, after three to four months.

The second man Shyama Muni said that the cow is there with him but not giving milk in the desired quantity. He said that due to his poor economic condition, maintenance of the cow is not possible for him. He did not avail himself of the facilities from the nearby Veterinary hospital to reproduce a calf but left the cow to he crossed with a country bull. As such there is a country calf available to him.

When the third man, Uchaba Dalai was interviewed, he replied that due to his poor economic condition he could not maintain the cow and left it in the open to move freely to search for food.

From the above three cases it is observed that :

(a) The beneficiaries are uneducated and they are not provided with proper guidance either by the bank offices or by the technical personnel of the Block.

(b) The RGB branches in most of the places have inadequate staff to visit the field. Posting of Field officers at the branches is an essential task for RGB. The Bank Manager who performs many functions cannot do the work satisfactorily and do Justice to his duties in relation to the beneficiaries.

(c) For reasons of lack of proper management and understanding and lack of proper interest, the beneficiaries fail to generate the desired level of income from the loans.

Unless .he Government officials and trained workers of the block level organisat ons play an effective role, the uneducated ignorant and poor beneficiaries cannot get income from the loan and loans cannot be repaid for recycling the credit by the Gramya Banks.

Problems of Deposit Mobilisation

There is lack of deposit mobilisation by RGB branches in the rural sector in comparison with branches of commercial Banks in the district. "The richer sections of society who alone have the major potential for depositing their surplus funds with these banks do not feel interested in doing so in view of the lending policies of the banks."[15]

The total deposits mobilised by the different banks of the district was 26853.59 lakhs and the deposit mobilised by RGB was Rs. 1552.82 lakhs as on March 1991. The RGB deposit constituted only 5.78% of the total deposit of the district.[16] The deposits of Sikiri and Samarjhala branch of RGB in Hinjilicut Block together constitute only 0.12% of the total RGB deposits during March 1991. As such most of the branches of RGB in the rural sector are not capable of mobilising a good amount of deposits[17]. By 1992 March, the deposits of both Sikiri and Samarjhola branches of RGB were above the quantity advanced. The Sikiri branch had deposits of Rs. 2127,000 while the amount advanced was Rs. 1785,000. Similarly in Samarjhola branch the deposit was Rs. 2406,000 while the advances were Rs. 1690,000. The excess deposits over the advances are causing loss to the bank as the cost of deposits are to be met through investments only. Ofcourse RGB as a whole diverts the excess deposits from surplus branches to some other defict branches for a general balance. The C.D. ratio during most of the periods remained below 100% or the said branches. The overall profit-loss situation is a correct explanation to study on viability of the bank rather than the branch wise explanation of profit-loss position. RGB being the bank for target groups, the number of accounts in deposit and borrowals are more but the per account business is low.[18]

The Government should give some encouragement to the RGB branches by directing the public institutions and offices of the block and villages to operate monetary dealings. The RGB deals only with small borrowers. It is the poor villagers very own bank'. The level of business of RGB branches compared to that of commercial banks in rural sector is much lower. Thus by opening the Government accounts the position of RGB in fund mobilisation may be improved to some extent. The RGB has mobilised Rs. 1923.23 lakhs of deposit in 125837 accounts by 31st March 1992. The deposit growth (outstanding) in the said year over the previous year is 27.52%.[19]

A better mobilisation of deposits will improve the capacity of lending of RGB.

Problem of Credit Assessment and Credit Utilisation

The question of credit assessment becomes a vital one because the granting of farm loans cannot be done on the basis of normal commercial considerations to which a banker is accustomed. It is a purely personal assessment and the assessor's experience of local conditions plays a vital role. The problems of credit assessment has already been discussed in chapter three. The uniformity in scale of finance and in the quantity of loan to every individual beneficiary in all the branches may cause somewhere an overfinance and elsewhere an underfinance. In this regard the scholar has examined the case of a beneficiary of Sikiri Village.

An amount of Rs. 5000/- was provided as loan under IRDP scheme to Sri Nityananda Routa S/o Sri Juro Routa of Sikiri village. A cart was provided to the person at the cost of Rs. 3050/- and the balance amounts i.e., (Rs. 5000 - Rs. 3050) = Rs. 1950 was not sufficient for the purchase of bullocks and for the insurance of the Bullocks. As per the statement of Sri Routa, an amount of Rs. 760/- was the extra payment borne by him. The Bank people recommended the case to the Block Development Officer in this regard. But the BDO has expressed his inability to extend the loan as the scale of finance prescribed did not allow the same.

Case of Multiple Loans to Beneficiaries

The main purpose of Service area Approach is to restrict the beneficiaries (Loanees) in the credit operation of a particular Bank branch for better credit discipline and administration. But, even after the adoption of Service Area Approach, some people take simultaneous loans from different sources and they generally do not repay them in time. They can be called as the professional loanees. They only know the techniques of taking loans through their personal touch or by the use local political influence. In this regard, the village Saradhapur in Hinjilicut block is a glaring example. Sri Kora Behera S/o Khetra Behera has availed a loan from RGB Samarjhola branch on 19.8.1983 for an amount of Rs. 1,500/-. The same was not repaid by him and the overdues by 1990 June stood at Rs. 2448/-. It is found from the field study that the same person has availed different loans from different sources. By the said date (1990 June) the overdues of Sri Behera at LDB Chatrapur was Rs. 5006/-, at Indian Overseas Bank, Kukudakhandi was Rs. 3,940/- and at Co-operative Primary society of Saradhapur village was Rs. 3791/-. The concerned person did not repay the loans of RGB but got the ARDRS benefit during 1989-90 as a result his overdues has come down to Rs. 1410/- only. He had paid only one instalment in 1986 of Rs. 275/-. He got notices from the bank several times for the repayment and also a registered notice was sent to him on 12.10.92 (As enquired from bank). But the beneficiary has not responded to any of these efforts to contact him by the Bank.

In the same way in Saradhapur village (a) Sri Bhaskar Das S/o Muni Das (b) Labanya Sahu S/o Dusa Sahu and (c) Lokanath Sahu S/o Tanka Sahu have also opened different loan accounts in different nearby banks including RGB and they too continue with overdues in all the banks.

Shortcomings of Service Area Approach

Thus the objectives of Services Area Approach (SAA) have practically failed in such cases. However, by restricting the area of operation of banks to a particular command area, thc borrower's choice has been restricted. Under S.A.A., the borrowers lose their right to choosing their bans and on the other hand "the profits and profitability of some bank branches might suffer on account of the implementation of the Service Area Approach. This problem will definitely be experienced in states, which are relatively overbanked."[20]

Problems of Competition Among the Banks

The RGB opens its branches at places where the branch of some commercial banks already exist. RGB also opened branches in the villages where Co-operative bank branches exist in nearby areas. There is unnecessary competition among the banks. For example at Sikiri, there is an RGB branch and just in front of the RGB branch there is a branch of S.B.I. Again within a three kilometer distance at Hinjilicut there exists a branch of Andhra Bank, UCO Bank and Berhampur Central Co-operative Bank. The RGB branches of Sikiri and Ralabu are at a distance of 3/4 kilometers from each another. Thus the area is overbanked.

The RGB has limited resources and limited bank staff in comparison to a bank branch of a nationalised bank. The Samarjhola RGB branch is surrounded in an area of 3 sq. km. a branch of S.B.I. at Saru, I.O.B. at Kukudakhandi. However 90% of the RGB branches are found at unbanked and underdeveloped areas of the district.

Problem of Remittance Facilities

It is a general problem for RRBs that the remittance facilities to the customers are very poor at the branches as they operate in a limited area. The RGB is a small bank which confines its operation to a specific area and to specific persons. The scope of business profit is limited for the bank. It is observed from the field study at Sikiri village that the cultivators of betelvine send their products to very distant places outside the state. To maintain easy financial transactions and better remittance facilities, they like to keep deposits at the SBI branch of Sikiri rather than in the branches of RGB in Sikiri. In a competition for mobilising deposits, the SBI branch has the superiority over the RGB branch in the said village.

The Problem of Non-Coordination

The RGB lends to the beneficiaries under the schemes like IRDP, ERRP (which is not there any more now) ITDP, SC and ST and several other Government sponsored programmes. Which lending programmes are carried out by the district authorities at the initial stage the block level organisations join the hands with bank personnel to achieve the target of lending. Similarly, the extension officers of the block, the veterinary surgeon, the IPO and other technical staff take a lot of interest in order to achieve the loan targets. But afterwards, excepting the bank officials, no other official pays any attention to the collection of dues. The above remarks are passed by the Bank managers of Ralaba, Sikiri and Samarjhola branch of RGB of Hinjilicut block in the interviews with this scholar on 4.3.1993 and 5.3.1993.

The bank managers of aforementioned branches were of the view that the Government should also fix responsibility for meeting the recovery targets on all the Blocks and other developmental agencies of the district and the responsibility of collection of overdues should not be left to the bank alone. But as things stand, when the scholar net the BDO on 21.4.1993 and asked him about his official co-operation and co-ordination in the affair he said that they regularly organise recovery camps and whatever recovery is found is mainly due to the efforts of the block authorities. The Banks are not able to collect their loans especially from the weaker sections by their own effort.

The beneficiaries whom the scholar interviewed in different places at different times, have regularly reported that the agricultural department, the veterinary department and the Block authorities are not prompt in providing the needed inputs to the borrowers for undertaking their activities and they do not provide the technical guidance.

Problems of Overdues and Poor Recovery Performance

The mounting overdues of RGB is a serious constraint and it affects the viability of the institution. The overall position of overdues and a comparitive overdue analysis of RGB with other financial institutions of the district has already been discussed in chapter - 5. In the present chapter constraints that arise from overdues will be studied with the help of case studies at the branch level and a branch level overdues position is being studied in detail.

"According to the opinion of the working group on RRBs the overdues whether they are in respect of agricultural loans or other loans are due to default which is either wilful or non-wilful."[21] Locking of funds in overdues has resulted in non-recycling of funds and greater dependence on re-financing agencies.[22]

Due to the debt relief schemes and regular assurances in this regard by different Governments and political parties, the defaulters in the rural sector got good encouragement and bank overdues are increasing continously. It is learnt from the people of 'Sasana Ambagaon' of Hinjilicut block that some people obtain loans from the schemes from which they can get more loans. Afterwards, they never repay the amounts, hoping that the "Governments under pressure from the political parties will give debt relief according to election assurances. The ARDRS (Agricultural Rural Debt Relief Scheme) of 1990 is a recent debt relief programme which has injected a feeling into the minds of beneficiaries not to pay the dues and to wait for such schemes to come into force. The scheme has benefitted the defaulters only. As for example, Ganga Nayak S/o Pipra Nayak of Sasana Ambagaon has taken a loan of Rs. 9380/- during November 1983 for energisation of a dugwell. He also availed the subsidy for Rs. 2993/-. During his instalments of repayments he has paid Rs - 2000/- to RGB of Samarjhola. He has also got debt relief of Rs. 2080 according to the ARDAS - 1990. After receiving all these benefits, the concerned beneficiary did not pay any amount and the overdues are mounting. The Bank has sent many reminders and legal notices. These notices have not been responded to by Sri Nayak.

In some cases the influence of defaulters sometimes discourage other persons to repay the loans. In this regard the cases of RGB Sikiri branch may be cited here (loans granted on 19.7.1991 to five numbers of Bullock Cart)

The beneficiaries are :

(1) Prakash Chandra Pradhan S/o Ganapati Pradhan

(2) Gouranga Nayak S/o Dandapani Nayak

(3) Abhimanyu Jena S/o Ganapati Jena

(4) Devaraj Nayak S/o Kartika Nayak

(5) Satrughana Nayak S/o Khalli Nayak

The first three persons after availing the loan disposed of the Bullock Carts without informing the Bank and they did not pay any instalment to the Bank. The other two persons purchased the Bullock Cart and also availed the ancilliary benefits and these two beneficiaries were willing to pay their instalments. The scholar has interrogated the bank officers and found that the first three persons have persuaded the other two persons not to pay any instalment and this was accepted by the rest.

Sri Devaraj Nayak and Satrughna Nayak stated in their interview that the bank cannot take steps against the defaulters, they also do not bother being called defaulters. The statement of these two persons in that "when nobody is repaying the loan why should we pay ? It is Government money .... why should you bother to repay it ?"

The Bank has written letters on 30.7.1991 pointing out thereby the lapses of the beneficiaries. The Bank advised the beneficiaries to return the whole amounts as the first three persons did not utilise the loan productively. The copy of the letter was also sent to the Head Office of RGB and the BDO. The head office has also written letters to the BDO of Hinjilicut. But after all these efforts, there was no recovery. As such , the other two beneficiaries have also followed the foot steps of the first three wilful defaulters and they also became the wilful defaulters.

The Sikiri branch on 26.11.1991 disbursed loans to eight mobile vendors and eight cycles were purchased by the bank and the beneficiaries were provided with a set of weights and balances for business.

(1) Lokanath Sahu

(2) Magati Pradhan

(3) Devaraj Mallik

(4) Deva Pradhan

(5) Rama Krishna Nayak

(6) Ananda Gouda

(7) Abhimunyu Panda

(8) Kalu Charan Sahu

The cost of each cycle was Rs. 1000/-. The first five persons after getting the cycles disposed of each for Rs. 800/- per cycle. Observing this, the other three persons also disposed of their cycles at a later stage.

The Wilful Defaulters & Non-Wilful Defaulters

After verification, the Branch Manager of the Sikiri branch has informed the matter to the BDO and head office on 16.12.1991. But no positive result has resulted from such actions. As such, the bank manager felt that he could not do anything to punish the defaulters of loan. In the same way the beneficiaries do not feel it is necessary to repay the loans. The loans are not also utilised for the purpose for which the same was given. It is found from all the above case studies that the wilful defaulters are 90% and only 10% of defaulters are non-wilful defaulters.

All the 27 beneficiaries of Jarado branch (Table 6.1 and 6.2) had dues and all the cases were found to be wilful defaulters. The wilful defaulters refer to the beneficiaries who have the capacity for repayment but they deliberately do not repay the loan.

Twenty three beneficiaries were interviewed in the villages i.e. Giria, Sikiri and Kharida to whom the RGB branch of Sikiri has given loans financed (table 6.3, 6.4 and 6.5). Out of 23 beneficiaries wilful defaulters were 13 which constitutes 56.52% of the total beneficiaries and 86.66% of the total defaulters. Only two beneficiaries are non-wilful defaulters as in table 6.3. The Sr. No. 2 of Table 3.6 Sri Brundavan Ch. Palo has taken a direct loan for Rabi Crop and his crops got affected in the flood of 1990. The same loan has been converted into a term loan and he could not pay any instalment due to his poor economic condition. On the other hand, another non-wilful defaulter (Sr. No. 8, Table 6.5) i.e., Sri Haria Nayak whose properties are also damaged in the flood and due to his poor economic condition coud not feed properly the she bufallow.

Out of 23 beneficiaries interviewed from the branch of Sikiri (loans granted during 1989) only eight of them have repaid and closed the accounts. The repayment and closure of account among the sample cases of 1989 loanees at Sikiri branch constitute only 35% while the defaulters (both wilfully and nonwilful) constitute 65%.

In Jarado village some beneficiaries after obtaining the loans neither repaid the loans nor continued staying in the village. Certain additional cases besides the cases of table 6.1 and 6.2 are presented here.

The Problem of Absconding of Loanees From the Village

Smt. Appi Nahakani wife of late Devaraj got a loan on 9.9.1983 in loan No. 83/43 under agricultural term loan (Allied) for Rs. 2200 for the purpose of Goatry and availed the benefit of subsidy for Rs. 733/-. She neither did pay any instalment nor was available in the village. After learning of this case from the branch Manager, Mr. Pradhan, the scholar went into the village during the sample survey and found her husband's brother in her house. He told that Smt. Nahakani has been absconding with 2 of her children. He expected that she may be at Bhubaneswar and might be doing manual labour.

Similarly Gobardhan Nahak S/o Sambari Nahak has been provided with a loan by Jarado branch under the IRDP for the purpose of Goatry for Rs. 1800 on 18.4.1983 vide Loan No. 83/27 and repaid Rs. 120/-. He got subsidy of Rs. 450/- and the outstanding due by December 1988 was Rs. 2158.95. But when the scholar wanted to meet the concerned loanee, the villagers informed him that ; he had left the village for doing manual work as a labourer in a Colliary and all the assets acquired were disposed of.

In the same way Pana Nahak S/o Late Kaibala Loan No. 84/9 of the date 12.5.1984 got loan for Rs. 2000/- and having outstanding due of Rs. 1680-15 has left the village to collieries, leaving no asset.

Having studied such type of cases it is felt that, unless the beneficiaries feel the importance of loans and unless they utilise them for production, the expansion of credit to the door-steps of villagers becomes meaningless.

The overdue position of RGB branches under the case study are presented in table 6.6 for a comparison :

TABLE - 6.6

Year	*RGB As a whole*	*Sikiri RGB Branch*	*Samarjhola RGB Branch*	*Jarado RGB Branch*
June 1990	62%	92%	76.4%	46%
June 1991	65%	70%	78.3%	68%
June 1992	60%	50.4%	80.3%	-

Source : RGB Head Office, Statistics Section, RGB Branch and Samarjhola, Sikiri and Jarado (Branch Managers)

It is found that the percentage of overdues to demand in RGB as a whole always remained above 60%. In the year 1990 in June, it was actually 62% but after the Debt Relief Adjustment it has come down to 50%.

In the year 1990 June, the Sikiri branch had a poor recovery performance and the percentage of overdues in case of Sikiri and Samarjhola was above the overdues of the RGB as a whole. On the other hand, the overdues of Jarado was less than the overdues of the RGB in general.

During June 91, all the three concerned branches were above the average overdues percentage of the RGB sector. By June 1992 Sikiri branch was below the percentage of the whole RGB sector while Samarjhola was much higher than the whole RGB sector. The information on Jarado branch coud not be collected for the said year.

The overdues is a problem which affects not only the RGB, it is a general problem affecting all the banks of the rural sector. The overdues position of all the banks of Ganjam District upto June 1990 has been discussed in Chapter 5 of this thesis by analysing the data of the Table 5.15. However, the Table 6.7 of this chapter provides the overdues position of the different banks of the district as on June 1991. Thus after a year's difference i.e., by June '91 the overdue position of RGB has increased to 65% from 4936% of the year June '90. The percentage to the demand for recovery has increased to more than 15% within a year in the case of RGB. In the same way by comparing the data of table 5.15 and table 6.7, the differences of overdues of other banks can be obtained.

TABLE - 6.7

(Overdues Position of All the Banks of the District)

(As on June 1991)

Sl. No. No.	*Name of the Banks*	*Overdues percentage to the demand*
1	2	3
1.	Allahabad Bank	40
2.	Andhra Bank	90

(Contd.)

TABLE 6.7 (Contd.)

1	2	3
3.	Bank of Baroda	70
4.	Bank of India	83
5.	Canara Bank	31
6.	Central Bank	97
7.	Indian Bank	77
8.	I.O.B.	66
9.	Punjab National Bank	74
10.	S.B.I.	55
11.	S.B. Hyderabad	98
12.	Syndicate Bank	88
13.	Union Bank	75
14.	United Bank	63
15.	UCO Bank	84
16.	Vysya Bank	11
17.	Vijoya Bank	90
18.	R.G.B.	65
19.	A.C.C. Bank Ltd.	98
20.	B.C.C. Bank Ltd.	67
21.	O.S.L.D. Bank	99
Total overdue percentage 70%		

Source : Andhra Bank, (Lead Bank), Regional Office Berhampur and From Statistical Section of RGB Head Office, Berhampur (Ganjam).

It is found from the table 6.7 that, when the total overdues of the district by June 91 was 70% to its demand, it was 65% for RGB. It is also seen from the table that some banks have higher percentage of overdues in comparison to RGB in the said year.

Overdues and the Benefits of Guarantee Corporations (DICGC)

Thus lending in the rural sector is a risky and non-profitable work for the Banks. The non-recovery is causing a big headache especially to RGB for its viability. To some extent on the basis of the coverage of Credit Guarantee Corporation Scheme (CGS), the bank is eligible to get some portions of recovery, by claiming the same from Credit Guarantee Corporation. The credit Guarantee Corporation of India Ltd. was incorporated on 14th January 1971 under the Indian Companies Act, 1956 with a view to afford a measure of protection to Banks and other financial institutions in extending credit to borrowers of small means.

The credit guarantee corporation of India Ltd. has been acquired by the Deposit Insurance Corporation with effect from 15th July 1978 and Deposit Insurance Corporation has been renamed as Deposit Insurance and Credit Guarantee Corporation (DICGC).

The DICGC in the initial period was covering the Guarantee for 90% of the defaulter's loan. But from 1.3.1980 it was 75% and from 1.1.85 it has reduced to Rs. 75,000 or 60% of the defaulter's loan.[23]

The Financial Claims and Settlements of RGB at DICGC and ARDRS

The Rushikulya Gramya Bank during the period 1991-92 has submitted claims for the sum of Rs. 84.05 lakhs covering 6201 Accounts and the DICGS has so far settled claims to the tune of Rs. 14.30 lakhs covering 508 No. of Accounts. Similarly, the bank has put up claims under the scheme of ARDRS - 90 amounting to Rs. 104.17 lakhs for 8098 beneficiaries. Against the claim the bank has been provided with Rs. 75.10 lakhs from the Government of India.

Problems of Negative Income

The RGB is incurring continous losses which can be seen from the sample branches from the table 6.8.

TABLE - 6.8

Profit and Loss of Sample RGB Branches

(In Rupees)

Year	*Jarado Branch*	*Sikiri Branch*	*Samarjhola Branch*
1988-89	Loss 49,000 (-)	Loss 16,000 (-)	Loss 21,609 (-)
1989-90	Profit 8,000 (+)	Loss 17,000 (-)	Loss 59,293 (-)
1990-91	Loss 64,000 (-)	Loss 109,000 (-)	Profit 12,000 (+)
1991-92	Not Available	Loss 114,000 (-)	Loss 138,604 (-)

Source : RGB - Branch (concern)

From the above table it is seen that during 1989-90 the Jarado branch has made a profit of Rs. 8,000/- and in 1990-91 the Samarjhola branch has made a profit of Rs. 12,300. These three branches in all other years have been incurring losses. The RGB Sikiri branch in all the four reporting years was incurring losses. On the other hand, the overall losses of RGB of Ganjam district as discussed in the previous chapter was continuously rising . The RGB branch being a small bank for a small man in a small area, has to play a big role for development in its command area and has to protect its viability as a banking institution.

The Problems of Staff

"Agricultural lending is the main constituent of credit activity at rural branches. Inadequacy of field staff in relation to the volume of work load, and utilisation of their services for general work are rather not unusual at the branch level. It is absolutely essential that time and services of the field staff are effectively used."[24] The Sikiri and Ralaba branches of RGB are very much understaffed. In both the branches only one officer i.e., the branch manager and one clerk-cum-cashier were available with a class IV employee. The branch manager is to play a dual role of BM and the field officer. It is learnt from those branch managers that due to heavy Banking operations they are forced to neglect the field work most of the time.

The officers posted in the rural areas must be young, energetic and well-trained in the lines of better disbursal of rural credit. They should not be frequently transferred as they need time to be acquainted with the locality and the local people. They should have their residence at the place of their posting. But, it is found that all the bank staff of Ralaba, Sikiri and Samarjhola of Hinjilicut block are not staying at their respective stations. All of them daily commute over long distances.

When the scholar raised this particular matter, the members told very politely that neither they get good accommodation nor there exists any educational facilities as is required for their children. Most of them also said that due to the absence of proper medical facilities in those area they are forced to stay out-side the places of their posting.

Most of the RGB staff do not get opportunities of appropriate training. "One of the factors for inefficient banking of RRBs is partly attributed to inadequate training of staff."[25] However 38 officers, 18 field staff and 30 clerks i.e. in total 86 staff of RGB out of 342 staff have undergone different trainings and courses by the end of 1991-92 financial year.[26] This constitutes 25.14% of the total staff of RGB.

The detailed staff position of RGB in Ganjam district by 31st March 1992 has been explained in chapter 3.

The per employee business for 1989-90 was Rs. 8.48 lakhs, for 1990-91 it was Rs. 10.20 lakhs and in 1991-92 it was Rs. 11.23 lakhs.[27]

Most of the Bank staff would like to stay in rural sector only as a temporary stop-gap arrangement. The Bank officials of RGB like to be posted in the semi-urban areas and urban areas to that they can move to the station daily. In the rural branches dedicated and committed staff are required. "Who must mix with the rural people, who should be performers and who should create banking awareness among the villagers. Their lending should continuously create success stories and their banking education should inculcate the saving habit amongst the rural poor. The two assets for Banks are good staff and their capacity to give good service. Good staff giving good service in rural and semi-urban branches are bound to get good business, while making the areas served economically prosperous."[28]

The success of RGB is very much dependent on the involvement and sincerity of the staff. Now, with the demands of the employee association of all RRBs the salary structure of RGB has been improved and they are paid at par with the staff of other nationalised banks. Their fitment into new scale of pay from 1.9.1987 has been approved by the Ministry of Finance, Department of Economic affairs (Banking Division, Jeeban Deep, Parliament Street, New Delhi-110001, vide letter No. 11-3/90-RRB(I)/dated 22.2.1991 (Mr. Lokanath Pradhan, Branch Manager, Samarjhola Branch (RGB) Enquiry)

The trade unionism among RGB employees appeared on the scene around 1977. In staff service regulations, employees who served in RRB in 1975-77 were neither confirmed in the service nor their provident fund contributions were deducted from the salary. Their salary structure was much below that of their counterparts in other commercial banks. They were given the salary of the State Government (District Level Organisations) in accordance with the principle of low cost Banking. This led to Frustration among the RRB staff. V.S. Vyas had warned earlier "Merely bringing down the pay-scales of the bank functionaries of having "non-decolam" look - desirable that these are - do not ensure a cultural affinity with the rural people.[29] Bhabatosa Dutta warned, "The argument about the cost - structure, involving pay-scales and staffing pattern is not reality very strong. It will be difficult to maintain for a long time two types of pay scales in each area for similar work. It will not be possible to get the work done only by local recruits and there will have to be a regular flow of personnel between the parent banks and their rural offices, weather these offices are direct branches or subsidiaries. The problem is there and is not likely to be completely resolved by having a separate cadre for rural subsidiaries. As has been experienced in other spheres, there will emerge soon a strong pressure for merging the cadres."[30]

However with the appearance of trade unionism at last the staff has got their demand acceded to by the authorities. Their demands were (1) Equal pay for equal work, (2) Recognisation of the All India unions of RRB by the Government (3) Uniform service conditions (4) Worker's participation in management (5) Training of personnel (6) Promotion Policy, (7) Withdrawal of deputed officers of sponsor bank after a particular period (8) Uniform transfer policy, (9) Regularisation of daily wage workers (10) Security arrangements (11) Officiating allowances (12) Facilities to office bearers of this union (13) Festival/consumption loans (14) vehicle loan and above State Government Guide lines etc. From the staff of RGB (Enquiry).

With the limited area of operation, the promotional opportunities for the employees of RRB are limited. For providing greater movement of personnel from lower cadres to higher cadres, the direct recruitment has been limited. Branches attaining a particular level of business, say 2 to 2.5 crores, should be headed by a senior manager who is to be equivalent to the cadre of an area manager of a Commercial Bank.[31]

Administrative Problems

The problems pertaining to the functions of the chairman, the members of Board of Directors the inter-relationship between rural banks and sponsor banks and control and supervision of branches may be regarded as administrative problems. The chairman of a Regional Rural Bank is the Secretary to the Board of Directors and the Chief executive of the Bank. He is the head of the RRB organisation, Liasion Officer, Audit and Inspecting Officer, Administrative Officer, Personal Officer, Establishment Officer, Recruitment Officer and follow up the Recovery Officer, with the result that most of his time is consumed in procedural and routine matters and little time is left for development and planning.[32] To assist him in all the matters, a general manager has also been appointed in Rushikulya Gramya Bank.

The Chairman and the General Manager are deputed from the Sponsor Bank (Andhra Bank). The other Deputed Officers are two Rural Development Officers (RDO) to monitor the rural planning and development cell and two other officers to ward the inspection cell as per the recommendation of the Kelkar Committee. The deputation from the sponsor bank is felt essential with a view to extend to the RRB the expertise, wisdom and culture of the Sponsor bank gained through long experience. The Regional Rural Bank art is silent about qualifications and experiences of the chairman, giving a long rope of discretion to the sponsor bank in his appointment.[33]

The Deputation staff are like guests and they do not have generally much involvement. The post of chairman always continues with uncertainity and they are to continue for period for three years only. Secondly, the act is also silent about the qualifications of the board of directors. Here the Government, politicians, local politics play a dominent role in the selection of members rather than any experience or Qualification. Thirdly, the problem arises on the relationship between a rural bank and its sponsor bank. Some times the misuderstandings between the sponsor bank and the RRB in different activities takes place and the sponsor bank creates a complex of superiority over the RRBs.

After the revision in the salary structure of RGB equivalent to the staff of the nationalised Banks, there is no meaning in keeping the RRBs as subordinate banks of sponsor banks. The RRBs either be merged with the sponsor bank or there must be a national level rural bank with the merger of all the RRBs of India. This will ensure better discipline, more resource facility, good coordination in the rural credit operation.

The objective of lower cost and rural base appointments are no more considered as an important need after the new pay structure of the RRBs.

"The non-viability of RRBs has been a matter of concern for quite sometime now. The Agricultural Credit Review Committee (ACRC) which examined the issue and came to the conclusion that RRBs should be merged with their sponsor banks but this recommendation was not implemented as it would alter the basic character of the RRBs. The Narasimham Committee recommended the creation of rural banking subsidiaries of public sector banks to take over the rural branches of banks and had left the option open to RRBs and their sponsor banks as to whether they should be merged on a voluntary basis with the sponsor banks rural banking subsidiaries. "The position of the majority of RRBs has, however, deteriorated to such a level that early remedial measures are necessary. Out of 196 RRBs, only 44 RRBs, were able to manage marginal profits while 152 banks were working at a loss (the accumulated losses amounting to Rs. 550 crores) and 134 banks have eroded a part of their deposits." (RBI Bulletin Jan. 1993 p.8.)

On account of NIT award the pay and allowances of employees of RRBs are likely to go up by 60 to 65 per cent. In the light of the foregoing, the Government of India have proposed merger of all RRBs into a National Rural Bank (NRB). A steering group of representatives of the Government, major sponsor banks, NABARD and Reserve Bank of India recommended as follows :

(a) NRB should comply with capital adequacy norms. The paid up capital should be Rs. 500 crore and should be held by Government of India. (51 per cent) NABARD (25 per cent) financial institutions/public sector banks (15 per cent) and the RRB employees (9 per cent).

(b) In order that the new bank should start on a clean slate, in addition to the losses of Rs. 550 crore, workedout with reference to the March 1992 working results, the additional losses of the RRBs during 1992-93 estimated at Rs. 300 crore may also have to be made good by Government of India in addition to NIT award arrears estimated at Rs. 220 crore and bad debts of about Rs. 198 crores.

(c) To enable NRB to increase their corporate lending it was recommended that the Statutory Liquid Ratio (SLR) requirements may be reduced from 25 per cent to 20 per cent.

(d) Regarding the organisational structure it was felt that the Head Office of the NRB should be either in Pune or Hyderabad and it should function through 15 zonal Offices. The Head Offices of existing RRBs will be regional offices of NRB with necessary adjustments regarding number of branches under the control of each Regional Office. The Group also recommended that the existing staff of sponsor banks should continue with NRB on a deputation basis.

No decision has been taken on the final set up of the proposed NRB. Apart from the problems posed by the very large size and logistics of the proposed institution, it would be necessary to focus attention on the burden on the Government for funding including past-losses, the drawing of a balance between viability of operations and reasonable cost of credit, the question of recovery prescription of prudential norms and appropriate rates of interest on deposits and lending institutions."[34]

Conclusion

In the case studies undertaken in Pursottmapur block and in Hinjilicut block taking the branches of Jarado, Sikiri and Samarjhola it is found that the Jarado branch during 1985 (From the Sample analysis). created employment to the extent of 77% and provided an average monthly income of Rs. 246.15 for the beneficiaries. In creation of employment the Jarado branch could not reach 100%. The branch could not make 100% utilisation of loans. More than 90% of the defaulters of the branch are willful defaulters.

On the other hand, from the case study of Sikiri branch in Sikiri village the employment generation from loan was 80% and the average income from the loan was 500/- per month. In the Giria village the loan was utilised 100% creating 100% of employment for the beneficiaries and creating an incremental income of Rs. 780/- P.M. per beneficiary. Similarly in Kharida village out of eight beneficiaries taken for consideration five of them are women beneficiaries. The loans have created monthly average incremental income of Rs. 590/- and provided employment of 90% to the beneficiaries.

As a whole the Sikiri branch by providing loans (to sample cases) created employment for 90% of the beneficiaries in the year 1989 and could generate an incremental average income of Rs. 625/- per month. As such the branches of RGB have brought a change in the traditional economic conditions of the rural poor of the blocks. But the development of rural sector does not depend upon cheap credit and other economic factors alone. It has to be associated with several other factors like communication, knowledge, persuasion, decision, change in attitude and socio-psycho cultural factors. "Though credit is a sine qua non for rural development, banks should not be treated as mere landing institutions. The efforts of the bankers should also concentrate on building up of awareness in the rural people to bring in the desirable changes in the attitude, knowledge and skill."[35]

The non-utilisation of loans in case of the Government sponsored programmes like IRDP is more in percentage. The non-utilisation of loan for the purpose for which the same was granted causes fall in income, employment and output. The misutilisation and overdues percent is more at Sikiri branch on IRDP (as told by BM and verfied in the considered cases like dairy and croploan). The overdues of IRDP for Sikiri bank by June 90 was 96.5%, in June 1991 it was 83% and by June 1992 it was 71%.[36] The cases of mobile vendors provided with cycles are also one of the glaring examples of the IRDP Loan.

The RGB is facing a lot of constraints and its viability as a financial institution is in doubt. In deposit mobilisation the targets are not achieved. The Bank like any other RRB in Orissa, is very much dependent on the external sources for its lending operation. The refinances from NABARD and sponsor bank constitute the major source of capital while the deposits of small villagers are not a very encouraging source of business. As such the RGB may follow the following suggestions.

1. Wide Publicity has to be accorded to various deposit schemes by the sponsor bank.

2. Government offices at the block level may be persuaded to keep and operate their accounts through the RGB.

3. The rural people in the Ganjam district are still depending upon the informal sources of credit. They should be well educated and be informed about the advantages of this institutional finance. The literacy programmes should also cover the people to be educated on this line.

4. The daily collection of deposit schemes may be introduced. The Puri Gramya bank has introduced this and scored a soccess.[37]

5. Depositors should be given due importance while considering the grant of direct loans.

6. The RRBs may be allowed to offer small gifts to depositors during deposit mobilisation campaingns.

7. The RRBs may be placed on the same footing as commercial banks for collection of pensions of Government and semi Government retired officials in the rural sector of Ganjam district.

The deposits of RGB is increasing from time to time but the percentage of deposits to the total deposits of the district and the percentage of deposit to the total RRB deposits of the state is very negligible. 77% of the total deposit of RGB are found from rural sector and 16% deposits from semi urban areas of the Ganjam district by December 1990. In the same way 85.13% of total lending was operated in rural sector and 11.90% of total lending was in the semi urban areas of the district by 1990.[38]

The business of the branches of RGB is confined to a limited service area and to the target groups of the rural mass. Thus, the branches are not able to make profit. The magnitude of overdues is ever-increasing due to non-repayment of loans by the weaker section either willfully or due to genuine difficulties. While illiteracy, ignorance and poverty are the three important factors responsible for the weaker sections not repaying the loans, deliberate and clear unwillingness to repay becomes to other reason of overdues. The ARDRS has increased the burden of overdues creating a feeling that non-repayment of instalments is preferable as in future there may be debt reliefs. Similarly, the persons who do not repay become the ideal examples for others not to repay the loans. The influence of village politics is also a major constraint on recovery of loans. A non-wilful defaulter is the person, who despite his best of intentions is not in a position to repay the loan instalment due to circumstances beyond his control such as natural calamities, fall in prices of the output, uneconomic holdings, etc. It is the class of these people who have paid some instalments at good times and could not pay some instalments due to their present weak economic conditions.

The reasons of poor recovery are as follows :

(1) There is no clear guideline from the Government on the follow-up action. As such, the bank managers only issue notices and then they are either forced to recommend the head office to write off the loan or to claim the same from DICGC. Generally very few cases are taken up for legal actions. No case of legal action could be found from the Branch Managers of the branches of RGB from any of the three samples taken (Sikiri, Samarjhola and Jarado).

(2) Sometimes, the offices of the bank are pressurised by the local politicians to sanction loans in favour of their own persons and those beneficiaries neither use them for increasing income, employment and production nor they like to repay the instalments of loan.

(3) 90% of the beneficiaries are of target group, those that exist below the poverty line. If they cannot generate income from loan, recovery is not possible for RGB.

(4) The RGB has no link with the DIC and it is not providing loans to DIC sponsored beneficiaries.

To improve the recovery of loans of RRB, the Government should take steps through media publication and recovery targets should be kept for every year involving the BDOs in their block. The recovery should not be an affair of bank staff but also all such rural development agencies of Government of the district. In this respect it is noticed from the case study made at Sikiri village the scholar observed that the RGB and the block officials do not posses good co-ordination and co-operation among themselves.

The evidence of this may be taken as the cases for which the bank has made letters for recovery and the statement of BDO on the recovery camps. However rural development is not possible by mere distribution of money power by the banks, but possible through a systematic co-ordination and planned activities of all the developmental agencies of the district under the leadership of the Lead Bank, which is the sponsor bank of the district. The overdue percentage is more incase of IRDP and other Government sponsored programmes. In case of direct loans (seen from the case study) it is not so much.

RGB being an institution for the weaker section may continue with a loss for a shorter period. It is not a charitable institution. Thus it cannot continue with continuous losses. It has to survive and for the same reason it has to make profits. With the increase in the expenditures over the income, the RGB together with seven other RRBs are continuously incurring losses. (Our of the total of nine RRBs of the State).

The DICGC and ARDRS has provided some amounts to wards the defaulters by settling cases of overdues. The coverage of DICGC has been reduced from time to time. In the initial period it was 90% but now it has come down to 60% in covering the risk of loans in favour of the defaulters. On the other hand the percentage of overdues are ever increasing. Thus, there comes a great challange against the viability of the RGB due to the mounting overdues and continuous losses.

The officers posted in rural areas do not stay at the places of posting. They daily move from distant places due to their personal difficulties and accommodation problems. The success of RGB in very much dependent upon the involvement and sincerity of the staff. The deputed staff are the temporary guests to RGB and the chairman has a three year tenure and has a lot of responsibilities. The salary structures of RGB has got changed due to the growth of trade unionism and subsequent proliferation of demands. They are now getting the salary at par with the sponsor bank (which is a nationalised bank). The RGB is no more a low cost organisation. When other commercial banks with the staff of comparable salary can do better business and credit deployment, deposit mobilisation is comparatively better than RGB, there is no need for keeping the separate identity of the rural bank. The following may be taken as suggestions. These suggestions are already under active consideration.

(1) The RGB and all other RRBs should merge together into one national institution and their recruitment should be made at the national level for increasing the efficiency of the staff and to avoid local influences. As an alternative to this suggestion, the banks may also be merged with the sponsor bank and the rural branches must continue with the objective of serving for the target and weaker section of the society.

(2) The rural branches should deploy their credit to both the target and non-target group in the ratio of 60% and 40% respectively and in the urban sector in 40% and 60% respectively.

(3) The officers and the staff of the rural branch should get adequate training and the credit estimates credit planning should be done through scientific surveys from time to time.

(4) Strong actions should be taken against the beneficiaries who misutilise the loan and dispose of the assets.

(5) Easy instalments should be fixed by the bank according to the economic conditions of the beneficiary.

(6) The developmental agencies of the Government should cooperate with the bank personnel to sanction loans and to help in the recovery. The targets of recovery should also be fixed for the blocks.

(7) If possible mobile rural banks on vehicles may move daily to the interior villages for disbursing the loans, collecting the deposits and for making recovery. They should also make field inspection and educate the beneficiaries. The nominee of the district administration and technical persons with some police-

man may once or twice in a month visit along with the bank staff. This will not only increase the recovery position and deposit mobilisation but also increase the proper employment of loans for generating the additional income and purchasing power of the weaker sections of the people in the rural locality. The problem of under finance and overfinance must be looked into through personal touch with the beneficiaries.

(8) Accomodation facilities and incentives for the rural staff has to be provided by the organisation for creating an interest among the staff to serve in the rural areas.

(9) The promotional facilities in the RGB are very much limited. Thus, the district recruitment should be confined to the posts Clerks and Field Officers and for the post of Branch Manager and Area Manager etc. to be appointed from among the existing staff on promotion.

(10) The deputation of staff to RGB should not continue forever. It should come to an end sooner or later and the guardianship of sponsor bank in all the affairs of RGB should be restricted within desired limits.

(11) Debt relief sanctions should not be a regular practices. It should be discouraged.

(12) Additional concessions and benefits should be given to the depositors and borrowers of the rural bank.

(13) It is found from the interviews with the Bank Officials of Sikiri village of Hinjilicut block that the cultivators of bettelevine send their products to distant places, outside Orissa. To maintain easy financial transactions and better remittance facilities, they like to keep deposits at the branch of SBI but not at RGB. Thus the remittance facilities of RGB and the RRBs has to be extended for the benefit of the beneficiaries.

However, the proposal for establishing a National Rural Bank (NRB) is under active consideration and if the same is established then it will be a special rural banking organisation at the national level. This will generate a new hope among the beneficiaries and the staff of RRBs and RGB in Ganjam district. The NRB should come out with realistic hopes and without the defects of RRBs. It should be a viable institution without the liability of loss but should not aim at economic profit alone, but provide social profitability and real economic development of the rural sector.

References

1. Wadva, Charan, D., *Rural Banks for Rural Development*, Delhi, Bombay, Caluctta, Madras, Macmillan Company Ltd., 1980, P. 164.

2. "Block Profiles", *ACP Ganjam (Andhra Bank)* 1991-92, P. 44

3. Ibid.

4. Ibid, PP. 44, 45.

5. *ACP Ganjam (Andhra Bank)*, 1988, P. 27.

6. ACP Ganjam, (Andhra Bank), Berhampur, 1991-92, p-36.

7. ACP Ganjam, (Andhra Bank), Berhampur, 1988, p-28.

8. ACP 91-92, *Op.cit*, p-36.

9. Worked out from the data of ACP 91-92, p-36.

10. Ibid.

11. As reported by the B.M. Sikiri, Dec. '92.

12. Lall G.S., (Edited), "Regional Rural Banks", *The journal of Banking studies*, Vol. X, No. 3, July-Sept., 1987, p. 177.

13. Bhatnagar, J.S., "Future of Rural Finance in India", *IBA Bulletin*, Vol. X, No. 12, December, 1988, p. 223.

14. Ibid.

15. Wadva, Ch. D. *Op Cit*, p. 156.

16. Lead Bank Sources (Enquiry).

17. B.M. of Sikiri and Samarjhola branch RGB (Enquiry).

18. Jethwaney, Sonika, "Regional Rural Banks", *IBA Bulletin*, Vol. X, No. 12, (rural Development Special Issue), Dec. 1988, p. 247.

19. Annual Report RGB. 1991-92.

20. Ganesan, S. "Service Area Approach to Rural Lending - Problems in implementation" *IBA Bulletin* Vol. X, NO. 12, Dec. 1988, p. 238.

21. V. Ananda Kumar, "Performance of Regional Rural Banks", *Rural Economy of India* (Edited by Murty & Narayana), Delhi, Mital publications, 1989, p. 289.

22. Government of India, Report of the working group on RRBs, 1986, p. 28.

23. Mr. Dharma Rao, Branch Manager, Hinjilicut, Ganjam.

24. Dandekar, M.N. "Toning up Rural lending for development" *IBA Bulletin*, Vol. X, No. 12, Dec. 1988, p. 231.

25. Jethewaney, Sonika, *Op cit*, p. 249.

26. Statistical section, Head Office, RGB (Enquiry Feb '93).

27. RGB Annual Report 1991-92.

28. Rao, B. Ramachandra, "Quality of Personel for Rural Banking", *IBA Bulletin*, Vol. X, No. 12, Dec. 1988, p. 273.

29. Wadva, *Op Cit*, P. 162.

30. Ibid, pp. 162, 163.

31. Reddy, L.B., "Increasing Efficiency of RRBs", *IBA Bulletin*, Vol. X, No. 12, Dec. 1988, p. 245.

32. Verma, M.L., *Rural Banking in India*, Rajendra Printers, Jaipur (Rajasthan), 1988, p. 198.

33. Ibid.

34. Restructuring of Regional Rural Banks (RRBs), Proposal for establishment of National Rural Bank (NRB), R.B.I. Bulletin, Jan. 1993, (Supplement) pp. 8, 9.

35. Rannorey, S.R. and Padmanabhaiah, E.V., "Extension Activities by Banks in Rural Area" *IBA Bulletin*, Vol. X, NO. 12, Dec. 1988, p. 271.

36. B.M. Sikiri, Interview, Feb. '93.

37. Verma, M.L., *Op cit*, p. 129.

38. Statistical section, RGB, Head Office, Berhampur (Enquiry).

7

Summary, Findings and Conclusion

The main objective of this work is to assess the working of the RRB in the Ganjam district of Orissa and to pinpoint its short-comings in fulfilling the avowed purpose for which it has been created. In this respect, the working of other financial institutions of the rural sector of Ganjam district has been examined to make a comparative study of their relative working in the provision of credit for the uplift of the rural poor in the district. The nature and functioning of the banking system has indeed undergone a radical transformation since nationalisation, both in quantitative and in qualitative terms. As a result of this, measures were taken for a massive extension of banking facilities to unbanked areas covering in particular the rural populating and increasing flow of bank credit to priority sectors consisting of agriculture, small-scale industries, small transport operators, professionals, the self-employed and weaker sections of society including those living below the poverty line. As such, the Rushikulya Gramya Bank (RGB) as the RRB of Ganjam district came into operation from the year 1981. The Andhra Bank, which is the lead Bank of the district, is the sponsor bank of RGB.

In the first Chapter of this work, the discussion pertained to an overview of the study. In this connection it traces the origin and gensis of rural development. In explaining the concept of Rural Development, the stages of evolutionary process of rural development, different poverty alleviation programmes, the social control over the banks, bank nationalisation, Lead bank Scheme and the need for establishing the Regional Rural Banks (RRBs) are discussed. The First Chapter of the thesis being an introductory chapter highlights the following :

(a) Importance of the Study.

(b) The Scope and Objectives of the Study.

(c) Hypotheses adopted for testing.

(d) Methodology used in economic analysis.

(e) Limitations of the study and,

(f) The Plan of the Study.

In the fitness of things the working of RGB has been analysed and finally assessed in the context of the rural economy of Ganjam district which constitutes the area of its operation. In the second chapter, the rural economic scene of Ganjam district of Orissa has been analysed.

Ganjam, which means the granary of the world, is rich in agricultural resources but is industrially backward. It has 86% of rural population which is higher than the national average. The work force of the district constitutes 34.75% and the scheduled caste/scheduled tribes account for 24% of the total population of the district. The agriculturists constitute 42.14% of the work force, the agricultural labourers constitute 32.46%. As per 1991 census, the workforce engaged in organised sector is only 4.76% of the total work force. It is estimated that 1.40 lakh persons were either underemployed or unemployed in the organised sector of the district. The marginal farmers of the district constitute 86.44% of the total number of farmers.

The Ganjam district is administratively divided into eight sub-divisions, fourteen tahasils and twenty nine blocks. It has good potentialities of mineral, forest, fishery, animal husbandry, horticulture, sericultural and Water Resources.

The net area sown in the district is less than the state average and also the national average. The percentage of net area irrigated to net area sown at the district level as on 1980-81 was 54.17% and the same has been steadily increasing from year to year. The district has 11,655 hectares of canals, 81,235 hectares of tanks, 12485 hectares of wells and 19,827 hectares of irrigation from other sources. The fertiliser consumption was 57 kgs per hectare during 1991-92 which is less than the national average. The district has 3366 kms of metal roads, 79 kms of broad gauge railway line and 45 kms of narrow gauge railway line. There is a small port at Gopalpur and a small airstrip at Rangeilunda. So far 3055 Villages have been electrified. The Jayashree Chemical Ltd. and Co-Operative Sugar factory of Asks are the two prominent large-scale industries of the district.

As on March 1992, there were seventeen Commercial banks with 143 branches, 75 branches of RGB and 27 branches of Co-operative banks having C.D. ratio of 52%, 102% and 105% respectively.

An examination of the broad features of the rural economy of Ganjam district to a great extent reflects the main characteristics of the state and the nation. The study of the various features of the rural economy of the Ganjam district provides ample justification for induction of the Regional Rural Bank (the Rushikulya Gramya Bank). The RGB being a special organisation meant for the rural sector and the target groups has to provide much needed cheap capital to the marginal farmers, landless labourers, village artisans and other professionals and help them in improving their standard of living.

In an agriculturally dominant district like Ganjam, having high irrigation potential, better prospects of multiple cropping and possibilities of high fertiliser in-take by land any development effort clearly spellsout the crucial importance of cheap credit which can be provided by the RGB because it is specially designed to serve such objectives.

The Third Chapter of the thesis highlights the need for correct credit estimation and the different credit agencies extending such credit to the rural sector of Ganjam district. It is not an easy task to estimate the credit needs of rural farmers as it varies from region to region, season to season and crop to crop. There is no media to collect accurate statistical information. The rural people need credit both for production and consurmption purposes or occupational and non-occupational purposes. Besides the agricultural credit needs, there are many other needs for rural people. As such any single estimate of rural credit cannot correctly reflect the credit needs. Singh and Gupta provided a model of microlevel credit estimate with the remark of its unsuitability at the macro level.

The credit setup of rural Ganjam consists of the following financial institutions.

(a) Co-operative Banks.

(b) Scheduled Commercial Banks.

(c) Rushikulya Gramya Bank (RGB)

NABARD being the apex body of rural refinance has a district level office at Berhampur. It prepares the potential linked Credit Plan which becomes the background paper for the district Credit Plan and also it keeps a tab on rural institutional financing in the district.

In estimating the credit needs the lead bank, (Andhra Bank) plays a pivotal role by preparing the Annual Action Plan and Annual Credit Plans. Targets fixed for every sector and for every branch of the bank are the estimations of credit on the basis of available financial resources. The credit estimates which are made by the bank are more supply oriented than demand-based. But to make a correct estimate of genuine credit needs of the various types of rural people is not easy. As such the Credit plans prepared by the Lead Bank are to be accepted even though there are certain drawbacks. One of the shortcomings is that it does not prepare the plan according to the needs of rural people but on the basis of resources at the disposal of the banks. The Annual Credit Plan for the year 1985 is a sample year, which was taken up for explaining the credit estimation of the Lead Bank.

The preparation of Credit Plans and estimating the credit through Service Area Approach have made the district Credit Plans more sensible and realistic as they are to be prepared right from the branch level. The branch manager of each bank at the village level with the help of the B.D.O. and other officials is to play an important role in making a proper socio-economic survey and in preparing the Credit Plans. The addition of Village Plans at the Block level and the Block Plans at the district level finally provide the District Credit Plan for each year.

In the fixation of credit outlays, the RGB's contribution to the district forms a very negligible part, but the same is increasing quantitatively from year to year. In a comparison between the achievement and the estimated credit outlay, the RGB's performance is better than the performance of other financial institutions of the district.

The RGB being an organisation for the poor of rural Ganjam should not feel satisfied by the percentage of achievement but should increase its allocation of credit quantitatively. It should increase its contribution to the district credit allocations (estimate).

In the Fourth Chapter, the lending techniques and operations of RGB are discussed sectorwise. The RGB being a purpose-oriented financial institution dealing with small borrowers of the target groups of people cannot make profit. Its main aim of business is not the same as that of the other Commercial Banks working in the district. RGB has limtied resources and limited staff to cater to the financial need of under-privileged poor people. As the clients of the RGB are poor, illiterate, ignorant and belong to the weaker section, the recovery and return for the banks is not very encourging and, as such, its business profits are limited.

The RGB has lent only 6.9% of the total lending of all RRBs of Orissa by the end of March 1990. Even though Ganjam is relatively a bigger and more developed district than many others, it has a very low percentage of performace among the RRBs of Orissa. It occupies 6th position out of 9 RRBs of the state in lending during 1989-90.

In sectorwise lending, the RGB's contribution to the district in the agricultural sector during the period 1990-91 constituted only 14.46%. The RGB branch has lent Rs. 2.17 lakhs of average agricultural loan in comparison to Rs. 11.94 lakhs by a branch of Commercial Bank of Ganjam district during the period 1990-91. It is seen that the role of RGB in agricultural sector in particular is not an insignificant one, but not a very impressive one. Its contribution to district lending compared to other RRBs in the state is very negligible.

Ganjam district is industrially backward and the performance of RGB in this sector is very limited. It has lent 1.19% of the total lending of the district in the industrial sector during the period 1990-91. Amont the 9 RRBs of Orissa during the period 1989-90, it has lent only 0.78% to this sector.

The performance of RGB in the service sector is very satisfactory. The achievement curve of RGB has always remained above the target curve of RGB upto 1990-91. In the total lendig to the sector of the district by all financial institutions the contribution of RGB alone constitutes 37.44%, while all other institutions together contributed 52.56% to the services sector during the period 1990-91. But the contribution of RGB among the RRBs of the state to this sector is only 5.39% for the period.

The RGB has followed the objectives of social justice in the promotion of economic development and confined its lending operations to the target people on a priority basis. The role played by RGB in the priority sector is satisfactory. In the year 1990-91, the RGB has advanced 92.43% of its total advances to the priority sector. The percentage of advances made to the weaker section in relation to the total advances during 1989-90 was 74.47% out of a total of 7133 beneficiaries in 1989-90, the beneficiaries in the priority sector were 67840 and out of them 58605 beneficiaries belong to the weaker section. It provides loans to the target group mainly through two sponsored programmes i.e., (i) ERRP and (ii) IRDP.

In the priority sector it lends to the people under the following programmes.

1. Twenty Point Programme.
2. Integrated Rural Development Programme (IRDP).
3. Economic Rehabilitation of Rural Poor (ERRP).
4. DRI Loans.
5. Better use of irrigation Water.
6. Loan to Small Scale Village and Cottage Industry.

7. Biogas.
8. S.C.F.C.C. etc.

Generally, the RGB gives loan in kind rather than in cash. The loans are repaid with simple interest if they are returned within the stipulated period and compound interest is charged if the payment is done after the said period. The rate of interest of RGB loan ranged from 9.5% to 10.5% to 11.5% for non-agricultural purposes. The period repayment ranges from 1 to 3 years or more in case of agricultural loans and it ranges from 1 to 5 years in case of loans to the service sector. However from 9.10.91, the rates of interest were linked to the quantity of loans and were charged differently to the priority sector and non-priority sector.

Even though the RGB is increasing its role in lending, the quantitative achievements are not very satisfactory either in the district or in the state by the RRBs. The RGB for its survival needs a sound capital structure. The lending activities of the bank will be effective and will proceed along desired lines only when the institution is financially strong. The inflow and outflow of funds must be set into a regular cyclical rhythm.

RGB being a small bank for small men has a very limited capital to cater to the needs of the people. Its share capital comes from the constituents i.e., the Central Government, State Government and Sponsor bank in the ratio of 50:15:35 for the total of 50 lakhs, while the authorised capital is one crore rupees. Because of the continuous losses, the RGB lost the significance of the "Reserve Fund". It mostly depends upon the deposit refinances and recoveries of past loans for redeploying it in lending cum investments. By 1991-92 RGB with its 75 branches in 1833 villages has mobilised deposits of Rs. 1923.21 lakhs in 125837 accounts. The average deposit per branch of an RGB was Rs. 5.67 lakhs in Dec. 1981 and had gone up to Rs. 25.64 lakhs by the end of March 1992.

By increasing the number of deposit accounts in more and more villages, the RGB is improving its deposit mobilisation, but its share in the deposit mobilisation of the whole banking sector in the district is not satisfactory. It is only 6% of the deposits of banking sector in Ganjam by

March 1991. The percentage growth of deposits of RGB has always remained below the percentage growth of the district. In deposit mobilisation the RGB occupies 6th position among 9 RRBs of the state during 1989-90. It has contributed 7.27% of deposits mobilised by all RRBs of Orissa during the period 1989-90, while the Cuttack Gramya Bank has contributed 24.61F% of deposits and remained at the top. In many of the year under study the RGB also failed to achieve the targets of deposit mobilisation. Both in a quantitative analysis at the district level and in a comparative study of the RRBs of the state in deposit mobilisation the RGB's performance is found to be insignificant. As such, the performance in this line cannot be treated as satisfactory.

Refinance constitutes a major source of capital for RGB. It gets refinances from NABARD and from sponsor bank. NABARD provides refinance for lending in Government sponsored programmes. NABARD has provided refinance of Rs. 1155.96 lakhs out of the refinance limit of Rs. 2005.00 lakhs during the years 1980-81 June to 1990-91 July (10 years). It is seen that the RGB could not avail itself of the refinance facilities to the maximum extent. The amounts drawn were less than the limits sanctioned. The RGB has repaid to NABARD Rs. 685.15 lakhs and the outstanding due to NABARD is Rs. 470.82 lakhs by June 1991. During the year 1991-92, out of the total limit of Rs. 315 lakhs, the RGB has drawn Rs. 180.32 lakhs in ST and Rs. 247.99 lakhs in MT i.e. a total of Rs. 428.31 lakhs. It shows an increasing role of RGB in Government sponsored programmes. On the other hand, the sponsor bank (Andhra Bank) has provided Rs. 935.25 lakhs as refinance limits but the RGB has drawn only Rs. 423.92 lakhs during the said ten year period.

By the end of March 1992, the sponsor bank has an outstanding refinance claim on RGB for Rs. 237.05 lakhs. The refinance of NABARD and Sponsor Bank are the most important sources of finance of RGB as deposits are not encouraging, recovery percentage is less and losses are regular. Recovery of loans is a general problem to most of the banks in district. By June 1990, the general overdues for the banks of the district was 59.6% while for RGB it was 50%. The debt relief schemes also encourage default and due to the non-recovery recycling of funds has not been possible.

The cost of banking has gone up due to the rise in salaries and other expenditure. The accamulated losses for RGB by the end of March

1992 was Rs. 417.18 lakhs.

Thus the capital structure of RGB is weak and for capital resources RGB is precariously dependent on refinances from outside.

In the Sixth Chapter a detailed analysis of the case studies has been made. From the case study at Jarado Branch of RGB it is found that the loans of 1985 have helped create employment to the extent of 77% and provided an average monthly incremental income of Rs. 246.15 for the beneficiaries. More than 90% of the beneficiaries were found to be wilful defaulters.

The Sikiri branch by providing loans to the beneficiaries of Sikiri, Giria and Kharida has created employment for 90% of the beneficiaries in the year 1989 and could help generate an incremental average income of Rs. 625/- per month. In this way, the RGB's role in creation of income and employment is not unsatisfactory. It stands for the weaker section of the rural sector. But rural development is dependent not only on cheap bank credit but also on many other factors, such as infrastructural facilities and the educating of the rural population in motivating them to avail bank finance. Unless factors like communication, proper co-ordination, knowledge, persuasion, change in attitude and socio-psycho cultural factors develop among the rural people and in rural areas the mere extension of credit in abundance, when people do not know how to make good use of it, will not solve the problem ; rather it will increase the difficulties of the banks.

The non-utilisation of loans in case of the Government sponsored programmes lime IRDP is more in evidence. The overdues of IRDP of Sikiri branch by June 1990 was 96.5%, in June 1991 it was 83% and by June 1992 it was 71%. It shows a decreasing trend. But unless the overdues come down substantially the banks cannot be financially solvent.

In the same way different problems of the RGB are discussed through case studies. In Saradhapur village and in Anbagaon village people take loans from different banks and under different programmes but they donot repay them.

The DICGC and ARDRS meet the unrecovered overdues to some extent. But these schemes should not be resorted to again and again as it promotes the tendency for nonrepayment ; and, what is more, they do not constitute a real source of capital for RGB.

From the profit/loss analysis of the bank as a whole in Chapter 5 and from the study of the sample branches done in Chapter 6 we find that there is continuous loss for RGB. This creates a problem for the viability of the bank.

As regards the problem of staff, the RGB employees do not stay in the stations where they are posted for various reasons stated in an earlier part of the study and they do not have any genuine involvement in the problems of the people of the localities. The recruitment is not fair. In acceding to the demands of the disgruntled employees the salary scales have been revised upward to bring them on par with the sponsor bank employees. As a result one of the reasons for the creation of RGB's is no more valid.

There is no proper co-ordination between the sponsor bank and the RGB. The deputed staff do not have proper involvement and regard themselves as temporary guests. The Chairman has many responsibilities and his duties are not fixed. He has been deputed from the parent institution for a period of three years. This creates many administrative and organisational problems.

The problem of mounting overdues which has become chronic has denied the bank resources through recovery for recycling. Added to this the high cost structure resulting from revised salary, rising interest cost and other administrative costs have seriously affected the profit position of the bank and endangered its viability. This is the inescapable conclusion that emerges from the analysis of capital structure and lending for income generation and employment creation as done in Chapters 5 and 6 of the study respectively. But the Narasimham Committee has gone a step further and came up with the idea of creating a new national level institution called the National Rural Bank through the merger of all RRBs in the country. This view has received the active consideration of the Government of India. It also felt that this is the only alternative and the NRB should emerge as a special Bank to protect the basic aims of RRBs i.e. rural development and uplift of the rural poor and weaker sections.

Testing of Hypotheses

The hypotheses adopted in the plan of the study have to be tasted to ascertain their validity.

Hypothesis - I

(1) *"The credit needs for rural development cannot be effectively met without tailor-cut, specially designed banking institutions like the Regional Rural Bank."*

The Regional Rural Banks are established with a special objective i.e., to promote rural development. Rural development lies at the root of all development as India is a country of villages. The development of villages again mean the economic development of the marginal farmers, rural artisans, agricultural labourers and economically weaker sections. Poverty alleviation programmes are to be assisted by bank finance and subsidies. The specially designed banks like RGB in Ganjam district have been providing cheap loans to such target groups.

The commercial banks and co-operatives are also playing an effective role for rural development. But the aim of this tailor-cut organisation is meant particularly for the persons who are not in a position to take loans as per the customary banking practices due to their poor economic condition and non-possesion of assets. Furthermore, the co-operatives have not come upto expectation in helping the weaker sections because of their poor capital base. Of late the co-operatives have become hot beds of politics and benefits are cornered by the affluent sections.

The RRBs being district level organisations, can be trusted to take banking closer to the rural households on a priority basis. The RGB in this respect has provided finance to the priority sector. It advanced to the priority sector and the same has been flactuating between 90% and 100% of the total advances of RGB during the years under consideration. The RGB has been established to fill the gap of rural credit needs of the target group people which the commercial banks and co-operative could not meet due to organisational and other reasons. The RGB has played a substantial role in the agricultural and in the service sector lending. Its role in industrial sector is not an encouraging one.

The average agricultural loan of a branch of RGB has always remained below the achievements of an average branch of the commercial banks of the district. The reason is that RGB as lent only to the target group farmers, while the commercial banks advanced to the target group to a very negligible extent and extended their credit to a larger extent to the non-target group of farmers (i.e., Large and Medium farmers).

The RGB in the years 1983, 1986, and after 1989-90 has not even achieved its targets in the agricultural sector. In a comparison between the RGB's percentage achievement and the percentage achievement of the district, the RGB was in a better position upto 1985 and also in the years 1987 and 1988. In the year 1989-90, the performance of RGB was not a good one and it remained below the percentage of achievement of the district.

The performance of RGB as a specially designed tailor-cut organisation is most satisfactory in the service sector. In the service sector the RGB's achievement has always remained above the target and the contribution of the RGB forms a substantial part in the district lending.

In the industrial sector, the achievement of RGB was satisfactory in the years 1984, 1985 and in 1986 but thereafter there is a big gap between the targets and achievements.

In the agricultural and industrial sectors the contribution of RGB in the district lending is not a satisfactory one and the contribution of RGB to the RRB sector of the state in any of the lendings is not an encouraging one.

In the priority sector, the RGB advances to the target people under the schemes of twenty point programme. The Integrated Rural Development Programme (IRDP), Economic Rehabilitation of Rural poor Programme (ERRP). Differential rate of interest scheme, village and cottage industries promotional schemes. In the programmes for the better use of irrigation water, loans are given to the target people on priority basis for Dugwell, Pumpset and Energisation of pumpsets or Dugwells. Under the scheme of justice to scheduled caste and scheduled tribes loans are provided to such people. Loans also are provided for biogas plants in the villages by RGB.

By 1991-92, 7592 beneficiaries got an advance of Rs. 211.15 lakhs and the outstanding amounts of RGB and IRDP loans was 539.74 and the number of beneficiaries was 25649. The IRDP loan constitutes 13.90% of the total priority sector. Under the ERRP loan, the RGB provided Rs. 3.23 lakhs as loans to 180 target group persons in 1990-91 and the outstanding loans to the beneficiaries, which constitutes 0.69% of the total advances in the year 1990-91.

In the agricultural-allied sector, the loans for irrigation were provided for dugwell in 107 accounts for Rs. 7.34 lakhs and the outstanding loan in this sector of the RGB by 31.3.91 was Rs. 37.76 lakhs. In the same way, in 195 accounts loans were provided for pumpsets for Rs. 14.26 lakhs and the outstanding amounts were Rs. 50.81 lakhs. In small scale, village and cottage industries, in 205 accounts only 4.14 lakhs were provided to target group artisans and other people in the period under report. The outstanding loans of SSI sector of RGB during the said time was Rs. 15.76 lakhs. In Biogas, in 4.3 accounts Rs. 8.96 lakhs was provided and the outstanding amounts were Rs. 14.98 lakhs and similarly for scheduled caste and scheduled tribes, the loan provided under the head of SCFCC was Rs.267.21 lakhs outstanding with the accounts of 17459.

Thus the bank as an organisation specially built for the poor and weaker sections of the society is playing an increasingly important role. But the rate of increment and the quantity of loans form a very small proportion of the total credit in all the sectors of the district and amount the RRBs of the state. The RGB by increasing its branches from 7 in 1981 to 75 in 1991-92 has covered 1817 villages. The average deposit per branch of RGB was Rs. 2011 thousand and the average advance per branch was 2212 thousand. As such, the RGB has come to the doorsteps of the rural people. But its role will be more effective only when the share of RGB increases in the district lending of the state and among the RRBs. The RGB is yet to play an effective role in the district as a separate organisation for the target groups of the district. As such, a close examination of all the relevent facts strengthens the validity of the hypothesis.

Hypothesis - II

(2) *"That it is not enough to provide credit on easy, convenient terms and at lower rates of interest to create sustained growth in the rural sector which would secure distributive justice, there is need for proper credit disbursement on a selective basis and also for monitoring of bank-financed activities and timely repayment of loans."*

Efforts for rural development do not end with the supply of easy loans and subsidies to the beneficiaries. By lowering the rate of interest neither the demand for loan can be created among the uneducated underprivileged and unskilled target group beneficiaries, nor even can the loan amounts create more income and employment for the beneficiaries, when they do not have any idea about the proper use of the amounts. The loan amount must reach the right person at the right time for right purpose. The beneficiaries should repay the loans in time for recycling them for future use by the bank.

The RGB doesnot have adequate demand for loan from the prospective beneficiaries in agriculture and industry as targets fixed for these sectors by the bank are not achieved in many years. The most important reasons for the same are listed below.

(1) People are uneducated.

(2) Developmental agencies do not play an effective role in educating the people.

(3) Bank Officials do not stay in the villages and they do not keep personal touch with the people.

(4) There is no proper co-ordination between the sponsor bank and RGB and the RGB and other developmental agencies of the district.

(5) The loans are inadequate in many cases.

(6) They are not disbursed at the right time and even if the loan got

sanctioned the development agencies do not supply the needed materials or animals at the right time.

All relevant facts in this respect are studied in Chapter 6 under the sample cases. The bank can be a viable institution only when the recoveries are successfully carried out. The recoveries are less than the demand and the overdues are always increasing not only in the case of RGB but in respect of all the financial institutions working in the district. A major contributory factor to the unsatisfactory recovery position is indiscriminate lending done without ascertaining the genuine purpose of borrowing. Besides, there are no follow-up measures to monitor the proper deployment of loans. The government agencies and financial institutions do not act in co-ordination. So results of lending are not commensurate with the lending operations. The preceding analysis proves the hypothesis.

Hypothesis - III

(3) *"That use of credit will be effective when provided as per planned assessment of requirements prepared in consonance with Rural Development Programmes."*

The use of credit will be effective when provided as per the planned assessment of requirements prepared in consonance with rural development programmes.

In Chapter 3 the problems of credit assessments have been examined in detain and it has been pointed out that the scale of finance fixed by DRDA plays a vital role while estimating the needs of the farmers and artisans and other beneficiaries.

The cases of underfinance is a common occurance in RGB lending which results in the ineffectiveness of the use of loans. These are also discussed with case studies in Chapter 6. All these go to prove that the hypothesis number 3 is very much valid.

Hypothesis - IV

(4) *"That there is a need for proper co-ordination of the working of rural credit agencies for planned supply of credit to the rural sector."*

In a multi agency credit structure, some times the beneficiaries multiply their loans from different banks and misutilise them very often. The cases of such incidence are also discussed in Chapter 6. Thus the Service Area Approach can become effective only when there is a proper co-ordination and co-operation between the different banks and the developmental agencies of the block and the district. The follow up actions after the loan must be carried out with the co-operation of the administrative agencies and the bank in the rural area. Similarly, before approving the loans the developmental agencies should provide proper training and guidence to the prospective beneficiaries. This is found very much wanting in the administrative financial set-up in Ganjam district as discussed in Chapter six. The analysis conducted in the study lends credence to the hypothesis.

Limitations of the Study

The study broadly covers the period 1981 to 1991. However in trying to give a correct perspective to some aspects of the study some times the temporal boundaries have been exceeded and data pertaining to years outside the reference period have been considered. The date collected from different sources and different agencies some time do not tally. Such examples are provided in the thesis at different points. The performance of RGB in Ganjam district has been examined on the basis of the role of RGB to the specific target group. The case studies are conducted to ascertain viability and income generation potential of lending operations of Jarado branch of Purushottampur block and Sikiri and Samarjhola branch of Hinjilicut block of Ganjam district.

The study is essentially an economic study of the working of RGB in Ganjam district. The relevant facts and data are collected from the Andhra bank (sponsor Bank) Regional Office, the Head office of RGB, the District NABARD office, District Industry Centre, the office of the DRDA Chatrapur, the Deputy Director of agriculture, Ganjam. The Deputy Registrar of co-operatives, Berhampur in person and through interviews of the different officials. The district credit plans, the annual reports of RGB, the Action Plan of DRDA and DIC Ganjam, the RRB statistics of NABARD and PLCP of Ganjam were utilised for collection of different relevant data and facts needed for analyses in the thesis.

Conclusion

It is revealed from the detailed study of the performance of Rushikulya Gramya Bank in Ganjam district that the bank has played an effective role, though at a slow pace and is responsible for creating income and employment for its beneficiaries. However the achivement is no 100%.

The viability of RGB is in danger due to the ever-increasing losses. The bank has to be allowed to lend to the richer sections. This will also improve the deposit mobilisation and the resources position of the RGB. The RGB provides consumption loans but this is very insignificant. The limits on such loans may be relaxed so that a better income for the bank can be derived from the higher rate of interest charged on such loans. The RGB can add to its income if, following the Kelker Committee Report, it is allowed to lend to public bodies like ST/SC Corporations, Housing Boards, Village Panchayats, etc.

It can also substantially reduce its cost if refinance funds are made available to it at a lower rate of interest by NABARD and the sponsor Bank. Such a recommendation was made by the RBI Study Team (1981) which was endorsed later by the Kelker Committee (1986).

The conversion of crop loans into term loans should be made only when there are natural calamities. It should be avoided under all other circumstances. In order to bring into being a uniform policy, while granting loan directly by the managers, a scale of finance is necessary, which should be laid down by the technical committee at the district level.

It is learnt from the interviews with the bank staff that the subsidies are not provided at the right time. The undue delay in the payment of subsidies by the government organisations creates a lot of difficulties. This should be avoided. The subsidies may be provided to the Regional Rural Banks in advance.

The collection of overdues should be done generally by the Bank Officers and the Administrative Officials of the block. The block office should bear a certain responsibility in recovery of loans.

The remittance facilities have to be introduced in the RGB.

Introduction of remittance system by bank drafts will popularise the RRBs and their utility in the area may be increased.

The Government and semi-Governmental organisations, Panchayats, Blocks and NACs and other wings of the district authority should be made to carry out their business transactions with the RGB. This will improve the resources position of RGB.

The Gift systems and prize systems to encourage heavy deposits in the RGB is to be introduced for encouraging the deposit mobilisation. The door-to-door collections on a daily basis may be introduced by the RGB as it is done in Puri Gramya Bank.

However, the non-viability of RGB is not a peculiar problem in Ganjam district. It is a general problem affecting the nation as a whole. As such, the merger of all the RRBs is needed immediately to form a National Rural Bank under the authority of NABARD and RBI.

The recruitment to the Officers' cadre must be done on an all-India basis and better accomodation for the bank staff is needed at the rural stations.

Rural credit is a long standing problem in India and radical measures to tackle the problem have been adopted at regular intervals ever since the enactment of the Co-operative Societies Act in 1904. From the inception of the co-operative movement via socialisation of banks, bank nationalisation finally to the induction of RRBs in 1976 it is a long history of woeful tales. But a study of the institutional set-up of rural credit in the nation as a whole or any of its states or any part thereof shows that the co-operatives, commercial banks and regional rural banks constitute a trio which can successfully deliver the goods. If they have not succeeded so far it is because they are not made to work to their full potential and they fail to reinforce each other through proper co-ordination of their activities in their effort to promote the common cause. In this large credit set-up the RRBs have a place of their own, which is rather crucial, as they are supposed to assist the vulnerable sections of the rural population.

The study reveals that the RGB has proceeded in the right direction but failed to go a long way. Some of the problems it faces are common to all RRBs in the state as well as the country as a whole while others are peculiar to the area in which it operates. There are quite a number of suggestions made in this study which are suitable for replication elsewhere, whereas others are particularly meant for removing the peculiar constraints in the working of the RGB so that it comes to play a more meaningful role in the rural development of Ganjam District.

Annexures

Annexure - 1
List of Branches of Rushikulya Gramya Bank

Head Office : Berhampur

Sl. No.	Name of Branch	Date of Opening	Sl. No.	Name of Branch	Date of Opening
1.	Berhampur	14.02.81	38.	Khandava	27.02.84
2.	Chirikipadasasan	5.06.81	39.	Dhunkapada	25.04.84
3.	Samarajhola	26.08.81	40.	Balipada	27.04.84
4.	Sumandi	31.08.81	41.	Sunapur	28.04.84
5.	Paralakhemundi	18.12.81	42.	Asurbandha	30.04.84
6.	Kesapur	22.12.81	43.	Kadua	12.05.84
7.	Kamuni	30.12.81	44.	Allada	15.05.84
8.	Garandi	12.01.82	45.	Mahanandapur	16.08.84
9.	Nalabanta	02.04.82	46.	Goiba	31.08.84
10.	Aska	02.04.82	47.	Hatiotta	12.09.84
11.	Padmanavapur	02.04.82	48.	Sourachachinna	13.09.84
12.	Budhambo	10.05.82	49.	Mangalpur	20.09.84
13.	Hadubhangi	15.05.82	50.	Narayanapur	25.09.84
14.	Palurgarh	25.05.82	51.	Sikiri	19.10.84
15.	Adava	01.06.82	52.	Turubudi (D)	12.11.84
16.	Bhanjanagar	17.07.82	53.	Ralaba	01.01.85
17.	Pandia	20.07.82	54.	Luhagudi	14.01.85
18.	Chatrapur	21.07.82	55.	Kulangi	30.01.85
19.	Khariaguda	23.07.82	56.	Baghala	31.01.85
20.	Ramgiri	03.08.82	57.	Thuruburei	11.02.85
21.	Uppalada	24.08.82	58.	Gazalabadi	15.02.85
22.	Pratapur (P)	25.08.82	59.	Khallikote	25.02.85
23.	Dengaosta	27.08.82	60.	Manitara	26.02.85
24.	Jarado	02.09.82	61.	Sidhewar	23.03.85
25.	Raipur	24.09.82	62.	Turubudi (P)	24.03.85
26.	Pankatabadi	24.06.83	63.	Talasara	25.03.85
27.	Angaragoan	27.06.83	64.	Birlkote	26.03.85
28.	Panchabhuti	15.07.83	65.	Kharnipada	27.03.85
29.	Bomikoi	05.08.83	66.	Madhupalli	28.03.85
30.	Kanaheipur	23.08.83	67.	Tarasingi	29.03.85
31.	Humuki	27.08.83	68.	Jeerango	30.09.85
32.	Bandhaguda	15.12.83	69.	Gayaganda	25.09.87
33.	Gautami	19.12.83	70.	Pratapur (J)	29.07.88
34.	Badabarasingi	21.12.83	71.	Bonka	25.09.89
35.	Humma	24.12.83	72.	Adapada	09.03.89
36.	Gurunthi	29.12.83	73.	Chelligada	22.03.89
37.	Chikili	16.01.84	74.	P. Ramachandrapur	27.03.89
			75.	Koinpur	29.03.89

Area Office : ASKA

Annexure - 2

Performances of Financial Institutions in Implementation of ACP as on 31.03.91 (1990-91)

(Rs. in Lakhs)

Name of the Financial Institute	*Crop Loan*		*Agril Tera Loan*		*Allied to Agl.*		*S.S.I.*		*Services*		*Total*		
	Target	*Achie.*	*Target*	*Achie.*	*Target*	*Achie.*	*Target*	*Achie.*	*Target*	*Achie.*	*Target*	*Achie.*	*%*
1	2	3	4	5	6	7	8	9	10	11	12	13	14
Alld. Bank	2.25	4.21	10.18	3.49	11.56	15.78	6.67	3.95	10.38	22.18	41.14	49.61	120
Andhra Bank	109.37	111.77	52.76	32.11	28.06	29.66	100.18	22.49	138.10	177.74	428.47	371.67	87
B.D.B.	3.40	0.84	2.65	2.48	2.91	1.11	2.01	0.85	2.50	3.77	13.47	9.05	67
B.O.I.	12.55	8.96	12.88	9.15	26.12	15.85	10.95	6.26	14.65	11.86	77.25	52.08	67
Canara Bank	33.50	72.81	14.81	22.76	11.12	19.58	3.28	5.39	61.59	54.73	124.30	175.27	141
C.B.I.	4.70	2.40	1.30	2.25	0.42	2.63	6.05	3.00	5.75	5.56	18.22	15.84	87
Indian Bank	60.08	89.88	28.70	16.26	19.32	46.87	14.60	13.49	40.27	56.93	162.97	223.43	137
I.O.B.	62.13	43.46	15.10	21.59	22.56	13.10	15.75	19.88	36.49	22.55	162.06	120.58	74

(Contd.)

Annexure 2 (Contd.)

1	2	3	4	5	6	7	8	9	10	11	12	13	14
P.N.B.	5.00	1.85	6.76	1.23	1.70	1.00	1.30	0.99	6.30	3.26	21.06	8.33	40
S.B.I.	177.65	223.85	115.46	119.64	88.32	48.22	124.22	59315	127.38	63.67	633.03	514.53	81
S.B.H.	–	0.02	–	0.23	–	–	5.00	2.60	2.00	10.90	7.00	13.75	196
Synd. Bank	17.71	10.78	9.43	2.12	5.54	4.52	7.81	4.41	9.93	14.69	50.42	36.52	72
J.B.I.	0.20	–	0.30	–	2.04	0.84	6.85	1.30	15.21	8.81	24.60	10.95	46
United Bank	21.29	7.70	18.48	9.69	19.14	6.67	28.50	12.95	109.59	34.20	197.00	71.21	36
UCO Bank	31.00	34.86	15.15	5.15	68.48	14.65	10.30	5.15	24.10	19.43	149.03	79.24	56
Vijaya Bank	–	2.81	–	–	5.00	2.43	37.00	0.83	48	–	90.00	6.07	7
Vysya Bank	–	0.10	–	–	1.30	2.74	3.00	3.67	5.70	12.45	10.00	18.96	189
Total	540.83	616.30	313.96	248.15	313.59	223.65	383.47	166.36	658.04	522.63	2210.02	1777.09	80
R.G.B.	249.05	108.36	133.82	74.99	107.88	47.71	34.30	4.14	115.85	489.31	640.90	724.51	113
A.C.C.B.	486.70	34.44	26.30	–	0.08	–	–	–	–	77.13	510.08	111.57	22
B.C.C.B.	573.24	178.85	20.30	3.45	5.15	29.11	–	–	8.35	65.32	607.04	276.73	46
O.S.C.L.D.B.	–	–	56.04	28.98	13.25	3.04	–	–	–		69.29	32.02	46
O.S.F.C.	–	–	–	–	–	–	195.00	176.98	100.00	152.20	295.00	327.18	112
CR. Total	1846.85	937.95	550.42	355.57	439.95	303.51	612.77	347.48	882.24	1306.59	4332.33	3251.10	75

Annexure - 3

Industrial Sector Lending : Different Financial Institutions of Ganjam District of Orissa

(Rs. in Lakhs)

Period	R.G.B.			Comm. Banks			Co.Operatives			OSFC			Total Lending of Ind. Sector		
	Target	Ach.	% of Ach.	Target	Ach.	% of Ach.	Target	Ach.	% of Ach.	Target	Ach.	% of Ach.	Target	Ach.	% of Ach.
1983	28.32	4.8	16.94	145.35	125.35	86.15	20.9	74.77	357.75	114.35	90.59	79.22	308.92	295.39	95.62
1984	3.46	11.53	333.23	192.00	139.01	72.40	21.03	82.37	391.67	145.94	114.82	99.23	362.43	377.73	104.22
1985	4.00	7.33	183.25	123.73	136.58	110.38	59.59	38.68	64.91	262.00	232.57	88.76	449.32	415.16	92.39
1986	5.00	6.95	139.00	160.00	120.16	75.1	125.00	268.57	214.85	210.00	195.63	93.15	500.00	591.31	118.26
1987	15.00	9.07	60.43	155.61	182.49	117.27	140.00	47.5	33.92	230.5	474.49	205.85	541.11	713.55	131.86
1988	16.00	10.68	66.75	169.85	254.56	149.87	75.00	55.6	74.13	257.76	104.92	40.72	518.61	425.81	82.10
1989-90	33.44	3.85	11.51	392.37	501.79	127.88	–	140.28	–	195.00	130.32	66.83	620.81	776.24	125.03
1990-91	34.30	4.14	12.06	383.47	166.36	43.38	–	–	–	195.00	176.98	90.75	621.77	347.48	56.70
1991-92	35.96	2.38	6.61	415.56	153.76	37.00	136.40	118.32	86.74	220.00	125.38	62.69	787.92	399.84	50.74

Sources : Annual Credit Plan, Andhra Bank, Lead Bank Ganjam District Berhampur (Ganjam)

Annexure - 4

A Comparative Statement of Data on Lending in Service Sector in Ganjam District

(Rs. in Lakhs)

Years	R.G.B.				Commercial Banks				Cooperatives				OSFC				Distt. Credit Plan of Ganjam			
	Target Ach.	Ach. Cont.	% of Ach.	% of Cont. to dist	Target	Ach.	% of Ach.	% of Cont. to dist.	Tar-get	Ach.	% of Ach.	% of Cont. to dist.	Target	Ach.	% of Ach.	% of Cont. to dist.	Target	Ach.	% of Ach.	% of cont to dist.
1983	2.39	21.4	895.39	6.66	198.71	284.22	143.03	88.47	14.3	2.63	18.53	0.82	57.95	12.98	22.39	4.04	273.35	321.25	117.52	100
1984	29.24	59.36	203.00	11.86	173.32	339.42	195.83	67.84	16.61	80.31	483.5	16.05	47.65	21.23	44.55	4.24	266.82	500.32	187.511	100
1985	35.00	58.43	166.94	7.32	206.25	609.01	295.27	76.37	60.00	46.82	78.03	5.87	60.00	83.17	138.61	0.42	361.25	797.43	220.74	100
1986	42.9	155.06	361.44	18.44	248.3	487.12	196.18	57.95	75.76	63.16	83.36	7.51	90.00	135.18	150.2	16.08	456.96	840.52	183.93	100
1987	80.00	255.15	318.93	21.66	404.00	625.5	154.82	53.11	74.54	68.15	91.42	5.78	147.49	228.82	155.14	19.43	706.03	1177.62	166.79	100
1988	85.00	349.59	411.28	26.47	428.38	777.74	181.55	58.90	74.8	116.57	155.84	8.82	160.00	76.48	47.8	5.79	748.18	1320.38	176.47	100
1989-90	93.48	456.02	487.82	32.95	591.64	703.08	118.83	50.81	–	156.18	–	11.28	100.00	68.35	68.35	4.93	785.12	1383.63	176.23	100
1990-91	115.85	489.31	422.36	37.44	658.04	522.63	79.42	39.99	8.35*	142.45	1705.98	10.90	100.00	152.20	152.2	11.64	882.24	1306.59	148.09	100
1991-92	111.54	65.38	58.61	11.34	747.58	269.94	36.10	46.61	5.70*	158.19	2775.26	27.45	100.00	85.59	85.59	14.33	964.82	576.10	59.71	100

(Contd.)

Annexure - 4 (Contd.)

N.B. Column 2, 3, 6, 7, 10, 11, 14, 15, 18 and 19 Rupees in lakhs. (Targets and Achievements)

Column 4, 8, 12, 16 and 20 are the % of achievement over their own target.

Column 5, 9, 13, 17 and 21 are the % of Contribution in Service Sector to the District Credit Plan of the Service sector, Ganjam.

Source : Credit Plans : Andhra Bank, Berhampur, Ganjam

* For B.C.C.B. only.

Annexure - 5

RRBS and Commercial Banks Orissa

As on Dec 1990 *(Rs. in Lakhs)*

Districts	*Regional Rural Banks*			*Other Scheduled Commercial Banks*			*All Scheduled Commercial Banks (Including RRBs)*		
	Offices	*Deposits*	*Credit*	*Offices*	*Deposits*	*Credit*	*Offices*	*Deposits*	*Credit*
1. Bolangir	66	8.34	25.00	32	42.55	33.24	98	50.90	58.24
2. Balesore	63	12.10	10.55	106	144.12	103.35	169	126.22	113.90
3. Cuttack	121	41.43	50.00	245	469.46	330.98	366	510.88	380.98
4. Dhenkanal	48	10.71	11.11	74	108.46	58.07	122	119.17	67.18
5. Ganjam	75	14.42	15.66	141	223.37	127.58	516	137.8	143.24
6. Kalahandi	62	6.50	15.56	41	33.57	39.58	103	40.07	55.14
7. Keonjhar	35	4.46	5.76	49	56.32	53.11	84	60.79	58.87
8. Koraput	90	27.41	37.26	60	83.25	70.49	150	110.66	107.75
9. Mayurbhanj	55	9.15	10.34	72	71.57	49.55	127	80.72	59.89
10. Phulbani	15	1.02	1.36	44	26.51	18.90	59	27.54	20.26
11. Puri	100	20.14	24.26	171	621.55	627.7	271	632.69	651.96
12. Sambalpur	73	8.13	18.68	115	192.62	119.30	188	200.75	137.98
13. Sundargarh	16	1.23	1.38	92	244.62	132.25	108	245.85	133.63
Orissa	819	165.04	226.92	1242	2278.98	1762.11	2061	2444.04	1989.03

Annexure - 6

Banking Key Indicators as on 30-09-1992
Ganjam District

(Amt. in Lakhs)

Name of the Bank	*No. of Branches*	*Total Deposits*	*Total Advances*	*Direct Agril. Adv.*	*Total P.S. Advances*	*Total W.S. Advances*	*Total DRI Adv.*	*C.D. Ratio*	*% of Col 5 to 4*	*% of Col 6 to 4*	*% of Col 7 to 6*	*% of Col 8 to 4*
1	2	3	4	5	6	7	8	9				
Allahabad Bank	02	389.04	193.03	82.30	155.33	73.89	6.39	50	43	80	48	3.31
Andhra Bank	32	5868.75	2061.70	489.67	1355.99	124.85	20.56	35	24	66	31	1.00
Bank of Baroda	02	324.70	230.12	32.17	97.38	36.05	0.72	71	14	42	37	0.31
Bank of India	07	600.92	753.39	549.79	671.30	95.08	6.59	125	73	89	14	0.87
Canara Bank	05	1485.59	687.48	300.04	547.35	–	8.52	46	44	80	–	1.24
Central Bank of India	02	589.60	197.30	20.03	126.10	50.20	1.45	33	10	64	40	0.73
Indian Overseas Bank	10	1678.25	971.66	363.75	684.89	619.67	17.99	58	37	70	90	1.85
Punjab National Bank	03	148.11	94.31	15.25	56.00	–	3.02	63	16	59	–	3.21
S.B. of Hyderabad	01	189.35	29.53	0.08	16.93	–	0.16	16	27	57	–	0.54
S.B.I.	41	11834.04	6071.14	1848.75	3922.95	2597.89	60.31	51	30	65	66	0.99
Syndicate Bank	05	872.26	469.91	123.86	309.00	–	7.19	54	14	66	–	1.53
UCO Bank	06	844.39	764.30	309.36	673.47	–	9.63	91	40	88	–	1.26
Union Bank	02	351.44	171.80	48.45	111.48	18.65	2.12	49	28	65	17	1.23
United Bank	10	1116.71	569.30	140.70	400.26	26.37	3.50	51	25	70	65	0.61
Vijaya Bank	01	284.02	164.43	17.06	87.66	–	0.26	58	10	53	–	0.16
Vysya Bank Ltd.	01	281.14	57.46	0.10	14.12	2.84	0.29	20	17	25	20	0.50
Indian Bank	13	1864.80	1053.86	402.15	671.59	254.88	7.62	57	38	64	38	0.72
Total of Commercial Banks	143	28693.11	14540.72	1743.51	9901.80	4437.37	156.32	51	33	68	45	1.08

(Contd.)

Annexure 6 (Contd.)

1	2	3	4	5	6	7	8	9				
R.G.B.	75	2091.85	1912.04	816.59	1912.04	–	8.40	91	43	100	–	0.44
A.C.C.B. Ltd.	11	687.78	934.17	–	648.64	–	–	135	–	69	–	–
B.C.C.B. Ltd.	17	1420.50	1482.80	–	1072.96	–	–	104	–	72	–	–
O.S.C.A.R.D.B. Ltd.	05	–	–	–	–	–	–	–	–	–	–	–
Total	33	2108.28	2416.94	–	1721.60	–	–	115	–	71	–	–
OSFC	1	–	1930.87	–	1930.87	–	–	–	–	100	–	–
Grand Total	252	32893.24	20800.60	5560.10	15466.31	4437.37	164.72	63	27	74	29	0.79

Andhra Bank (Agenda Note) Dist. Level Review Committee
23rd December 1992

Bibliography

(a) Books

A.V. Ananda Kumar — *"Performance of Regional Rural Banks"* Rural Economy of India, Mital Publications Delhi, 1989.

Andhra Bank — *Hand Book on Service Area Approach,* Andhra Bank Central Office, Hyderabad.

Carver, T. — *Rural Economics,* Thakar Sprink & Co., Calcutta 1960.

Desai Vasant — *A study of Rural Economics,* Himalaya Publishing House, Bombay, 1983.

Dhingara I.C. — *Rural Econòmics,* Sultan Chand and Sons, Delhi, 1986.

Desai SSM — *Rural Banking in India*, Himalaya Publishing House, Delhi, 1986.

Desai B.M. — *Rural Financial Development,* Centre for Management in Agriculture, I.I.M. Ahamadabad, 1989.

Das and Chatarjee — *The Indian Economy its Growth and Problems*, Book land Private Ltd., Calcutta, 1967.

Dutta, Rudra & Sundarm, K.P.M. — *Indian Economy*, S. Chand & Company (Pvt.) Ltd., Delhi, 1986.

Elias, A.H. — *Operational Problems of Rural Banks*, Vora & Co., Publishers, Pvt. Ltd., Bombay, 1967.

Gupta, S.C. — *Development Banking for Rural Development*, Deep and Deep Publications, Delhi.

Ghosh Alok	*Indian Economy its nature and problem*, The World Press Pvt. Ltd., Calcutta, 1987.
Grewal, P.S.	*Rural Banking in India*, Kalyani Publishers, Delhi, 1985.
Gupta, A.K. and Shroff M.	*Rural Banking : Learning to unlearning an Action Research Enquiry*, Centra for Management in Agriculture, I.I.M., Ahemadabad, 1990.
Khandewal, Anil K.	*Hand Book on personal Management and Industrial relation for Rural Banks*, Rawat Publicatons, Jaipur, 1987.
Karve, D.G.	Rural Development, Reserve bank of India Bombay 1959.
Kamal Suri and S. Gangadharan (Edited Hannan Ezekid)	*The Economic Times' Statistical Survey of the Indian Economy*, Vikash Publishing House Ltd., Delhi, 1984.
Lall, G.S.	*Rural Economics*, H.P.J. Kapoors Publication, Delhi, 1984.
Misra S.K. and Puri, V.K.	*Indian Economy its Development Experience*, Himalaya Publishing House, Bombay, Nagpur, Delhi, 1988.
Murthy, N.L. and Mital Narayana	*Rural Economy in India*, K.V. Publications, Delhi, 1989.
Mathur, D.P.	*Public Sector Banks in Indian Economy*, Sterling Publishers (Pvt.) Ltd. New Delhi, 1978.
Mahajan, V.S. (Ed.)	*Studies in Indian Banking and Finance*, Vol. I Deep and Deep Publications, Delhi, 1989.
Ministry of Information and Broadcasting, Government of India.	*India, 1990.*

Naidu L.K. (Ed)	*Bank Finance for Rural Development* Ashish Publishing House, New Delhi, 1986.
Patel A.R. and Khankoje D.D.	*Rural Economics*, Sultan Chand & Sons, Delhi, 1985.
Patel, Sah, D'Mello.	*Rural Economics,* Himalaya Publishing House, (on behalf of IBA) Bombay, 1987.
Pillai and Sarangadharan	*Rural Economics,* Himalaya Publishing House, Pvt. Ltd. Bomhay, 1987.
Reddy, A. Rangarajan	*Agricultural Development Rural Credit and Problems of its recovery,* Mital Publications, Delhi, 1990.
Sadhu, A.N. and Singh, Amarjeet	*Fundamental of Agricultural economics,* Himalaya Publishing House, Delhi, 1989.
Subramanya, K.N. (Ed)	*Modern Banking in India,* Deep and Deep Publications New Delhi, 1982.
Sundarm J.D.	*Rural Industrial Development,* Vora & Co. Publishers Pvt. Ltd. Bombay, 1970.
Singh Garudev and Ashokan, S.R.	*Institutional Finance in Rural India : Efficiency and Efficacy,* Centre for Management in Agriculture, I.I.M. Ahemadabad, 1988.
Sharma, D.P. Tokhi, M.R.	*Rural Banking in India Sterling,* Rural Publishers, New Delhi, 1975.
Thekkamali, S.S.	*Rural Development and Social Changes,* Sangita Printers, Delhi, 1983.
Verma, M.L.	*Rural Banking in India,* Kuber Associates and Publishers Jaipur 1988.
Vyas, M.R.	*Financial Performance of Regional Rural Banks*, Arihint Publishers, Jaipur, 1991.

Venkataratnam M. *Social Banking An attack on poverty and unemployment*, Andhra Bank Central Office, Hyderabad, 1987.

Verma, S.A. *Post independence change in Rural India*, Inter India Publication, Delhi, 1980.

Wadva, Charan D. *Rural Banks for Rural Development-An Analysis of working of Regional Rural Banks in India with two case studies*, The Macmillan company of India Ltd., Delhi, 1980.

Bureau of Statistics and Economics, Govt. of Orissa, Bhubaneswar. District Statistical Hand Book, Dist. Ganjam.

(b) Journals and Articles

Abdul, Noorbasa and M. Jyoti "*Viability of Regional Rural Banks - A case Study*" Yojana Vol. 33 No. 9 May (16 to 31) 1989.

Annonymous *Reports on trend and Progress of Banking in India (July - June, 1988-89),* RBI Bulletin, Supplement, October, 1989.

Annonymous *Reports on trend and progress of Banking in India*, (1991-92, July - June) RBI Bulletin, Supplement January, 1993.

Annonymous "*Project Approach to Agricultural Development*". Andhra Bank Staff College, Hyderabad.

Annonymous "*Guidelines for effecting satisfactory repayment of Agricultural loans*". Andhra Bank Staff college, Hyderabad.

Annonymous Note on Integrated Rural Development

programmes. Andhra Bank, Staff College, Hyderabad.

Annonymous "*Rural Development strategy in 6th plan*". Andhra Bank staff college, Hyderabad.

Annonymous "Project Approach to Agricultural Development", Andhra Bank Staff College, Hyderabad.

Annonymous "*Guidelines for effecting satisfactory repayment of Agricultural loans*". Andhra Bank Staff College, Hyderabad.

Annonymous *Note on Integrated Rural Development Programme.* Andhra Bank, Staff College, Hyderabad.

Bhatnagar, J.S. "*Futures of Rural finance in India*", IBA Bulletin, Vol. X, NO. 12 December, 1988.

B. Saty Murty "*Banks costs and Profitability concepts evaluation Techniques and statistics for improvements*", The journal of the Indian Institute of Banks. Vol. 61, No. 3 July-Sept. 1990.

Badatya Kishorhari "Role of Rushikulya Gramya Bank in Ganjam". The Ganjam Economic review. Vol. 5, January, 1993.

Govt. of India Rural Banking/enquiry committee.

Govt. of India CARAFICARD, RBI, 1981.

Ghosh, D.N. "*Commercial Banking lessons from Indian Experience*", The Indian Institute of Bankers. Vol. 60. No. 1, January, March, 1989.

Iyer, V.R. Faculty Member	"NABARD - Functions and working" College of Agricultural Banking. Reserve Bank of India, Pune.
Jyotilok, Guha	*"Development of weaker sections Role of Social Scientist",* Kurukhetra. Vol. XXXVIII, No. 8, May, 1990.
Jethwaney, Sonika	*"Regional Rural Banks - a review".* IBA Bulletin Vol. X, No. 12, December, 1988.
Jhoshi, Nabin Chandra	*"Regional Rural Credit Delivery System".* The Journal of the Indian Institute of Banking, Vol. 57, No. 3. July, Sept. 1986.
Kumar, Geeta	*"Recovery ethics in Rural lending".* IBA Bulletin Vol. X, No. 12, December, 1988.
Kulshresta, U.C.	*"The role of lead Bank in Branch expansion a case study".* The Indian Economic Journal Vol. 34, No. 1, July-Sept., 1986.
Kulkarini, J.R.	"*Important Provisions of Banking Regulation Act,* 1949 and RBI Act, 1934 - Applicable to Regional Rural Banks". College of Agricultural Banking RBI, Pune, December, 1985.
Lal, G. (Ed.)	*"Rural Finance : The Multiagency approach".* The Journal of Banking studies Vol. X, No. 3, July - Sept., 1987.
Malhotra, R.N.	*"India's Monetary Policy and the role of Banking system in Economic Development"* - IBA Bulletin, March, 1990.
Malhotra, R.N.	*"The role of Banking in rural Development."* The Journal of the Indian

Institute of Bankers Vol. 57, No. 3, July - Sept., 1986.

Malhotra, R.N. *"The role of Banking, in Rural Development".* RBI Bulletin, Vol. XL., No. 9 Sept., 1986.

Malhotra, R.N. *"Service Area Approach"*, RBI Bulletin, Vol. XLIV. No. 9, Sept. 1990.

Marwaha, M.G. *"Lead Bank Scheme"* College of Agricultural Banking, RBI, Pune.

Ojha, P.D. *"Regional Development and the role of Banks"* RBI Bulletin, Vol. XLIII, No. 1., January 1989.

Ojha, P.D. *Service Area Approach - a new challange:* Banks. The Journal of the Indian Institute of Banks. Vol. 61, No. 1, January - March 1990.

Ojha, P.D. *"Banking and Economic Development in India".* RBI Bulletin, Vol. XLI, No. 1, January, 1987.

Ojha, P.D. *"Agricultural Credit Institutions - India, their structure and role in development."* RBI Bulletin, Vol. XL, No. 2, February, 1986.

Patnaik, Dhanalaxmi *"Development of Commercial Banks in Ganjam".* The Ganjam Economic Review. Vol. 5, January, 1993.

Panda, J. *Recovery of Agricultural Advances in Orissa - A study of State Bank of India.* Ganjam Economic Review Vol. 3, February, 1991.

Pradhan, K.C., Patnaik, Pradip, Tripathy, S.N. *Role of Rushikulya Gramya Bank Financing Rural Development,* Ganjam Economic Review, Vol. 5, January - 1993.

Panda, Prabhakar — *Rural Development - Some important aspects of the role of Banks.* Orissa Review, Government of Orissa, November, 1981.

RBI — RBI Bulletin, March, 1991.

Rangarajan, C. — *"Banking Development since, 1947."* RBI Bulletin, Vol. XLIII, No. 1, January, 1989.

Reddy, L.B. — *Increasing efficiency of RRBs*, IBA Bulletin, Vol. X, No. 12, December, 1988.

Rao, B. Ramachandra — *"Quality of personel for Rural Banking".* IBA Bulletin, Vol. X, No. 12, December 1988.

Rannory, S.R. and Padmanava, E.V. — *Extension activities by Banks in Rural India*, IBA Bulletin, Vol. X, No. 12, December, 1988.

Singh, R.K.P.
Singh, B.B.
Singh, R.P.N. — *"Financial viability of Commercial and Regional Rural Banks in Bihar - a case study".* The Journal of Indian Institute of Bankers, Vol. 58, No. 2, April - June, 1987.

Satymurty, B. — *"Bank cost and profitability concepts, Evaluation, Techniques and strategies for improvement".* The Journal of the Indian institute of Bankers, Vol. 61, No. 3, July, Sept., 1990.

Sethy, S. Vasudev — *Some issues on Rural Development.* The Journal of Indian Institute of Bankers, Vol. 59, No. 3, July - Sept., 1988.

Srivastava, Lalima — *Role of Institutional finance in Agricultural Development of Uttar Pradesh (Doctoral Work)*, Allahabad University, Allahabad, 1982.

Sardesai, A.V. Faculty Member — *"Institutional arrangements for Rural India."* College of Agricultural Banking, RBI, Pune.

Singh, V.B. — *"A study on Cooperative Credit and its impact on C.D. Programmes in selected districts of U.P. (Doctoral work)*, Allahabad University, Allahabad, 1976.

Sardesai, A.V. Faculty Member — *"Rationale and development of Regional Rural Banks."* College of Agricultural Banking, RBI, Pune.

(c) Reports/Souvenir/Government Periodicals

Annonymous — Jaipur Nagaur Anchalika Bank.

Annonymous — Rushikulya Gramya Bank in the Service of the Rural Poor.

Misra, S.N. — *Swakhyar Ganjam Sundar* Ganjam, 1992.

Patra, K.C. — *"Brakishwata Fisheries Development in Ganjam"*, Ganjam, 1990.

Patra, K.C. — *"Construction of Harabhangi Irrigation Project - step in Economic Development of Ganjam"* Ganjam, 1990.

Pradhan, Gourhari — *"A decade DRDA, Ganjam, Chatrapur"*, Ganjam, 1990.

Patnaik, P.C. — *"Glimpses of Cooperative activities" in Ganjam Dist. Swakhyar Ganjam Sundar*, Ganjam, 1992.

Panigrahi, Nalinikanta — *"Post-nationalisation of Banking Scenaries".* Ganjam, 1990.

Rushikulya Gramya Bank, Andhra Bank, Regional, Office.	Annual Reports ; from 1981. to 1991-92.
	Annual Credit Plan and District Credit Plans from 1980-81 to 1991-92
NABARD, District Office, Bhubaneswar.	Potential Linked Credit Plan, Ganjam, 1993-94.
DIC, Ganjam Berhampur,	Annual Action Plan (1988-89 to 1992-93).
DRDA, Chatrapur	Annual Action Plan, IRDP, 1987-88, Chatrapur, Ganjam.
Syndicate Bank	The role of Banks in National life Manipal, 1968.
NABARD, Bombay.	RRB Statistics (1989-90).
Government of India.	Reports of Working Group on Rural Banks, 1986.
Central Office, Andhra Bank, Hyderabad.	Manual of Lead Bank Scheme.
Government of India.	RRB Act, 1976.
Government of India.	RRB (Ammetment) Act, 1987.
Government of India, Ministry of Rural Development.	IRDP, Manual 1986.